DETROIT PUBLIC LIBRARY

3 5674 00978909 1

D0141926

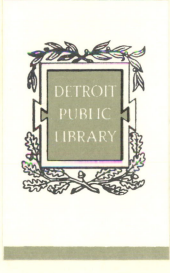
DETROIT
PUBLIC
LIBRARY

RELEASED BY THE
DETROIT PUBLIC LIBRARY

The Judicial Power of the United States

THE JUDICIAL POWER OF
THE UNITED STATES

The Eleventh Amendment in

American History

JOHN V. ORTH

New York   Oxford
Oxford University Press
1987

R 347.7312 O77j

JUL 9 '87   C.1

OXFORD UNIVERSITY PRESS

Oxford   New York   Toronto
Delhi   Bombay   Calcutta   Madras   Karachi
Petaling Jaya   Singapore   Hong Kong   Tokyo
Nairobi   Dar es Salaam   Cape Town
Melbourne   Auckland

and associated companies in
Beirut   Berlin   Ibadan   Nicosia

Copyright © 1987 by John V. Orth

Published by Oxford University Press, Inc.,
200 Madison Avenue, New York, New York   10016

Oxford is a registered trademark of Oxford University Press

All rights reserved. No part of this publication may be reproduced,
stored in a retrieval system, or transmitted, in any form or by any means,
electronic, mechanical, photocopying, recording, or otherwise,
without the prior permission of Oxford University Press.

Library of Congress Cataloging-in-Publication Data
Orth, John V., 1947–
The judicial power of the United States.
Bibliography: p.   Includes index.
1. United States—Constitutional law—Amendments—11th.
2. Judicial power—United States—History.   3. Jurisdiction—
United States—History.   4. State bonds—Law and legislation—
United States—History.   I. Title.
KF8735.078   1987   347.73'12   86–8424
347.30712
ISBN 0–19–504099–6

1 3 5 7 9 8 6 4 2

Printed in the United States of America

R
SE

To

THE HON. JOHN J. GIBBONS

United States Court of Appeals
3rd Circuit

Katie's godfather

and

the godfather of this book too

Preface

"No part of a book is so intimate as the Preface. Here, after the long labor of the work is over, the author descends from his platform, and speaks with his reader as man to man, disclosing his hopes and fears, seeking sympathy for his difficulties, offering defence or defiance, according to his temper, against the criticisms which he anticipates." With these words Harvard President Charles W. Eliot introduced the Harvard Classics collection of *Prefaces and Prologues to Famous Books* (1908). Were another such volume ever compiled, the present preface would find no place in it. But President Eliot's words bear repetition here because of the simple truths they so eloquently express. In the first place, despite its placement at the beginning of a book, a preface really comes last; that is, it is composed "after the long labor of the work is over." Oftentimes a preface is not fully comprehensible without reading the rest of the book. Also a preface is written in a more intimate style; the author addresses the reader, as President Eliot said, "man to man," or as we would say today, "person to person." Finally in a preface the author reveals more of himself: he pens his apologia or thumbs his nose, "according to his temper."

In a preface an author is invited to avow his hopes. Mine are to explain one of the most obscure parts of the Constitution and to do it in terms understandable to the educated public. The Eleventh Amendment concerns the jurisdiction of federal courts, an esoteric topic normally reserved for legal audiences. As our nation approaches the two-hundredth anniversary of the drafting of the Constitution it is well to notice its technical aspects as well as its great generalities. We all know that courts must give the generalities concrete meaning in particular cases. When courts are open and when they are shut (which is what lawyers mean when they say a court does or does not have jurisdiction) concerns all citizens, not just the legal community.

Eleventh Amendment law is hard to explain. Despite its brevity—less than fifty words—the Amendment itself is far from clear, and the cases that have elaborated (or embroidered) its meaning are peculiarly complicated. The principal historical cases concern, in fact, state debts in the form of bonds. For dryness and technicality no subject can rival public finance, except perhaps federal jurisdiction. To explain the one as developed in cases involving the other is a fearful task indeed. Can these dry bones be made to live? God knows! In an attempt to enliven my subject I have deliberately chosen a literary style that is unusual in the treatment of topics of such moment. Sparse use of technical terms and reference to works of popular fiction will strike those accustomed to legal treatises as unserious, even racy. In defense I say that its aim is to make the book more readable.

Thirty years ago, in the *Harvard Guide to American History,* Samuel Eliot Morison, President Eliot's kinsman, lamented the fact that historians no longer wrote for the educated public. Adopting a "scientific" style and addressing only their professional colleagues, historians forfeited the large audiences that had profited from the works of their great nineteenth-century predecessors. "When John Citizen feels the urge to read history," observed Morison, "he goes to the novels of Kenneth Roberts or Margaret Mitchell, not to the histories of Professor this or Doctor that." In law much the same thing has happened. Whereas Blackstone once wrote for gentlemen, and early American judges justified their decisions to a large readership, modern lawyers have withdrawn into a professional ghetto. Communicating only with one another, legal writers, including too many judges, have adopted a form of shorthand decipherable only by trained votaries. The law has suffered in the process. Encoded in the crabbed style is too often a crabbed doctrine, oversubtle and absurdly technical. John Citizen has been left out again; this time with no one to turn to. To hold this reader's attention while explaining the Eleventh Amendment, I quote his favorite authors—including Margaret Mitchell. I do this fully aware that the legal profession usually punishes such departures by simply ignoring them. If that is to be my fate I accept it—according to my temper—with a polite *defi*.

Chapel Hill, N.C.   J. V. O.
June 1986

Acknowledgments

To Judge John Gibbons I owe the most stimulating professional experience of my life: the chance to spend 1977–78 as his law clerk. To him I also owe the basic idea of this book: that the peculiar complexity of Eleventh Amendment law is traceable to the constitutional implications of the Compromise of 1877.

To C. Vann Woodward, the modern authority on that Compromise, I owe encouragement to continue my research. That so distinguished a scholar would read and comment upon unsolicited articles by an unknown author continues to amaze and inspire me.

To my friend Henry Brandis, Graham Kenan Professor of Law Emeritus at the University of North Carolina, I owe the inestimable benefit of a critical reading of the present manuscript by a scholar with high standards who nonetheless respects my right to make my own mistakes (after he has pointed them out).

Bits and pieces of this book have previously appeared in various places. The thesis was first stated in a lecture at Tulane Law School, published in the *Tulane Lawyer* vol. 2 (1980), pp. 2–15. Further details were given in the *North Carolina Law Review* vol. 59 (1981), pp. 747–66; in the *University of Illinois Law Review* (1983), pp. 423–55; and in a collection of essays edited by David J. Bodenhamer and James W. Ely, Jr., *Ambivalent Legacy: A Legal History of the South* (1984), pp. 106–22. The present copyright holders are respectively: Tulane University School of Law, the North Carolina Law Review Association, the Board of Trustees of the University of Illinois, and the University Press of Mississippi. To all of the above, acknowledgment is due for permitting me to reuse parts of my work.

A Note on Notes

Numbered notes appear at the end of the book, not at the foot of the page, and contain citations only. Sources are provided for all quotations except for quotations of the Eleventh Amendment. These notes will be of interest, if to anyone at all, only to professional scholars. In the rare instances in which the general reader would benefit from explanations of legal terms or from cross references to other parts of the book, footnotes marked by asterisks are used. For those interested in what I have read or for those who wish to do further reading of their own, a bibliographic essay is provided.

Contents

The Judicial Power of the United States

*The judicial power of the United States
shall not be construed to extend to any
suit in law or equity, commenced or
prosecuted against one of the United States
by citizens of another state,
or by citizens or subjects of any foreign state.*

THE ELEVENTH AMENDMENT

I

Introduction

In *A Christmas Carol* by Charles Dickens the grasping
Scrooge receives a series of visitors from the spirit world.
Disturbed by the ghostly comings and goings during what
seems an unending night, Scrooge begins to fear that he has
slept round-the-clock. To the alarmed miser the lost twenty-
four hours mean pecuniary disadvantage. The bills of exchange in his possession are payable "three days after sight
. . . to Mr. Ebenezer Scrooge, or his order." Unless presented on time, valuable commercial paper will become
worthless—or, to use the metaphor Scrooge uses, will become "a mere United States' security."[1] That American debts
had become a byword for worthlessness was due to the financial Panic of 1837. During the euphoria of Andrew Jackson's
second term as President, American states had borrowed
heavily on world money markets to finance internal improvements. When the inevitable downswing in the business cycle
occurred, the American economy, bereft of a central bank by
Jackson's hostility to the Bank of the United States, passed
quickly through contraction to collapse. Like Third World
countries today, the borrowers were tempted to default. After
a few impecunious states repudiated their bonds, American
credit abroad plummeted. Although the United States had
faithfully paid off the first national debt by 1835, the federal
government was unable to float a foreign loan in 1842, the
year before *A Christmas Carol* was published. "Not a dollar,"
said Baron Rothschild to the American emissary.[2]

3

A reader of the United States Constitution (drawn up in 1787) might well be surprised to learn that American states could repudiate their lawful debts. Among the sovereign powers surrendered by states on joining the Union was the power to pass any "law impairing the obligation of contracts."[3] Bonds sold to investors were certainly contracts of indebtedness obligating the borrower to repay. The right to repayment could, it seemed, be established in federal courts, the repositories of the "judicial power of the United States."[4] This power extended, in the language of the Constitution, "to all cases, in law and equity, arising under this Constitution," as well as "to controversies . . . between a state and citizens of another state . . . and between a state . . . and foreign . . . citizens or subjects."[5] If recognized in court the lender's right would, it seemed, be upheld by the "executive power"[6] vested in the President, who swore a solemn oath to "preserve, protect and defend the Constitution of the United States"[7] and who was charged with the duty of seeing to it that "the laws be faithfully executed."[8] All that seemed to be required, in other words, was that bondholders show their right to repayment. In the ancient language of the common law: *Ubi jus, ibi remedium*"[9]—or, in plain English, "Where there is a right, there is a remedy."[10]

Yet even a popular novelist on the other side of the Atlantic knew that repudiation in the 1830s and 40s was a fact. But however serious the threat repudiation posed to the rule of law and the credit of the United States in the first half of the nineteenth century, it posed an even greater threat during the second half of that century. By the outbreak of the Civil War the American economy had taken off into sustained growth; it had begun, in other words, the "drive to maturity" that reached completion at the beginning of the twentieth century.[11] During this critical period the legality of repudiation by American states became again a pressing problem. This time the dollars involved were greater by a factor of ten.

Still an underdeveloped country, the United States continued to depend on imported capital to finance internal improvements, the necessary precondition for industrialization. Repudiation threatened this vital economic lifeline. Furthermore the power of states to impair "the obligation of contracts" threatened the supremacy of national law, a principle only recently sustained on the bloody battlefields of the Civil War.

Although exacerbated by another financial crisis, the Panic of 1873, the fiscal problems that led to the second wave of repudiation were rooted in war. After their defeat the states of the Old Confederacy were subjected to a regimen of Reconstruction, rule by the Carpetbaggers and Scalawags of popular history. Already in difficulties with respect to antebellum debts, the impoverished governments nonetheless embarked on ambitious and costly programs of social change made even more difficult and expensive by disorganization and defalcation. Taxes had to be eked out by borrowing. Millions of dollars' worth of state bonds were sold, mostly to non-Southerners. As charges on the state fisc mounted, discontent with social experimentation grew. Only the unwavering support of the victorious North for the policy of Reconstruction could have remade the defeated South. When Northern resolve faltered, Reconstruction was doomed. In 1877, the necessary accommodation was reached: the South regained self-government, which meant in the circumstances rule by the indigenous white population. A concomitant of self-government was repudiation. The books were at last balanced by the simple expedient of writing off debts in the necessary amount.

Repudiation was possible only because the justices of the United States Supreme Court in the late nineteenth century denied the existence of the judicial power to negative it. Since judicial recognition of their rights was denied, the bondholders went away empty. Without a remedy there is no right, and repudiation became an accomplished fact. The *ratio deci-*

dendi most often advanced by the justices was the Eleventh Amendment, formally declared part of the Constitution by presidential proclamation in 1798. By its terms the Amendment restricts the jurisdiction of federal courts: "The judicial power of the United States shall not be construed to extend to any suit in law or equity, commenced or prosecuted against one of the United States by citizens of another state, or by citizens or subjects of any foreign state." These words had been interpreted in landmark decisions by Chief Justice John Marshall in the 1820s. Although states were immune from suit by two classes of plaintiffs, their officers were not. By a judicious reinterpretation of the Amendment in the late nineteenth century, however, the justices were able to preside over the massive repudiation of Southern state bonds.

The end of Reconstruction was, as it turned out, the central event in the history of the Eleventh Amendment. While Reconstruction lasted, the legislative and executive powers of the United States had been exercised in unprecedented ways. The end of Reconstruction meant the end of aggressive use of those powers in the South. The concomitant contraction of the judicial power of the United States was effected by the revitalization of the Eleventh Amendment. Declaring themselves without jurisdiction, the justices avoided the need to remedy the wrong of repudiation. The convolutions of legal doctrine, the economic motives and consequences, the political context in which events unfolded, as well as the enduring legacy of the past—all require extended treatment. Because of this complexity, it is well to begin with a brief summary of the argument, the plot if you will.

Introduction

The Argument*

Unlike the first ten amendments comprising the Bill of Rights which safeguard individuals, the Eleventh Amendment protects states. Always a dollars-and-cents proposition, the Amendment was adopted to overturn an early Supreme Court decision that an out-of-state plaintiff could sue a state in federal court to collect a debt. Fearful of suits by British creditors and American Tories whose property had been confiscated during the Revolution, the states amended the Constitution to deprive federal courts of jurisdiction over suits against states by citizens of another state or by foreigners. After the immediate economic threat had passed, the Supreme Court under the leadership of Chief Justice Marshall gave the Amendment a narrow interpretation; that is, the limitation on federal jurisdiction was itself limited. In a landmark case involving attempted state interference with the Bank of the United States, Marshall held that a suit against a state officer is not against the state itself if the officer is acting pursuant to an unconstitutional state law. In other words, if a state attempts to violate the federal Constitution, its officer can be sued in federal court notwithstanding the Eleventh Amendment.

As late as 1876 this interpretation was upheld by the Supreme Court. After 1877, however, the Supreme Court reversed the Marshallian approach and gave the Amendment a broad interpretation. The cases in which this occurred involved repudiation of Southern bonds. With one exception the states of the Old Confederacy were permitted to renege on their debts despite the Contracts Clause of the federal Constitution. Giving the Eleventh Amendment a generous interpretation the Supreme Court deprived federal courts of

* Summarizing as it does the detailed information in later chapters, the Argument is without notes. For full references see the relevant chapter.

7

jurisdiction over suits brought by creditors. Because states may close their own courts to claimants by virtue of the doctrine of sovereign immunity, the creditors were left without a remedy and therefore without a right. This sea change in constitutional interpretation coincided with the Compromise of 1877, the compromise that ended Reconstruction in return for Southern acquiescence in the inauguration of President Rutherford B. Hayes.

Louisiana and North Carolina, the two most heavily indebted states, led the way in invoking the Eleventh Amendment and sovereign immunity to protect themselves against suits by their creditors. In leading cases brought by out-of-state plaintiffs, officers of those states were permitted to invoke the Eleventh Amendment despite the unconstitutionality of state law. Because vast sums of money were involved, the bondholders' legal advisers determinedly sought plaintiffs whose suits would not be barred. Since the Amendment explicitly refers only to suits brought by "citizens of another state," they arranged for other states of the Union to sue on behalf of their citizens. This ingenious attempt was rejected by the Court. Next, creditors who were citizens of the debtor states attempted to sue their own states and state officers in federal courts. This route too was barred by the Court. Finally, a picturesque but futile attempt was made by a foreign sovereign to sue a state. With the failure of all these legal strategies Southern bonds became valueless.

The Compromise of 1877 was the bondholders' Appomattox. With Congress and the President committed to end Reconstruction there were no means by which the Supreme Court, even if it had been willing, could have forced Southern states to pay. Orders to raise taxes to pay unpopular debts would require more than a judge's say-so. It is one of the neglected ironies of history that federal judges firmly committed to the protection of property countenanced the repudiation of millions of dollars' worth of Southern bonds.

Still more ironic, Southern courtroom victories were won by arguing the cause of state sovereignty within a generation of the military defeat of that principle in the Civil War.

While Louisiana and North Carolina were pioneering safe routes to repudiation, Virginia was encountering judicial obstacles. The crucial difference lay in one term in the Old Dominion's contract with its creditors: the interest due on the bonds, represented by coupons, had been made receivable in payment of state taxes. Although a generation of Virginia lawyers devised imaginative means to evade this agreement, the state was never able to free itself entirely of debt. The reason speaks volumes about the nature of judicial power. While holders of Louisiana and North Carolina bonds had to sue the debtor states for their money, holders of Virginia coupons could tender them in payment of state taxes and then simply sit back. The state would be forced to sue them for the taxes it claimed. Under these circumstances federal courts did not need to rely on the political branches of government to enforce their orders but could protect creditors by a judgment that their taxes had in fact been paid. In these cases the Eleventh Amendment faded into the background.

While the Supreme Court was blinking at repudiation by most of the Southern states it was simultaneously insisting, at the peril of its logic, that cities and counties in the West could not shelter their own repudiations behind the Eleventh Amendment. The rationale was that municipal corporations did not share their parent state's immunity: the Amendment says states and in this case means it. As a result the South was relieved of its burden of debt, while the credit-hungry regions of the West were held to the highest standards of fiscal probity. The states of the Old Confederacy were permitted to slip back into a cash-crop economy seeking little foreign capital, while the credit ratings of borrowers in the nation's developing regions were simultaneously maintained.

After 1890, as the Supreme Court became more and more concerned about the threat that state governments in the hands of Populists and Progressives posed to corporate capitalism, it again reinterpreted the Eleventh Amendment. Once the politico-legal problems caused by the end of Reconstruction had been solved, the Court was free to reconstruct the Amendment. During the years from 1890 to 1908 it accepted two principal theories for avoiding the Eleventh Amendment: consent to suit and suits against state officers. Consent was premised on the theory that states could waive the Court's lack of jurisdiction. Despite the unqualified language of the Amendment—"the judicial power of the United States shall not be construed to extend . . ."—the Court read it to mean that it shall not be so construed *unless* the state consents. If the state waives its Eleventh Amendment immunity, then the judicial power does encompass the suit. In the same era the Court also revived the Marshallian tradition respecting suits against state officers. In a landmark case in 1908, it enjoined a state attorney general from enforcing an arguably unconstitutional law regulating railroad companies. Suits against officers were not necessarily suits against states. At the same time it heard an argument for yet another means of escaping the Eleventh Amendment: implied modification by congressional legislation pursuant to subsequent amendments—a theory it did not actually accept until 1976.

By the early twentieth century a complete set of contradictory precedents had accumulated. Although judicial policies and predilections continued to shape the law, they did so through ever-increasing technicalities and refinements. The distinction between municipal corporations and the parent state became blurred by the institutional complexity of modern state government. Eleventh Amendment immunity was extended to suits in admiralty, and foreign sovereigns were barred from suing states. Waiver was first enlarged by recognition of implied consent to suit and then contracted by stricter requirements for consent. Suits against officers generated a growing number of exceptions. A new understanding of sovereign immunity, involving a wholesale reinterpretation of legal history, was proposed. Finally a novel suggestion was made that state courts had a duty to hear suits barred in federal courts.

By the late twentieth century the law of the Eleventh Amendment exhibited a baffling complexity. In 1984, two law professors confessed to their students: "The case law of the eleventh amendment is replete with historical anomalies, internal inconsistencies, and senseless distinctions."[12] Marked by its history as were few other branches of constitutional law, interpretation of the Amendment has become an arcane specialty of lawyers and federal judges. Yet few legal doctrines affect modern American life as immediately as the rules governing the stretch of federal jurisdiction. Whether a state can be forced to repay its debt will depend on the meaning given the Eleventh Amendment—as will whether an individual can compel a state to desegregate its schools or reapportion its legislature. Whether, in short, a private citizen can make a state obey the federal Constitution will depend on the reach of "the judicial power of the United States."

II

Ratification of the Eleventh Amendment

On February 18, 1793, three years after its establishment, the United States Supreme Court decided its first important case, *Chisholm v. Georgia*.[1] Still sitting in Philadelphia, the nation's capital pending the move to Washington, the Court was composed of five justices: Chief Justice John Jay of New York and Associate Justices William Cushing of Massachusetts, James Wilson of Pennsylvania, John Blair of Virginia, and James Iredell of North Carolina. A sixth seat recently vacated by the resignation of Thomas Johnson of Maryland was not filled until two weeks later, when William Paterson of New Jersey was sworn in. The *Chisholm* case presented the justices with the momentous issue of the right of a private citizen to sue a state in federal court. Robert Farquhar, a citizen of South Carolina, had supplied war matériel to Georgia during the Revolution. Although the state had appropriated the necessary funds, the Georgia commissaries had failed to pay for the purchases. In the meantime Farquhar had died and the executor of his estate, Alexander Chisholm, also a citizen of South Carolina, attempted to collect the money from Georgia by suing for failure to pay as promised, an action technically known as *assumpsit* (that is, in Latin, "he undertook"). Rebuffed in the local federal court, then known as the circuit court, presided over by Justice Iredell,* Chisholm invoked the Supreme Court's original

* Circuit riding, that is, the duty of presiding over federal trial courts in the circuits assigned to them, was required of Supreme Court justices by

12

jurisdiction over "all cases . . . in which a state shall be party"[2] and commenced a new action against Georgia in the high court.

Chisholm's case was forcefully argued by Edmund Randolph, a onetime delegate to the Constitutional Convention. Although Randolph was then serving as Attorney General in President Washington's cabinet, the legal etiquette of the day did not prevent him from representing a private client as well. Randolph did not present the case as raising a federal question, that is, as one arising under the Constitution by virtue of a state law impairing the obligation of contracts. Instead he treated it simply as a controversy that could be litigated in federal court because it was between a state and a citizen of another state. Georgia for its part presented no defense. Although the governor and state attorney general had both been served with process, that is, notified of the claim against the state, neither put in an appearance because Georgia denied the right of the Supreme Court to call a state to account.

After giving the state a decent interval to repent its decision not to respond, the Court announced its decision. Following English practice, the justices delivered their opinions *seriatim,* that is, one at a time. Justice Iredell spoke first, although the lengthy opinion he delivered would now be termed a dissent. While recognizing that the Constitution extends judicial power to "controversies . . . between a state and citizens of another state,"[3] he observed that it does not specify what kinds of controversies are included. Turning to the Judiciary Act of 1789,[4] the federal law that established the courts of the United States, Iredell perceived no provision for actions against states in *assumpsit.* The Supreme Court was simply authorized to issue all writs "agreeable to the

---

the Judiciary Act of 1789. Temporarily abolished in 1801–02, the duty was not finally eliminated until 1891.

principles and usages of law."[5] Since in England no action in *assumpsit* would lie against the sovereign, Iredell reasoned that it was not permissible under American law to sue a state. In the absence of clear-cut congressional authorization he concluded that the Court lacked jurisdiction. Perhaps because he was familiar with the strength of feeling in Georgia, Iredell would have had the Court take the case only if Congress agreed that the judicial power extended so far. With the legislature on its side the judiciary might safely risk incurring the wrath of a state. In the last paragraph of his twenty-one-page opinion Iredell ventured a doubt about whether even Congress could permit a "compulsive suit against a State for the recovery of money,"[6] although he admitted that given his view of the case this expression of doubt was "extra-judicial."[7] So fearful was Iredell of the consequences of such a suit that he concluded his opinion with an appeal to the Almighty: "I pray to God, that if the Attorney General's doctrine, as to the law, be established by the judgment of this Court, all the good he predicts from it may take place, and none of the evils with which, I have the concern to say, it appears to me to be pregnant."[8]

The other justices took a broader view. Justice Blair held simply that states could be sued in federal court by citizens of other states. Justice Wilson thought the issue of no less magnitude than whether "the people of the *United States* form a NATION."[9] Answering his question in the affirmative, he concluded that state sovereign immunity was a thing of the past. Wilson buttressed this conclusion with a jurisprudential observation: a state, he said, is "an *artificial* person."[10] While it may acquire property, incur debts, and be bound by contracts, it remains a legal concept, not a living, breathing creature. "[W]e should never forget," he insisted, "that, in truth and nature, those, who think and speak, and act, are *men*."[11] God created man, Justice Wilson piously observed;

14

man created the state. Justice Cushing more mundanely concurred with Blair in holding that "controversies" in the constitutional sense included actions in *assumpsit*. He pointed out that under the Constitution, states were clearly liable to suit by other states of the Union or by foreign states, citizens, or subjects. If this decision was inconvenient, he added prophetically, the Constitution could be amended. Chief Justice Jay concurred in the judgment that the action could be maintained. All the justices except Iredell looked only to the Constitution. Finding that grant ample they saw no need to look at the statute book.

The opinion of the urbane Chief Justice, one of the American commissioners who had negotiated the Treaty of Paris with Great Britain ending the Revolutionary War, and thereafter Secretary of Foreign Affairs under the Articles of Confederation, deserves special attention. Jay noted that populous cities could be sued in federal court and asked: Why not states? Referring to Philadelphia, where the Court was then sitting, he said: "In this city there are forty odd thousand free citizens, all of whom may be collectively sued by any individual citizen. In the State of *Delaware,* there are fifty odd thousand free citizens, and what reason can be assigned why a free citizen who has demands against them should not prosecute them?"[12] Furthermore it was conceded on all hands that a state could sue another state's citizens in federal court. Georgia itself, the unwilling defendant in *Chisholm v. Georgia,* was at that very moment suing two citizens of South Carolina in federal court in *Georgia v. Brailsford.*[13] Turnabout, as the saying goes, is fair play. Jay reasoned that a national judiciary independent of the states was one of the principal benefits of the federal Constitution. Before the Constitution "[e]ach State was obliged to acquiesce in the measure of justice which another State might yield to her, or to her citizens; and that [was true] even in cases where

State considerations were not always favorable to the most exact measure."[14] Fairness and wisdom, he said, called for an end to that practice.

But uppermost in the mind of the diplomatist-turned-Chief Justice were reasons of state:

> the *United States* had, by taking a place among the nations of the earth, become amenable to the laws of nations; and it was their interest as well as their duty to provide, that those laws should be respected and obeyed; in their national character and capacity, the *United States* were responsible* to foreign nations for the conduct of each State, relative to the laws of nations, and the performance of treaties; and there the inexpediency of referring all such questions to State Courts, and particularly to the Courts of delinquent States became apparent.[15]

What Jay had in mind were provisions dealing with English merchants and American Tories in the Treaty of Paris, which he had helped negotiate. The Americans had agreed that "creditors on either side shall meet with no lawful impediment"[16] to the recovery of prewar debts and that the Continental Congress would "earnestly recommend"[17] that the states restore confiscated property. Congress had duly made the earnest recommendation[18] but most of the states had failed to respond. English creditors continued to find it difficult to collect their debts; in fact some states passed laws creating new impediments. So serious were American violations of the treaty that Jay, then Secretary of Foreign Affairs,

---

* It is worth noting that Chief Justice Jay, in keeping with then current usage, referred to the United States in the plural. As late as the drafting of the Thirteenth Amendment in 1865 the practice was continued: "Neither slavery nor involuntary servitude, except as a punishment for crime whereof the party shall have been duly convicted, shall exist within the United States, or any place subject to *their* jurisdiction." After the Civil War the practice began, which is now prevalent, to refer to the United States as a unit. To this day, however, foreigners still regularly use the plural.

had induced Congress to send a circular letter to the states censuring their breach of public faith and requesting repeal of the inconsistent laws.[19] What made the matter so serious, apart from the creditors' right to be paid, was the fact that the British refused to evacuate seven forts on the American side of the Canadian border until the United States fully complied. A year after *Chisholm,* President Washington named Chief Justice Jay envoy extraordinary to Great Britain to negotiate a new treaty.[20] The new accord, known to history as Jay's Treaty, provided for British evacuation of the frontier posts by 1796; the question of money owed to English creditors was referred to a joint commission.[21] When American dissatisfaction with the commission led to its breakup, high-level negotiations had to be resumed. In 1802, after further wrangling, the United States paid $2,664,000 to English claimants.[22]

Yet even if *raison d'état* formed the most persuasive part of his argument, the Chief Justice was concerned about a seeming inconsistency in his reasoning. The judicial power also extends, according to the Constitution, "to controversies to which the United States shall be a party."[23] Did Jay imply that the federal government, like a state, could be sued? His answer was a reluctant no: "[I]n all cases of actions against States or individual citizens, the National Courts are supported in all their legal and Constitutional proceedings and judgments, by the arm of the Executive power of the *United States;* but in cases of actions against the *United States,* there is no power which the Courts can call to their aid."[24] Without power to enforce a remedy, in other words, the Court could recognize no right.

The strong arm of the executive might well be needed if the Supreme Court's writ was to be made to run against a state. Feeling in Georgia ran high against the federal judiciary. In fact a bill passed by the state House of Representatives, although rejected by the state Senate, provided a Draconian punishment for anyone attempting to make Georgia pay:

> any Federal Marshal, or any other person or persons levying or attempting to levy on the territory of this State or any part thereof, or on the treasury or any other property belonging to the said State, or on the property of the Governor or Attorney-General, or any of the people thereof, under or by virtue of any execution or other compulsory process issuing out of, or by authority of the supreme court of the United States, or any other Court having jurisdiction under their authority, or which may at any period hereafter under the constitution of the said United States, as it now stands, be constituted; for, or in behalf of the before-mentioned Alexander Chisholm, Executor of Robert Farquhar, or for, or in behalf of, any other person or persons whatsoever, for the payment or recovery of any debt or pretended debt, or claim against the said state of Georgia; shall be, and he or they attempting to levy as aforesaid, are hereby declared to be guilty of felony, and shall suffer death, without the benefit of clergy,* by being hanged.[25]

The decision in *Chisholm* that the Supreme Court was open to suits against states was rendered in the aftermath of a vigorous national debate on fiscal policy. In 1790, Secretary of the Treasury Alexander Hamilton had presented the first Congress with a "Plan for supporting Public Credit."[26] He had proposed that the federal government pay its debt in full and assume as well most of the debts of the several states. After a bitter struggle his program was adopted, Jefferson's support being purchased with a promise to locate

---

* Benefit of clergy was originally the privilege of ordained churchmen to be tried for felonies only by church courts. For this privilege St. Thomas à Becket died a martyr's death in 1170. By the time of the American Revolution the principle meant, for felonies to which it still applied, that all persons whether in religious orders or not were exempt from capital punishment for the first offense. Felonies for which the exemption did not apply were expressly made "without benefit of clergy."

the nation's capital in the South. To many observers Hamilton's policy seemed to beggar the poor to pay the rich. Were the national debt still owing to the original lenders, the result would have been otherwise, but the securities had passed out of the hands of smallholders and into the pockets of the wealthy, often at ruinous discounts. Now the nation would be taxed to redeem the debt at par. The issue had been not merely a class issue, it had also been a sectional one. The debt had accumulated in the Northeast where a calculating mercantile ethos prevailed. South of the Mason-Dixon line an older, less exacting philosophy obtained. As distinguished modern scholars have observed: "The Virginia planter knew little of business and less of finance. A gentleman inherited his debts with his plantation, why then should debt trouble the United States? . . . To men such as these, in love with 'republican virtue' of the pristine Roman model and ignorant of not only public finance but of the simplest principles of accounting, Hamilton's system looked like jobbery and corruption. . . ."[27]

Chisholm was part of the high drama of public affairs. Four out of five justices made a clear statement of national unity and fidelity to treaties. In addition they staked out a large claim for the Supreme Court: the judicial power of the United States extends to disputes concerning the indebtedness of American states and that power is vested in the Court by the Constitution itself without the need for implementing legislation. As Justice Iredell had feared, the result was ignominy: the decision was speedily overturned. Since the majority had relied on the Constitution rather than on a statute, a constitutional amendment was required. As provided by the fundamental law itself, Congress may by a two-thirds majority propose amendments which become part of the Constitution when ratified by the legislatures of three-fourths of the states.[28] Because of delays to give Georgia a further chance to put in an appearance, final judgment in

Chisholm was not entered until February 14, 1794.[29] By March 4 of that year both houses of Congress had proposed the Eleventh Amendment. Not only were "citizens of another state" like Chisholm barred from suing a state, but foreigners also were ruled out of court: a state was immune from suit "by citizens or subjects* of any foreign state."

The Union included fifteen states at the time—the original thirteen plus Vermont and Kentucky—so approval by twelve was required. Jay's Treaty was simultaneously under consideration in Congress and popular hostility to the rights of British creditors and American Tories speeded ratification of the Amendment. By February 7, 1795, less than a year after its proposal, the requisite number of state legislatures had acted favorably.[30] But the presidential proclamation of ratification was delayed almost three years, until January 8, 1798,[31] the effective date usually given for the Amendment. Procrastination by the ratifying states in certifying their actions has been blamed for the delay.[32] There also seems to have been some confusion in the mind of Secretary of State Timothy Pickering about whether the Amendment had received the necessary approval before the admission of Tennessee on June 1, 1796.[33] But an attempt by the executive branch to secure a role in the process of constitutional amendment should not be ruled out. At the time it was still an open question whether the President's approval of the original congressional proposal was required. And it is unclear from the text of the Constitution which branch certifies that an amendment has lawfully been adopted.[34] The Washington

---

* A "citizen" is a member of a state owing allegiance to the government and entitled to the rights of membership. In monarchies a citizen is called a "subject." During the American and French Revolutions much emphasis had been placed on the distinction between citizens of a republic and subjects of a monarchy. Shortly after *Chisholm* was decided, the ambassador accredited to the United States from the French Republic, Edmond Charles Edouard Genet, ostentatiously insisted on being known as Citizen Genet. In France *citoyen et citoyenne* replaced *monsieur et madame*.

and Adams administrations, committed in all events to fiscal rectitude, were keeping nervous eyes on the international standing of the new Republic, which might be damaged by signs of inability to keep its house in order.

The validity of the Amendment was promptly challenged in *Hollingsworth v. Virginia,*[35] it was attacked on the ground that the congressional resolution originally proposing it had not been submitted to the President for his approval. The Veto Clause of the Constitution requires that "[e]very order, resolution, or vote to which the concurrence of the Senate and House of Representatives may be necessary . . . shall be presented to the President of the United States; and before the same shall take effect, shall be approved by him, or being disapproved by him, shall be repassed by two thirds of the Senate and House of Representatives. . . ."[36] While it is true that proposals to amend the Constitution require a two-thirds majority in the first place, it is also true that the President's participation in the process might be useful: he might, for example, raise objections that would change the votes of erstwhile supporters. More troubling perhaps to the justices was the fact that the first ten amendments comprising the Bill of Rights had been adopted without the President's formal approval. With one justice stating that the "negative of the President applies only to the ordinary cases of legislation,"[37] the Court without further elaboration held the Eleventh Amendment—and by implication the other amendments as well—"constitutionally adopted."[38] Indubitably part of the nation's organic law, the Eleventh Amendment exactly negatived the decision in *Chisholm* and precluded the use of that precedent by foreigners as well. The Court accepted its humiliation and kissed the rod, dismissing suits against states brought by individuals, including the still pending *Chisholm v. Georgia.* That Congress intended such a result may be inferred from the wording of the Amendment: it applies to suits "commenced or prosecuted" against a state. Although

21

Chisholm and suits like it had been commenced before the effective date of the Amendment, they could not be prosecuted thereafter. It is noteworthy that the Court did not dismiss a pending suit against a state in which a foreign sovereign had intervened.[39]

Ever since 1793 the question has been asked whether the decision in *Chisholm* was wrong, that is, whether the majority of the justices misunderstood the meaning of the Constitution. A century later the Supreme Court itself entered the historical debate. In 1890 in *Hans v. Louisiana*[40] a majority of the then sitting justices declared that the Founding Fathers had never intended to give the Court jurisdiction over suits against a state by whomsoever brought and that the decision in *Chisholm* had sent "such a shock of surprise throughout the country"[41] that the Eleventh Amendment had been promptly adopted to correct the error. The Amendment, said the Court, was nothing new; it merely restored the *status quo ante*. By virtue of this *ex cathedra* declaration, that view represents legal orthodoxy to this day. But it may be doubted whether justices who were no more than remote gleams in their grandfathers' eyes when the Constitution was drafted make better expositors of the original understanding than the first bench of justices. After all, Justices Blair and Wilson had both been delegates to the Constitutional Convention and had subsequently served in the ratifying conventions of their respective states. Justice Cushing had presided over his state's convention, and Chief Justice Jay, in addition to serving in New York's convention, had collaborated with Hamilton and Madison on *The Federalist,* the brilliant collection of papers intended to persuade New Yorkers to ratify the Constitution. Even Justice Iredell who had led the fight for the Constitution in the North Carolina ratifying convention made little of his doubts about the original understanding and rested his dissent on the Judiciary Act instead.

Nothing, it appears, had been said in public at the Constitutional Convention concerning the meaning of the key clause: "controversies . . . between a state and citizens of another state."[42] But evidence directly bearing on the original understanding of the Framers may be found in the argument on behalf of the plaintiff in *Chisholm* by Edmund Randolph and in the opinion in that case by Justice Wilson. Randolph and Wilson were two of the five members of the Committee of Detail that drafted the clause in 1787. Although Randolph's role as an advocate six years later lessens the value of his evidence, there is no reason to doubt Wilson's honest effort to construe the words correctly. After all, the justice had sworn a solemn oath to support the Constitution[43] and in 1787, at the Pennsylvania ratifying convention, he had expressed the view later propounded from the bench: "When a citizen has a controversy with another state, there ought to be a tribunal where both parties may stand on a just and equal footing."[44] Randolph too had argued the same point at the Virginia ratifying convention, explicitly recognizing the economic consequences: "I admire that part which forces Virginia to pay her debts."[45] What Randolph later argued in *Chisholm* seems to have expressed his own view as well as that of his client.

The decision, if such there was, to permit suits against states would have been in keeping with Americans' experience as English colonists. It is a commonplace that the idea of a written constitution embodying the fundamental principles of government was suggested by the charters that gave legal existence to the colonies. Colonial governments that were either municipal corporations or proprietorships were as subject to suit as were other corporations or individuals.[46] To assume that American states were expected to be immune when colonial governments were not is to forget that the War of Independence had been fought, among other things, to make government more accountable to the citizenry. Even after independence the states individually were never recognized as sovereign.[47] Sovereignty passed, according to the Declaration of Independence, directly from the British crown to the United States of America.

The strongest evidence that the decision in *Chisholm* was indeed wrong, that is, that the Court flouted the original understanding, was a statement to the Virginia ratifying convention by James Madison, a leader at the earlier Constitutional Convention. To an opponent of ratification who criticized the power apparently conferred on the Supreme Court Madison replied: "Its jurisdiction in controversies between a state and citizens of another state is much objected to, and perhaps without reason. It is not in the power of individuals to call any state into court. The only operation it can have, is that, if a state should wish to bring a suit against a citizen, it must be brought before the federal court."[48] If that was Madison's view in 1788, it had not been his view a year earlier, on the eve of the Constitutional Convention. Then he had written to George Washington that "an appeal should lie to some national tribunals in *all cases* to which foreigners or inhabitants of other States may be parties"; admiralty jurisdiction, he thought, should be "entirely within the purview of the national Government."[49]

Another name to conjure with among the spokesmen who attributed a meaning to the Constitution contrary to the one adopted in *Chisholm* is that of John Marshall. Supporting Madison, Marshall argued: "It is not rational to suppose that the sovereign power should be dragged before a court. The intent is, to enable states to recover claims of individuals residing in other states. I contend this construction is warranted by the words. But, say they, there will be partiality in it if a state cannot be defendant—if an individual cannot proceed to obtain judgment against a state, though he may be sued by a state. It is necessary to be so, and cannot be avoided. I see a difficulty in making a state defendant, which does not prevent its being plaintiff."[50] Unlike Madison, Marshall had not been present at the Constitutional Convention but his views deserve attention because as Chief Justice of the United States from 1801 to 1835 he became the chief expounder of the Constitution. It will appear, however, that Marshall's protestations about state dignity were not repeated from the bench.

Although not part of the record of any ratifying convention, Alexander Hamilton's views on federal jurisdiction have also been cited by critics of *Chisholm*. In his contribution to *The Federalist*, on which he collaborated with Jay and Madison, Hamilton—ever the financier—declared:

> It has been suggested that an assignment of the public securities of one State to the citizens of another, would enable them to prosecute that State in the federal courts for the amount of those securities; a suggestion which the following considerations prove to be without foundation.
>
> It is inherent in the nature of sovereignty not to be amenable to the suit of an individual *without its consent*. This is the general sense, and the general practice of mankind; and the exemption, as one of the attributes of sovereignty, is now enjoyed by the government of every State in the Union. Unless, therefore, there is a surrender of this immunity in the plan of the convention, it will remain with the States, and the danger intimated must be merely ideal. . . . [T]here is no color to pretend that the State governments would, by the adoption of that plan, be divested of the privilege of paying their own debts in their own way, free from every constraint but that which flows from the obligations of good faith. The contracts between a nation and individuals are only binding on the conscience of the sovereign, and have no pretensions to a compulsive force. They confer no right of action, independent of the sovereign will.[51]

Like Chief Justice Jay in his speculations concerning the suability of the United States, Hamilton feared that judgments would be unenforceable.

> To what purpose would it be to authorize suits against States for the debts they owe? How could recoveries be enforced? It is evident, it could not be done without waging war against the contracting State; and to ascribe to the federal courts, by mere implication, and in destruction of a preexisting right of the State governments, a power which would involve such a consequence, would be altogether forced and unwarrantable.[52]

Of course no one ever supposed Hamilton in favor of repudiation; as Secretary of the Treasury he later advocated and carried through the payment in full of national and most state debts.

The first Congress had the opportunity to clarify the extent of judicial power. Several states led by Virginia had proposed amendments at the time they ratified the Constitution, including a proposal to prohibit federal courts from hearing suits against states.[53] At the very least this indicated doubt about the reach of judicial power in the unamended Constitution. By implication the Virginians accepted Randolph's reading instead of Madison's and Marshall's. Winnowing the proposed amendments Congress selected a dozen, of which ten became in short order the Bill of Rights. But the suggested limitation on federal jurisdiction was not among them. At the same time Congress was debating the Judiciary Act, which incidentally had been drafted by Oliver Ellsworth, who had earlier served with Randolph and Wilson on the Constitutional Convention's Committee of Detail. With respect to suits against states, Congress did not significantly depart from the language of the Constitution: "[T]he Supreme Court shall have exclusive jurisdiction of all controversies of a civil nature, where a state is a party, except between a state and its citizens; and except also between a state and citizens of other states, or aliens, in which latter case it shall have original but not exclusive* jurisdiction."[54]

* The distinction between "exclusive" and "not exclusive" jurisdiction is

The language of the statute, notwithstanding Justice Iredell's labored reading of it in *Chisholm,* comports most naturally with the majority's interpretation of the Constitution.

Critics of *Chisholm* sometimes point to the wording of the Eleventh Amendment for evidence that it was meant to be merely declaratory of the original understanding. Unlike the Constitution itself which enumerates cases and controversies to which the judicial power of the United States "shall extend,"[55] the Amendment lists suits to which it "shall not *be construed to* extend." To suggest that this means the Constitution is not changed, only the particular construction put on it by the judges, is not very persuasive. More likely it means nothing special at all. The Fourteenth Amendment declares among other things that Southern war debts and slaveowners' claims for compensation "shall be *held* illegal and void,"[56] rather than simply that they shall *be* illegal and void. No one has ever attached any significance to this difference.

Critics of *Chisholm* have also stressed the celerity with which the states ratified the Eleventh Amendment and the across-the-board political support it received. Speedy adoption is not significant, however; action by twelve seaboard states need not be time-consuming. It is notorious that the near impossibility of amending the Constitution today is caused by the difficulty of aligning three-fourths of a fifty-state Union. State legislatures were less busy in the early days of the Republic and few items on their agenda were more important than state debts. Concerning the widespread political support for the Amendment, the key question involves the attitude of the Federalist Party, otherwise the most zealous defender of the supremacy of federal law and treaties as well

---

that in the former case the controversies may be adjudged only in the designated court, while in the latter case they may be decided there or in another court of competent jurisdiction. When the Supreme Court's jurisdiction is not original it is appellate.

as of fiscal probity. Even Federalist strongholds like Massachusetts ratified the Amendment in short order. Since the subsequent history of the party makes clear that it had not abandoned its most cherished policies, the Federalist stand on the Amendment was either aberrational or it sprang from a conviction of the Amendment's limited effect. As one modern scholar has shrewdly observed,[57] even before the ratification of the Eleventh Amendment an alternative to suing a state was already in train: whether or not a state could be impleaded, state interests could certainly be adjudged in suits between private parties.[58]

The search for the original understanding on state sovereign immunity bears this much resemblance to the quest for the Holy Grail: there is enough to be found so that the faithful of whatever persuasion can find their heart's desire. And, of course, the object of the search may prove equally illusory. Of the fifty-five men who attended the Constitutional Convention, not one seems to have said a word on the subject outside the meeting of the relevant committee. A few spoke up later on, in the course of ratification debates and in the Chisholm case. Of the hundreds of delegates to state ratifying conventions only a handful addressed the issue, most often to urge it unsuccessfully as a reason for refusing to ratify the Constitution. As a matter of fact most of the delegates seem to have given the matter no thought at all. What was true of the delegates was even truer of the voters who elected them. The understanding of the electorate let alone of the populace as a whole upon a topic so esoteric was undoubtedly nil. To attribute one view or another to them on the basis of the scattered and inconsistent remarks of their leaders is to engage in the purest legal fiction.

The safest course would seem to be to accept the plain meaning of the language used. As Blackstone observed earlier: "Words are generally to be understood in their usual and most known signification. . . ."[59] Or as the Supreme Court

later put it: "[I]f, in any case, the plain meaning of a provision, not contradicted by any other provision in the same
instrument, is to be disregarded, because we believe the
framers of that instrument could not intend what they say,
it must be one in which the absurdity and injustice of apply-
ing the provision to the case, would be so monstrous, that
all mankind would, without hesitation, unite in rejecting the
application."[60] This, of course, is the usual rule of interpretation unless it can be shown that words were used in a special sense and that no one was thereby misled. The Constitution refers to "controversies . . . between a state and
citizens of another state."[61] The argument that *Chisholm* was
wrong comes down to the assertion that these words always
meant and were intended to mean that states can sue citizens
of another state but not be sued by them. As Justice Blair
sensibly observed in *Chisholm,* a "dispute between A and B
is surely a dispute between B and A."[62] If that is the case
then *Chisholm* was right. It follows that the Eleventh Amendment in fact amended, that is, altered, the Constitution. Although at first blush this might not seem such a momentous
conclusion, its correctness would imply the error of later
Supreme Court decisions. Beginning in 1890, a century after
the Chisholm case, the Court officially adopted the view that
the Amendment, rather than amending the Constitution,
merely restated its original meaning. On that premise important developments of Eleventh Amendment law were to be
based. In the meantime, however, the interpretation of the
Amendment was left to the Supreme Court under Chief Justice John Marshall, the Virginian who had spoken up for
state dignity.

III

Early Interpretation

In the November 1800 election, the Federalist Party was routed from national office. President John Adams failed to win re-election and the Federalists lost control of Congress. In early 1801, with the clock ticking away on the Adams Administration,* the defeated President faced the difficult problem of filling the Supreme Court's vacant chief justiceship. Oliver Ellsworth, Chief Justice since 1796, had resigned for reasons of health in 1799. The President had first turned to John Jay, the former Chief Justice who had left the Court to serve as governor of New York. But Jay refused to be the once and future Chief Justice. "I left the bench," he wrote Adams, "perfectly convinced that under a system so defective it would not obtain the energy, weight, and dignity which are essential to its affording due support to the national government, nor acquire the public confidence and respect which, as the last resort of the justice of the nation, it should possess."[1] The reaction to *Chisholm* had doubtless contributed to Jay's disillusion.

At last Adams settled on his Secretary of State, John Marshall, a kinsman but political enemy of President-elect Thomas Jefferson. The forty-five-year-old Marshall was to dominate the Court until his death thirty-four years later.

* For most of American history, victors in the November national elections did not take office until the following March 4. The Twentieth Amendment, ratified in 1933, abolished the so-called lame-duck Congress, providing that congressional terms expire on January 3, and established January 20 as the date of the presidential inauguration.

30

Of the thousand decisions handed down during his tenure, the Chief Justice personally penned more than half. Under his leadership the justices abandoned the English practice of *seriatim* opinions, seen in *Chisholm,* and established the American tradition of "the opinion of the Court." Although his formal legal training was limited to a six-week lecture course at the College of William and Mary, Marshall proved himself a masterful jurist, able to exploit every latent judicial power, no matter how "defective" the system.

The Federalist Party, to which Marshall belonged, favored a strong central government, encouragement of industry, protection of property, and a well-ordered society. Once the Federalists had lost control of the legislative and executive branches of the national government, the judicial branch, staffed by Federalist appointees of Washington and Adams, was the party's last bastion. Soon after taking office, Chief Justice Marshall defended that stronghold and in the process greatly strengthened it. In 1803 in *Marbury v. Madison*[2] the Supreme Court made good its claim to review the constitutionality of federal legislation. While it remained for the Court in later years of Marshall's chief justiceship to defend similar claims to review state legislation[3] and the decisions of state courts,[4] *Marbury* stands as the most significant decision of the Marshall years; indeed it is hardly an overstatement to describe it as the most significant Supreme Court decision of all time.

While the power to review state actions is unmistakably important, there is nothing surprising about the highest federal court reviewing the acts of the Union's constituent members, particularly in light of the clause in the federal Constitution declaring the Constitution, laws, and treaties of the United States the "supreme law of the land."[5] But making good the Court's claim to review the acts of other branches of the federal government is something far different. The Constitution did not expressly provide for such review, neither did any statute. By the time of the American Revolution, English common law despite some earlier equivocal indications[6] was clearly settled against it.[7] Although a few precedents for judicial review of other branches existed in scattered American states,[8] the power was by no means conceded. And power, as Chief Justice Jay noted ruefully in *Chisholm,* is of the essence in jurisdiction.

Viewed in historical context *Marbury* is even more remarkable. Behind the litigation lay a political struggle involving prepotent powers. In the last days of the Adams Administration—later even than the appointment of Chief Justice Marshall—the President made a host of lesser judicial appointments,[9] the "midnight judges" of popular history. Least among his appointees were certain justices of the peace for the District of Columbia.[10] Although the commissions were signed and sealed, several were never actually delivered, among them those naming William Marbury and three others. Responsibility for the slip-up lay with John Marshall himself, who had still been acting as Secretary of State at the time.

In the famous case the would-be JPs asked the Supreme Court to compel delivery of their commissions. The plaintiffs' theory was simple: the Judiciary Act of 1789 conferred on the Court "power to issue . . . writs of mandamus,* in cases warranted by the principles and usages of law, to any . . . persons holding office, under the authority of the United States."[11] In an original action the plaintiffs sought a writ of mandamus against James Madison, Secretary of State in President Jefferson's new administration, requiring him to produce the commissions. The fact was, however, that the immensely popular President, outraged by Adams's attempt to pack the judiciary, was determined that the exec-

---

* The writ of mandamus, from the Latin word meaning "we command," was a common-law writ for compelling the performance of a public duty required by law.

utive branch would never yield. And the President's determination was matched by that of his supporters in Congress,
whose numbers increased at the 1802 midterm election. The
forces opposed to Marbury were resolute and resourceful, as
evidenced by the statute doing away with the 1802 term of
the Supreme Court[12] to delay the hearing of Marbury's case
and by the initiation of impeachment proceedings against
a federal district judge[13] to demonstrate the Jeffersonians'
power. It was widely believed—not least by John Marshall
himself—that the Chief Justice would be impeached and
removed from office if he supported the issuance of the
writ.[14] To no one's surprise, Marbury lost; indeed the commissions remain unaccounted for to this day. But to everyone's surprise the Supreme Court won its most stunning
victory.

The case had seemed to confront the justices with a cruel
choice. If they ordered Madison to deliver the commissions
and he refused, there would be no way to enforce the order.
Enforcement was the responsibility of the executive branch.
Alternatively, if they declined to issue the mandamus they
would be viewed as kowtowing to the all-powerful President.
Instead Chief Justice Marshall refused to issue the writ, but
for a reason that amounted to a claim of high prerogative—
a claim, furthermore, with which President Jefferson could
not interfere. The Court held the clause of the Judiciary Act
that Marbury relied on to be in conflict with the Constitution. The Act could be read to authorize original actions
seeking such a writ, but the Constitution expressly limits the
Court's original jurisdiction to "cases affecting ambassadors,
other public ministers and consuls, and those in which a state
shall be party"[15]; in all other cases the Court's jurisdiction is
appellate. Although the Judiciary Act could have been given
a more restrictive reading, Marshall deliberately reached out
for the broadest issue in order to make his point. Exceeding
constitutional limits, acts of Congress, even those conferring

additional powers on other branches of government, are unenforceable and void. While the Court established its power
to review congressional legislation, it did so in a context of
self-denial. Depriving itself of an apparent power, the power
of issuing writs of mandamus in original actions, it secured
for itself a far greater power, the power of judicial review.
Because of the realities of the judicial system, the decision
was not subject to revision by the politicians. What the Court
refused to do, neither President nor Congress could make
it do.

The power of judicial review put the federal judges and,
hence, for the time being, the Federalists in the game of
national power politics. From this perspective the Eleventh
Amendment, by limiting the jurisdiction of the national
courts, inhibited judicial power and thereby endangered the
dearest tenets of the Federalist faith. If the Court had no
jurisdiction over suits against states, it had no jurisdiction in
such cases to decide even questions of constitutionality. On
the bench Marshall forgot his emollient reassurances to the
Virginia ratifying convention; instead the Federalist Chief
Justice led the Supreme Court to defend—or, as it seemed
to Jefferson and the Antifederalists, to expand—its jurisdiction. In no important constitutional case did the Marshall
Court ever find itself barred by the Eleventh Amendment.

In 1809 in *United States v. Peters*[16] the opinion of the
Court, authored by the Chief Justice, declared that a state
cannot assert the Eleventh Amendment on behalf of an individual merely because it claims an interest in the dispute.
Like *Chisholm, Peters* involved a controversy stemming from
Revolutionary War days. In 1778, some sailors from the
American merchant marine who had been forced to work
on a British ship mutinied and seized the ship. Before they
could sail it to an American port, a Pennsylvania State vessel
overtook them and claimed the ship as a prize of war. Out
of the proceeds of the sale, state officers paid the seamen only

one-fourth and deposited the balance with Pennsylvania's treasurer, the celebrated scientist David Rittenhouse. Like many fiscal officers in the days before bureaucratic government, Rittenhouse held state funds in his own account. Although his term as treasurer expired in 1789 and he went on to serve as director of the U.S. mint, Rittenhouse never turned over the money to his successor and the funds were still in his estate at his death in 1796. In 1801, the Pennsylvania legislature directed the incumbent treasurer to secure the money from Rittenhouse's heirs, but at the same time Gideon Olmstead, one of the sailors, sued the heirs in federal court. In 1803, Federal Judge Richard Peters ruled in favor of Olmstead and entered judgment on his behalf. Pennsylvania refused, however, to accept the decision and threatened forcibly to resist any attempt to collect from the Rittenhouse heirs.

In 1808, Olmstead petitioned the Supreme Court for a writ of mandamus ordering Judge Peters to execute his earlier judgment, and a year later the Court granted the writ despite the state's claim to the money. This problem of the relationship between the state and a controversy, which emerged even while the Eleventh Amendment was under consideration, was to recur repeatedly as the Court interpreted the Amendment. The state is interested in some degree in every adjudication of rights respecting its citizens; when title to property is involved, the state's interest in future taxes, if nothing else, is implicated. When the defendant happens to be a state officer claiming to act under state law, the state's interest is immediate: orders to act or refrain from acting will implicate the state and may affect the balance in the state treasury. In *Peters* the Court held that even a significant state interest is not sufficient to trigger the Amendment's protection.

Decisions of the Supreme Court do not execute themselves, however, and Pennsylvania, like Georgia before it, was recalcitrant. The governor deployed the state militia around the Rittenhouse home, causing the neighbors to describe it as "Fort Rittenhouse." In response the federal marshal organized a posse composed of soldiers of the U.S. Army. The standoff ended when Pennsylvania backed down. For resisting the federal marshal, however, General Michael Bright of the state militia was tried and convicted in federal circuit court (although later pardoned by the President). At trial the Eleventh Amendment was again offered as a reason to deny federal jurisdiction; again it was rejected. But in *United States v. Bright*[17] a different reason was given by Justice Bushrod Washington of the United States Supreme Court on circuit. The justice, a nephew of President Washington, held that federal judicial power in this case, which derived from a dispute on the high seas, rested on admiralty law, the branch of law concerned with maritime controversies. The Eleventh Amendment applied, as it said, to "any suit in law or equity,"* not to the well-recognized category of cases of admiralty. This conclusion makes sense in light of the Founding Fathers' careful distinction in the Constitution between "cases in law and equity," on the one hand, and "cases of admiralty and maritime jurisdiction," on the other.[18] Interpreting the Seventh Amendment's guarantee of trial by jury in "suits at common law," the Court later held that cases in admiralty were not included.[19]

As a practical matter Justice Washington also pointed out

* "Equity" refers to the rules and principles developed since the Middle Ages by the English Chancellors in the Court of Chancery. In contrast "law" refers to the rules and principles developed by the common-law courts: King's (or Queen's) Bench, Common Pleas, and Exchequer. A punctilious lawyer might have objected to the use of the word "suit" to refer to proceedings at law as well as in equity. "Action at law" and "suit in equity" would have been more in keeping with tradition. The draftsman of the 1871 Ku Klux Klan Act, for example, was more careful: every person who under color of state law deprives anyone of civil rights "shall be liable to the party injured in an action at law, suit in equity, or other proper proceeding for redress."

that in the usual admiralty case, unlike the one before him, enforcement would present no problem. The object in dispute, a ship for example, would generally be in the possession of the court; such a proceeding is said to be *in rem,* that is, "against a thing," as opposed to *in personam,* "against a person." "In such a case," he observed, "the court need not depend upon the good will of a state claiming an interest in the thing to enable it to execute its decree."[20] Although the Supreme Court did not pass on the applicability of the Eleventh Amendment in admiralty until more than a century later, it was assumed by bench and bar in the meantime that *Bright* was correctly reasoned.[21] In fact in 1921 the Court decided that it was not.[22] *

In 1821 in *Cohens v. Virginia*[23] the Marshall Court faced another argument based on the Eleventh Amendment: that it lacked jurisdiction to review state criminal convictions because the writ of error by which such convictions were at the time reviewed was itself a "suit in law . . . commenced or prosecuted against one of the United States." Under this procedure the roles of the parties were nominally reversed, the state appearing as defendant and the erstwhile defendant appearing as plaintiff. The plaintiffs in this particular writ of error were citizens of the defendant state, so the Amendment did not apply according to its terms. The state's argument was that because the Amendment denied to foreigners and citizens of other states the right to prosecute suits against a state, it implied that federal courts did not have jurisdiction over suits against a state brought by its own citizens; otherwise the anomaly would result that a state could be sued in federal court by its own citizens but not by foreigners or citizens of other states. In an opinion written by the Chief Justice, the Court rejected this argument on the ground that process by writ of error was not a "suit . . . against one of

---

* The case in question, *Ex parte New York,* is discussed in Chapter IX.

the United States" within the meaning of the Amendment. The state had prosecuted its citizens; they in turn were merely carrying the matter to a higher court. But the Chief Justice also made plain that even if it had been a new suit, Virginia would not be able to rely on the Amendment in this case because it was not commenced or prosecuted "by citizens of another state."[24]

In the course of his opinion Marshall addressed several points concerning the Eleventh Amendment. The origin of the Amendment he matter-of-factly attributed to worries about money:

> It is a part of our history, that, at the adoption of the constitution, all the States were greatly indebted; and the apprehension that these debts might be prosecuted in the federal Courts, formed a very serious objection to that instrument. Suits were instituted; and the Court maintained its jurisdiction. The alarm was general; and, to quiet the apprehensions that were so extensively entertained, this amendment was proposed in Congress, and adopted by the State legislatures. That its motive was not to maintain the sovereignty of a State from the degradation supposed to attend a compulsory appearance before the tribunal of the nation, may be inferred from the terms of the amendment. It does not comprehend controversies between two or more States, or between a State and a foreign State. The jurisdiction of the Court still extends to these cases: and in these a State may still be sued. We must ascribe the amendment, then, to some other cause than the dignity of a State. There is no difficulty in finding this cause. Those who were inhibited from commencing a suit against a State, or from prosecuting one which might be commenced before the adoption of the amendment, were persons who might probably be its creditors. There was not much reason to fear that foreign or sister States would be creditors to any considerable amount, and there was reason to retain the jurisdiction of the Court in those cases, because it might be essential to the preserva-

tion of peace. The amendment, therefore, extended to suits commenced or prosecuted by individuals, but not to those brought by States.[25]

Concerning its effect Marshall pointed to an important distinction. The Constitution extends the judicial power of the United States to "all cases, in law and equity, arising under this Constitution, the laws of the United States, and treaties made, or which shall be made, under their authority"[26] as well as to "controversies . . . between a state and citizens of another state . . . and between a state . . . and foreign . . . citizens or subjects."[27] The former grant of jurisdiction depends on the nature of the dispute; it is known in legal shorthand as "federal question jurisdiction." The latter depends on the parties involved and is commonly called "diversity jurisdiction" because to qualify for it the parties must be of different, or diverse, citizenship. *Chisholm* itself, it may be recalled, had been treated as a diversity case, not as a federal question case. Marshall suggested that the Eleventh Amendment applied only to diversity cases. Anticipating the argument that states were entitled to sovereign immunity in federal question cases as well, he replied that sovereigns may consent to be sued and that the adoption of the federal Constitution amounted to such consent with respect to cases arising under the Constitution, laws, and treaties of the United States. However plausible the distinction pointed out by Marshall, his successors on the Court in the late nineteenth century were to reject it. Consent to suit, however, was to have a brighter future.

Also in *Cohens* Marshall recognized a potential difference between cases apparently similar. Using as an example an unconstitutional state tax on exports, Marshall asked: "Were a State to lay a duty on exports, to collect the money and place it in her treasury, could the citizen who paid it . . . maintain a suit in this Court against such State, to recover back the money?* Perhaps not. . . . Suppose a citizen to refuse to pay this export duty, and a suit to be instituted for the purpose of compelling him to pay it. He pleads the constitution of the United States in bar of the action, notwithstanding which the [trial] Court gives judgment against him. This would be a case arising under the constitution. . . ."[28] The economics are the same either way, of course, but the judicial power may get a purchase in the latter case that it lacks in the former. The difference would in fact separate the sheep from the goats half a century later.

Finally, in 1824, Marshall led the Court to confine the Amendment more narrowly than ever before. In *Osborn v. The Bank of the United States*[29] an officer of the state of Ohio had violated the federal Constitution by collecting an illegal tax from a branch of the national bank. Rejecting the argument that the officer shared the state's immunity from suit, the Chief Justice mapped a dual route around the Eleventh Amendment. The key to avoiding its effect was to sue not the state, as Chisholm had done, but to sue an officer of the state. Then the Court could exercise its judicial power either on the simple theory that "in all cases where jurisdiction depends on the party, it is the party named in the record,"[30] or on the grander theory that since a state cannot validly authorize an act contrary to the Constitution of the United States, any unconstitutional act must perforce be the act of some individual.

What Marshall did in *Osborn* was to reenact in America one phase of English constitutional history. From the simple fact of practical politics that the king could not be made to answer in his own courts, the English had derived the gran-

---

* Under the Constitution states are in general prohibited from taxing exports. If "absolutely necessary" for enforcing its inspection laws, however, a state may with the consent of Congress impose a duty on exports but in such cases the proceeds must be paid into the U.S. Treasury, not the state treasury. See U.S. Constitution, Article I, section 10, clause 2.

diloquent maxim: "The king can do no wrong"[31]—or, dressed up in Latin, *"Rex non potest peccare."*[32] Far from forming a basis for absolutism, however, this maxim actually became a cornerstone of constitutional monarchy. If the king cannot do wrong, but wrong has in fact been done, then someone other than the king has done it. An errant officer could not assert the sovereign's immunity. Marshall simply put this thinking to work in *Osborn* to minimize the extent to which the Eleventh Amendment insulates state officers from suit.

Only once during Marshall's long tenure did the justices accept a claim of immunity based on the Eleventh Amendment. In *Governor of Georgia v. Madrazo*[33] they modified the first branch of the doctrine in *Osborn:* "where the chief magistrate of a state is sued, not by his name, but by his style of office, and the claim made upon him is entirely in his official character, we think the state itself may be considered as a party on the record."[34] Insofar as this meant that the plaintiff must take care to sue an officer by name and not by title it added only a small technicality to the party-of-record rule. But *Madrazo* contained as well a suggestion of a real-party rule. Not only must the plaintiff sue an officer by name but he must also make a demand on him personally and not officially. Perhaps this is no more than a reference to the second branch in *Osborn:* that a state officer acting pursuant to a constitutional state statute may assert the state's immunity. The effect of such a rule is unobjectionable: if the Court heard such a case, it would have to recognize the defense that the officer was acting under a valid state law. Relying on the Eleventh Amendment, the Court merely turned the issue into a jurisdictional one.

For half a century the rule on the Eleventh Amendment laid down in *Osborn* held firm. Nor is it surprising that it did. Although Marshall's successor as Chief Justice, Roger B. Taney, was a Jacksonian, a believer in states' rights, and a defender of slavery, the judicial power of the United States

41

was not diminished during his twenty-eight years on the bench. The Amendment was cited in only five cases[35] and in none did the Court find itself ousted of jurisdiction. *Madrazo* was referred to in a majority opinion only once and then not relied on[36]; otherwise it came up in two dissents.[37] On the rare occasions that *Chisholm* was mentioned, the justices gave their opinions that it had been correctly decided and that the Eleventh Amendment had altered the Constitution, not merely restated the original understanding.[38] Taney, like Marshall but for different reasons, was a judicial nationalist. The Federalist Marshall believed in national supremacy and the protection of property; if the American states could be bound together in an economic union, he thought, the political branches could be relied upon to compromise the divisive issues, even the issue of slavery. The Jacksonian Taney, on the other hand, was convinced that the preservation of the Union depended upon the protection of slavery; it was the duty of the judicial branch, he believed, to teach the nation that slavery was not a subject for political compromise. Although this faith led Taney to endorse the Court's most damaging decision, the infamous *Dred Scott Case,*[39] he was certainly not inspired by any desire to diminish the judicial power of the United States.

Shortly after Chief Justice Taney was sworn in, the nation was wrenched by the financial Panic of 1837, the crisis that made "a mere United States' security" a byword for worthlessness with Charles Dickens's readership.[40] English investors were particularly hard hit and literary men gave voice to their outrage. The Reverend Sydney Smith, witty canon of St. Paul's, penned a "Humble Petition to the House of Congress at Washington,"[41] while the poet laureate, William Wordsworth, composed a sonnet on the subject. Addressing the Pennsylvanians whose state was among the first to default, Wordsworth recalled the Quaker virtues of the state's

founder and denounced "state-dishonour black as ever came /
To upper air from Mammon's loathsome den."[42] Later in a
prose note on another sonnet he acknowledged the Keystone
State's endeavors to resume payment and commended other
states to "follow the example now set them by Philadelphia
and redeem their credit with the world."[43] These lines incidentally seem to be the last composed for publication by the
great Romantic.

Unlike the burst of repudiation that followed Reconstruction and generated a series of cases involving the Eleventh
Amendment, this fiscal crisis fathered no Supreme Court
precedents. But the failure to make a federal case out of
default did not indicate that the lenders were indifferent to
their legal rights. The problem was how to invoke the judicial
power of the United States on their behalf. Although the
Judiciary Act of 1789 conferred diversity jurisdiction on the
lower federal courts,[44] the Eleventh Amendment barred suits
against states "by citizens of another state, or by citizens
or subjects of any foreign state." Federal questions could
be raised in the Supreme Court, but that tribunal could be
reached only by bringing one of the few original actions[45] or
by appealing from a decision of the highest state court.[46] It
was not yet established that the Supreme Court could review
a state court's refusal to decide for lack of jurisdiction.[47]

For help in their dilemma the creditors sought the best
advice money could buy. In 1839, Baring Brothers, the London investment bankers, consulted Daniel Webster, then
senator from Massachusetts, about whether defaulting states
could be sued on their bonds. The great lawyer's reply is
far from clear. While observing that states could not be sued,
any more than the United States or the English Crown,
Webster went on to say nonetheless that they "cannot rid
themselves of their obligations otherwise than by the honest
payment of the debt."[48] An explanation for this *non sequitur*
is that Webster seems to have been thinking in the first place

about suit in state courts. This could be prevented by the state's assertion of sovereign immunity. His second thought, however, seems to have concentrated on the creditors' rights under the federal Constitution. Apposite to this idea Webster noted that states "can pass no law impairing the obligation of their own contracts."[49] This reading of the Contracts Clause Webster himself had helped to establish twenty years earlier in the *Dartmouth College Case*[50] in which he had represented his alma mater in its struggle against state interference with its charter. As a practical matter, however, the lawyer-politician thought suability largely irrelevant: "The solemn obligation of a government, arising on its own acknowledged bond, would not be enhanced by a judgment rendered on such bond. If it either could not, or would not, make provision for paying the bond, it is not probable that it could or would make provision for satisfying the judgment."[51]

But moneylenders never like to take no for an answer. A more promising reply to their query came from another New Englander, Benjamin R. Curtis. A prominent Massachusetts lawyer, Curtis was later to serve as a Supreme Court justice, a position he resigned because of violent disagreement with the Dred Scott decision.[52] In 1844, at the behest of Baring Brothers, Curtis published an anonymous article on state debts in the *North American Review*,[53] the leading periodical of the day. At the time of writing, American states were in arrears on debts worth millions of dollars, the largest arrearages being owed by Mississippi, which was also the most recalcitrant to repayment. The litigation strategy revealed by Curtis took careful account of the Eleventh Amendment. Conceding that the Amendment bars federal courts from hearing suits commenced by "citizens or subjects of any foreign state," Curtis echoed the observation of John Marshall and others that no such bar is stated to apply to foreign states themselves. The Constitution extends judicial power "to controversies . . . between a state . . . and foreign states . . . ,"[54] and the Eleventh Amendment leaves this grant untouched. Curtis's idea was to assign bonds to a foreign state which could then invoke the Supreme Court's original jurisdiction over "cases . . . in which a state shall be party."[55] For reasons now obscure this idea was not acted upon at the time. But unpaid creditors have long memories, and ninety years later the Principality of Monaco attempted to sue Mississippi in the Supreme Court on some bonds that had been belatedly given to it. For reasons that will be examined in due course* the Court pointed to the Eleventh Amendment and sovereign immunity and found itself without jurisdiction over the case.[56]

Instead of the high-flying approach described by Curtis, the bondholders adopted a different strategy. In the election of 1852 the question of paying the bonds was submitted to the voters of the state of Mississippi. When they answered with a resounding "No," a suit against the state was commenced. Oddly enough, Mississippi was one of the few states at the time to waive its sovereign immunity and permit suits against itself in its own courts.[57] The lower court decided in favor of the bondholders and on appeal the state's highest court affirmed the decision.[58] Judgment was issued, could it be collected? The answer was no. Mississippi was the first state in the Union to provide for the election of judges[59] and at the next opportunity a prominent judge who had ruled for repayment went down to defeat.

A judicial attitude more appealing to Mississippians was described by a contemporary lawyer and humorist. In 1853, Joseph G. Baldwin, later a justice of the California Supreme Court, published a series of sketches on *The Flush Times of Alabama and Mississippi,* a minor classic of American humor with touches worthy of Mark Twain. Reminiscing about law and lawyers on the Southern frontier, Baldwin recalled:

* *Monaco v. Mississippi* (1934) is discussed in Chapter V.

Those were quashing* times, and they were the out quash-
ingest set of fellows ever known. . . . In one court, forth-
coming bonds, to the amount of some hundred thousands
of dollars, were quashed, because the execution was written "State of Mississippi"—instead of *"the* State of Mississippi," the constitution requiring the style of process to be
the State of Mississippi: a quashing process which vindicated the constitution at the expense of the foreign creditors
in the matter of these bonds, almost as effectively as a subsequent vindication in respect of other bonds, about which
more clamor was raised.[60]

The lenders did not join in the laughter, of course, since the
joke was at their expense. Nor would a later generation of
bondholders laugh when the United States Supreme Court
outdid the merry fellows Baldwin depicted.

* "Quash" is a legal term meaning to annul or cancel an obligation.

IV

Reconstruction and American Law

The power of the United States was made manifest on the great battlefields of the Civil War. The legislative powers vested in Congress—"to lay and collect taxes," "to borrow money," "to declare war," "to raise and support armies," "to provide and maintain a navy," "to make rules for the government and regulation of the land and naval forces," as well as "to make all laws which shall be necessary and proper for carrying into execution the foregoing powers"[1]—provided the legal authority for the war. The executive power, embodied in the President's role as "commander in chief of the army and navy,"[2] animated the legal authority, handled the finances, gave body to Union forces, directed and misdirected the troops in the field, and at last attained victory. During hostilities the judicial power of the United States was reduced to relative insignificance. *"Inter arma leges silent"*[3] ("When arms speak, the laws are silent") has become a legal maxim.[4] But great wars inevitably mark the polity that wages them. The American Revolution led after trial and error to the federal Constitution. The Civil War which was, as contemporaries quickly grasped, the "Second American Revolution"[5] led to profound changes in the Constitution and after trial and error to profound changes in American law in general. When the arms fall silent, the lawyers find their voices.

Northern victory in the Civil War resulted in three constitutional amendments, the first additions since 1804, and the first ever to increase the power of the federal govern-

47

ment.* The purpose of the Reconstruction Amendments, Thirteen through Fifteen, was to write the Northern war aims into the nation's basic law. The Thirteenth Amendment, ratified in 1865 as soon as hostilities were over, abolished slavery in the United States: "Neither slavery nor involuntary servitude, except as a punishment for crime whereof the party shall have been duly convicted, shall exist within the United States, or any place subject to their jurisdiction."[6] The Fourteenth Amendment, the most important in American history, was ratified in 1868. The first section created the concept of United States citizenship, as opposed to state citizenship; protected life, liberty, and property from interference by the states without due process; and guaranteed to all persons the equal protection of the laws. Although originally designed to safeguard freedmen's newfound rights, this section became the palladium of all Americans' civil rights; by extending the reach of national law it altered the balance of state and federal power for all time. The second and third sections of the Fourteenth Amendment were aimed at the political Reconstruction of the South, especially at giving the Republican Party, which had after all won the war, a chance at winning elections: a state that denied the vote to any of its citizens (read: Negroes) would have its representation in Congress reduced proportionally; and anyone who had broken an oath to uphold the Constitution of the United States (read: Confederates who had held state or federal office before the war) would be disqualified from further office holding unless relieved by a two-thirds vote of each house of Congress. The fourth section guaranteed the payment of the national debt, swollen by borrowing to finance the war, but wiped out the

---

* The Twelfth Amendment, ratified in 1804, made the election of the Vice-president a distinct contest, revising the original plan of giving the job to the runner-up in the presidential race. The necessity of the change had been demonstrated in the 1800 election when Thomas Jefferson and Aaron Burr, candidates of the same party for President and Vice-president, had received the same number of electoral votes.

complementary Southern war debt and prohibited compensation to the former slaveholders: "neither the United States nor any State shall assume or pay any debt or obligation incurred in aid of insurrection or rebellion against the United States, or any claim for the loss or emancipation of any slave; but all such debts, obligations and claims shall be held illegal and void."[7] Finally, the Fifteenth Amendment, ratified in 1870, guaranteed the right to vote without regard to "race, color, or previous condition of servitude."[8] By each amendment Congress was expressly given power to enforce its provisions by appropriate legislation.[9]

Congressional power under the Constitution, stretched to its fullest extent and augmented by the new Amendments, was expressed in a mass of Reconstruction legislation. The Reconstruction Act of 1867[10] divided the "rebel states" into five military districts ruled by major generals. The task of the military commanders was to reestablish loyal governments in the South. Conventions were called in each state to draft new constitutions, the results in almost every instance being improvements on the older organic laws. North Carolina's Constitution of 1868, for example, democratized state and local government[11] and enlarged the rights of women.[12] It overhauled the judicial system, abolishing the age-old distinction between actions at law and suits in equity.[13] As required by the constitution,[14] the first legislature under the new dispensation reformed the law of civil procedure, adopting the enlightened code drawn up by David Dudley Field.[15] Unlike other Reconstruction constitutions, North Carolina's survived the Conservative *revanche* that ended Reconstruction and continued to serve as the state's fundamental law for more than a century.

Not only did Congress use its awesome powers to reconstruct the South politically, it also aimed to reconstruct Southern society. For almost a decade it legislated to protect the newly freed slaves. The Civil Rights Act of 1866[16] guar-

49

anteed blacks the same right to life, liberty, and property "as is enjoyed by white citizens."[17] Because of doubts about its constitutionality, the guarantee was reenacted in 1870[18] after the ratification of the Fourteenth Amendment. To crush Southern opposition to Reconstruction, Congress enacted a series of enforcement measures popularly known as Force Bills. The first two[19] were designed to enforce the Fifteenth Amendment's guarantee of the right to vote; they imposed heavy penalties on anyone interfering with balloting by citizens "otherwise qualified by law to vote."[20] To ensure that these punishments were meted out federal courts were given exclusive jurisdiction.[21] The third Force Bill,[22] inspired by the activities of the Ku Klux Klan, and usually called by that eponym, declared the acts of armed combinations tantamount to rebellion and empowered the President to suspend the writ of habeas corpus. In addition, in what was to become the most important statutory provision guaranteeing civil rights, the Ku Klux Klan Act declared that every person who under color of state law deprives anyone of civil rights "shall be liable to the party injured in an action at law, suit in equity, or other proper proceeding for redress."[23] By this provision individuals were permitted to enforce their own rights without waiting for the public prosecutor. Finally in 1875, Congress sought to complete the legal revolution in the South with a social revolution; a final Civil Rights Act[24] imposed penalties on innkeepers, owners of conveyances for hire, and proprietors of establishments open to the public for discriminating against blacks.

To make effective the new order Congress reconstructed the judicial power of the United States as well. The process began with provisions in various statutes permitting removal to federal courts of cases commenced in state courts.[25] Although limited removal jurisdiction had been conferred by the original Judiciary Act of 1789,[26] the Reconstruction legislation greatly extended its scope. The decisive break with the past came in 1875, the year of the last Civil Rights Act. While the first Judiciary Act had granted the lower federal courts only diversity jurisdiction in civil cases,[27] the Judiciary Act of 1875 added federal question jurisdiction as well.[28] Although the latter had been conferred by the Federalist-sponsored Judiciary Act of 1801,[29] that Act had been repealed in 1802 by the Jeffersonians who restored the *status quo ante*.[30] Unlike its short-lived ancestor, the Judiciary Act of 1875 has survived to the present day. Federal courts have been in the front line of defense of constitutional rights ever since.

Even before the reconstruction of federal judicial power, however, the Supreme Court found itself at the center of the post-Civil War power struggle. Defeated on the battlefield, the South indomitably opened a new campaign in court. Georgia sued Secretary of War Edwin M. Stanton,[31] and Mississippi sued President Andrew Johnson,[32] each seeking to enjoin the enforcement of the Reconstruction Acts. The legal strategy was no more successful than the military had been. In rejecting Mississippi's claim, Chief Justice Salmon P. Chase, appointed by President Lincoln to fill the place left vacant by Taney's death in 1864, was candid about the realities of power:

Suppose the bill filed and the injunction prayed for allowed. If the President refuse obedience, it is needless to observe that the court is without power to enforce its process. If, on the other hand, the President complies with the order of the court and refuses to execute the acts of Congress, is it not clear that a collision may occur between the executive and legislative departments of the government? May not the House of Representatives impeach the President for such refusal? And in that case could this court interfere, in behalf of the President, thus endangered by compliance with its mandate, and restrain by injunction the Senate of the United States from sitting as a court of impeachment?

51

Would the strange spectacle be offered to the public world of an attempt by this court to arrest proceedings in that court?

These questions answer themselves.[33]

Because it lacked power, the Court found that it had no jurisdiction. Where there is no remedy, there is no right.

The relationship between law and power stood even more starkly revealed a few years later. The Northern cause in the Civil War had been financed in part by taxes but in even greater part by those old standbys, borrowing and inflation. In 1862, when Salmon P. Chase was serving as Secretary of the Treasury, the government had begun printing paper money unsecured by gold or silver but taking its value from a law declaring it "legal tender in payment of all debts, public and private, within the United States."[34] These notes, popularly known as "greenbacks," fluctuated in value as the military fortunes of the North rose and fell. In 1870, the constitutionality of the Legal Tender Act reached the Supreme Court, now presided over by Chief Justice Chase. Speaking for a bare majority of the justices, Chase against all expectations held that greenbacks were not legal tender for obligations entered into prior to issue and made the even more alarming suggestion that they were not legal tender for any purposes at all.[35] Two vacancies on the Supreme Court permitted President Grant to strengthen the government's case in favor of the currency. William Strong, Chief Justice of the Pennsylvania Supreme Court, and Joseph P. Bradley, a railroad lawyer from New Jersey, were both staunch Republicans and outspoken supporters of greenbacks. Promptly on their appointment the Court accepted a new Legal Tender Case and reversed its stand of barely a year earlier.[36] Half a century later, Charles Evans Hughes, then a law professor but soon to be Chief Justice, stigmatized the *Legal Tender Cases* as a "self-inflicted wound,"[37] comparable in the damage it did the Court to the notorious *Dred Scott Case*.[38]

While the Supreme Court was learning painful lessons about the nature of judicial power, the rebel states were experiencing the trauma of Reconstruction. Amid confusion and corruption the new regimes shouldered the task of rebuilding the South. In addition they inaugurated ambitious programs of social services, public education, and internal improvements. The idealistic aim was to create a new economy, one in which emancipated blacks would be offered an alternative to peonage. The practical means to this end was the sale of state bonds to raise the necessary capital. Buying on credit was the only possibility for the war-worn states of the Old Confederacy. During Reconstruction the debts of these states grew by more than a hundred million dollars.[39]

In historical terms Reconstruction was short-lived and a failure. Thaddeus Stevens—no less than Robespierre before and Lenin after—learned how difficult it is to reconstruct a society. Republican radicalism foundered on the Northern commitment to defend all property except slaves. After making small gains at first, the program of internal improvements lost momentum during the Panic of 1873 and the ensuing years of depression. Reconstruction governments failed to strike root and withered when federal nurture ended. As early as 1869, self-rule was restored in Virginia; in 1870 it came in North Carolina. In a few states such as Louisiana it was delayed until 1877.

Reconstruction was brought to a full stop by the presidential election of 1876. It was not so much the outcome of the balloting as the way the votes were counted and the means used to secure Southern acquiescence in the result that marked the turning point. The contest in November 1876 ended in deadlock. The Democratic nominee, Samuel J. Tilden, received a majority of the popular vote but was one vote short of a majority in the Electoral College. There was a contest over one Oregon elector and there were double and conflicting returns of electoral votes from Florida, South

Carolina, and Louisiana. To settle this dispute Congress created an unprecedented Electoral Commission, composed of fifteen members.[40] On the Commission were five Senators and five Congressmen; the ten politicians were equally divided between the parties. The remaining Commissioners were justices of the Supreme Court. Four justices—Nathan Clifford, Stephen J. Field, William Strong, and Samuel F. Miller—were named outright. These four, of whom the first two were Democrats and the second two Republicans, were empowered to choose a fifth. Given the composition of the Commission the fifth judge would decide the outcome. When Justice David Davis, widely tipped as the likely choice, precipitately resigned from the Court the job fell to Justice Joseph P. Bradley, one of the Republicans who had voted to reverse the first *Legal Tender Case*. His pivotal position on the Electoral Commission put Bradley in the eye of the political storm. It was later reported—and he never denied it[41]—that he had actually written out an opinion giving the election to Tilden. In the end, however, he closed ranks with his fellow Republicans and declared Rutherford B. Hayes President-elect.

The political maneuvers that preceded the inauguration of Hayes were as important as the process by which he was selected. The horse trading was detailed and complicated; the object was to rearrange American politics for years to come. In this it succeeded, though not in the manner intended by any participants. Hayes and his advisers hoped to convert those Southerners who had been Whigs before the war into loyal Republicans. In fact Southern Whiggery never revived; the South became solidly Democratic, and the Republican Party based its national hegemony on the Northeast and Midwest. The price of Southern acquiescence in the decision of the Electoral Commission was a share in government patronage and federal subsidies for internal improvements. But above all it was self-government for the South, known to contemporaries as "home rule," an application of the slogan contemporary Irishmen were using as they agitated for greater independence from Britain. Although Reconstruction bonds were apparently never referred to, the Compromise of 1877 altered the balance of power between the South and the national government in such a way that the bonds were inevitably affected. Federal troops were ordered back to barracks, while federal courts remained open. The issue would soon arise whether states of the Old Confederacy could be compelled to pay their lawful debts.

Congress wrote the new reality into the statute book by enacting the Posse Comitatus Act in 1878.[42] Since time immemorial law officers had relied on the *posse comitatus*, Law Latin for the "force of the county," whenever law and order was threatened. On the unruly frontier posses composed of able-bodied citizens were much in evidence. The mainstay of federal posses, on the other hand, had been soldiers from the U.S. Army. One such martial posse had outfaced the Pennsylvania militia under General Michael Bright at Fort Rittenhouse in 1809.* In 1878, however, Congress prohibited the routine use of regular army troops in the enforcement of court orders. Only when faced by "combinations too powerful to be suppressed by the ordinary course of judicial proceedings," and then only on the orders of the President, could the state militia be invoked in aid of the courts.[43] In the words of Judge John J. Gibbons, historian and jurist: "If any single piece of legislation may be said to embody the spirit of the Compromise of 1877, it is the Posse Comitatus Act. . . ."[44]

The compromise between Southern Democrats and Northern Republicans meant that Congress would pass no more Civil Rights Acts or Force Bills and that the President would no longer use military power to coerce the South. The po-

---

* See *United States v. Bright*, referred to in Chapter III.

litical decision to concede home rule left black Americans at the mercies of their former masters. As their newly won rights slipped away, blacks appealed to the Supreme Court, the proud defender of constitutional rights since the days of Chief Justice Marshall. In 1883 in the *Civil Rights Cases*[45] they were cruelly rebuffed. Invalidating the key provisions of the Civil Rights Act of 1875, the Court ruled that Congress lacked power under the Fourteenth Amendment to outlaw racial segregation in private accommodations. To Justice Joseph P. Bradley went the honors of explaining this result. "It would be running the slavery argument into the ground," he said, "to make it apply to every act of discrimination which a person may see fit to make as to the guests he will entertain, or as to the people he will take into his coach or cab or car, or admit to his concert or theatre, or deal with in other matters of intercourse or business."[46] He added: "When a man has emerged from slavery, and by the aid of beneficent legislation has shaken off the inseparable concomitants of that state, there must be some stage in the progress of his elevation when he takes the rank of a mere citizen, and ceases to be the special favorite of the laws, and when his rights as a citizen, or a man, are to be protected in the ordinary modes by which other men's rights are protected."[47] Bradley had only recently changed his tune on the Fourteenth Amendment. Before the fateful election of 1876, he had given it a far more generous reading.[48] In the words of Professor C. Vann Woodward, distinguished scholar of the period: "The decision constituted a sort of validation of the Compromise of 1877, and it was appropriate that it should have been written by Justice Joseph P. Bradley, the 'Fifth Judge' of the Electoral Commission."[49]

In its racial component the Compromise of 1877 proved long lasting. In 1890, with Republicans in control of both houses of Congress as well as the presidency an attempt was made to push through a new Force Bill giving the national government control over elections in the South.[50] But it failed. Too many Republicans were unwilling to unsettle the Compromise. The judicial expression of this sentiment came in 1896, in the notorious decision in *Plessy v. Ferguson*.[51] The object of the Fourteenth Amendment, the Court conceded, was "undoubtedly to enforce the absolute equality of the two races before the law, but," the Court continued, "in the nature of things it could not have been intended to abolish distinctions based upon color, or to enforce social, as distinguished from political equality, or a commingling of the two races upon terms unsatisfactory to either."[52] In consequence the Court found nothing wrong with a Louisiana statute requiring "equal but separate" accommodations on public conveyances.[53]

After the Plessy case, its reasoning, encapsulated in the transposed phrase "separate but equal," was used to justify Jim Crow in public schools and other state institutions as well as in private business. The message quickly got through. The key civil rights provision of the Ku Klux Klan Act figured in only nineteen decisions during its first sixty-five years on the books.[54] The racial component of the Compromise of 1877 stood up until the school desegregation decision in 1954.[55] Reviewing this sorry history, eminent historians have concluded: "Abandoned by Congress and the President, the Negro was now repudiated by the courts."[56] Making all due allowance for judicial bigotry, one may yet observe that civil rights for blacks had been hard enough to maintain when all the might of the U.S. Army had been deployed in the South. Once the troops were gone a cadre of federal judges kept a lonely vigil. Perhaps one should conclude that *because* the Negro was abandoned by Congress and the President he was also repudiated by the courts.

V

The Eleventh Amendment and the
End of Reconstruction:
Louisiana and North Carolina

During Reconstruction, when the full stretch of federal legislative and executive powers were brought to bear on the
South, it was easy for judges to exercise judicial power over
the states. With respect to the Eleventh Amendment this
meant the maintenance of the Marshallian tradition, first laid
down in *Osborn v. The Bank of the United States* half a century earlier. Although states could not be haled into court,
their officers could be, at least when they acted under unconstitutional statutes. After Reconstruction a growing number
of plaintiffs with claims against states were holders of Southern bonds. Most often in the dock were officers of Louisiana
and North Carolina. Between them the two states repudiated
debts totaling twenty-seven million dollars.[1] In the case of
Louisiana the repudiated debts had been contracted during
Reconstruction. North Carolina, on the other hand, while repudiating millions of dollars' worth of Reconstruction securities, also improved on the occasion by relieving itself of millions more of antebellum debt. When the legislative and
executive will to reconstruct the South failed, the judiciary
was forced to abandon the proud precedents of Chief Justice
Marshall. In a break with tradition the Court held that it was
without jurisdiction over a wide variety of suits against states.

58

The North Carolina state debt more than doubled in the five years after the end of the Civil War. On January 1, 1866, North Carolina owed $14,369,500; by October 1, 1870, its obligations had risen to $33,084,641.[2] Particularly reckless and dishonest financiering marked the Republican administration of Governor William W. Holden from 1868 to 1870. Millions of dollars' worth of state bonds bearing 6 percent interest were issued to railroads the stock of which was pledged as security. As North Carolina's Reconstruction Constitution of 1868 required most bond issues to be coupled with the simultaneous levy of a special tax to pay the annual interest,[3] the legislature enacted several special taxes; but it was confident that the revenue would not be needed because dividends on railroad stock held by the state would pay the interest on the bonds. Most North Carolinians were destitute at this time so the Reconstruction bonds were peddled, usually at a great discount, in the money markets of the Northeast and Europe. The disputes that arose over repayment raised obvious questions under the Contracts Clause of the federal Constitution. If the federal courts were ousted of jurisdiction it could only be because of the Eleventh Amendment.

North Carolina regained home rule in 1870 when the federal army of occupation was withdrawn and the Democratic Party returned to power. The state's conservative leaders, like those of the South generally, were referred to as Bourbons. The term means social and political reactionaries and comes from the name of the exiled French royal family whose scion forfeited the chance of restoration in 1871 by insisting that the white flag of Bourbon replace the Revolutionary tricolor. Needless to say, this is the same family of which Talleyrand is said to have quipped: *"Ils n'ont rien appris, ni rien oublié."* ("They have learned nothing, and forgotten nothing.")[4] On coming to power in 1870, the North Carolina Bourbons promptly took action against the Reconstruction bonds. The special tax acts were repealed and the money already collected was appropriated to the use of the state government.[5] Because the state constitution expressly prohibited the repudiation of the debt,[6] the legislature began the process that ended in 1873 with the popular approval of an amendment repealing the prohibition.[7] As if to make assurance double sure, the state treasurer was prohibited by statute in 1874 from paying any interest on the bonded debt of the state.[8] Unmistakably North Carolina was bent on repudiation. But the federal courts, the keepers of the Marshallian tradition, might have something to say about that.

Perhaps to avoid the bad odor of the special tax bonds, the parties challenging North Carolina's action sued first on some antebellum bonds that had been in default since 1869. These bonds, known as "construction bonds," had been authorized by the lily-white legislatures in 1849 and 1855 to finance the building of the North Carolina Railroad.[9] They were secured by a first mortgage on railroad stock owned by the state. Because the railroad was turning a nice profit at the time and paying dividends to the state, the litigators probably felt confident of recovering the arrearages. Recovery would also pay dividends, as it were, for holders of special tax bonds: the inviolability of North Carolina's obligations would be established and so would federal jurisdiction over the controversy. In 1871 in the lower federal court, still known as the circuit court, holders of construction bonds sued the railroad, its directors, and the state treasurer, asking for the appointment of a receiver to collect the dividends for the bondholders. The plaintiffs requested the sale of stock only if the dividends proved insufficient to pay the debt. At the commencement of the suit, captioned *Swasey v. North Carolina Railroad*,[10] it appeared that no stock certificates had ever been issued to the state. The court promptly ordered the issuance of the proper certificates to a receiver who was appointed to collect the dividends and pay them over to the bondholders.

As it turned out, the dividends were sufficient to pay current interest but not to discharge the arrearages and in 1874, the bondholders petitioned for the sale of the stock. The case was heard by Hugh L. Bond, Federal Circuit Court judge, and Morrison R. Waite, Chase's successor as Chief Justice, on circuit. North Carolina challenged the court's jurisdiction, but the Chief Justice on behalf of the court rejected the state's arguments. The Eleventh Amendment was inapposite, he said, because North Carolina although interested in the matter was not a party of record. To the contention that the state was a necessary party without whom the case could not be heard the Chief Justice replied: "If the state could be brought into court, it undoubtedly should be made a party before a decree is rendered, but since the case of Osborn v. Bank of U.S. . . . it has been the uniform practice of the courts of the United States to take jurisdiction of causes affecting the property of a state in the hands of its agents without making the state a party, when the property or the agent is within the jurisdiction. In such cases the courts act through the instrumentality of the property or the agent."[11] The "real question," according to the Chief Justice, was whether the court had jurisdiction over the property or the agent. Finding that it had jurisdiction over the property the court ordered an accounting and, if the state failed to pay in full by April 1, 1875, the sale of the security. The defendants appealed to the Supreme Court. Given the requirement of circuit riding still imposed on justices, the appeal was from Morrison R. Waite in one place to Morrison R. Waite in another; the Chief Justice wrote the opinion of the Supreme Court dismissing the appeal on the ground that the order was not final because the accounting had not been completed.[12] For an unexplained reason the plaintiffs did not force a sale and the receiver continued to collect the state's dividends on behalf of the bondholders.

What *Swasey* revealed about the status of the Eleventh Amendment—that the Marshallian tradition was alive and well—was twice confirmed by the Supreme Court. The two leading cases on the point, both involving Southern states, arose respectively out of disputes concerning railroads and state bonds, two fertile fields for litigation during the Gilded Age. In "one of the great railroad give-aways of the time"[13] the assets of the Memphis, El Paso and Pacific Railroad had been turned over to the Texas and Pacific Railroad in return for a nominal consideration. The losers were the bondholders in the Memphis, El Paso and Pacific, most of whom were French investors. The winner was the notorious Tom Scott, later president of the Pennsylvania Railroad and associate of John A. C. Gray, the court-appointed receiver of the insolvent Memphis, El Paso and Pacific line. Gray had been named by Justice Joseph P. Bradley, the railroad attorney appointed to the Court by President Grant. In an extraordinary proceeding in 1872 in his hometown of Newark, New Jersey, Bradley convened his Circuit Court for the Western District of Texas and approved Gray's handling of the receivership.[14]

In 1873, Gray defended before the Supreme Court the Memphis, El Paso and Pacific's title to its most valuable remaining asset, land grants from Texas. The antebellum Texas legislature had conditioned the grants on completion of a certain amount of construction, but the state's Reconstruction Constitution had declared all such grants forfeit.[15] Although the grantee had not built the lines promised, Gray asserted that the state's belligerency during the Civil War had rendered fulfillment impossible and that the Constitution could not divest the grant. On behalf of the railroad, Gray sued in federal circuit court to enjoin Texas Governor Edmund Davis from seizing the land. The governor, like his Georgia counterpart in *Madrazo* a generation earlier, asserted the bar of the Eleventh Amendment, but the circuit court rejected this defense and ruled in favor of Gray. Ignoring *Madrazo* the Supreme Court in *Davis v. Gray*[16] repulsed the attack on its jurisdiction and harked back to *Osborn*. That case, it held, stood for three propositions dispositive of the governor's claimed immunity:

(1) A Circuit Court of the United States, in a proper case in equity, may enjoin a State officer from executing a State law in conflict with the Constitution or a statute of the United States, when such execution will violate the rights of the complainant.

(2) Where the State is concerned, the State should be made a party, if it could be done. That it cannot be done is a sufficient reason for the omission to do it, and the court may proceed to decree against the officers of the State in all respects as if the State were a party to the record.

(3) In deciding who are parties to the suit the court will not look beyond the record. Making a State officer a party does not make the State a party, although her law may have prompted his action, and the State may stand behind him as the real party in interest. A State can be made a party only by shaping the bill expressly with that view, as where individuals or corporations are intended to be put in that relation to the case.[17]

Finding itself with jurisdiction the Court proceeded to the merits. It accepted the railroad's excuse for nonperformance and enjoined the governor from interfering with the railroad's title. Not even Chief Justice Marshall had given a state's claim of sovereign immunity such short shrift.

As late as 1876, the Supreme Court was still adhering to the *Osborn* rule. In *Board of Liquidation v. McComb*[18] the Court was confronted with an attempt by another state of the Old Confederacy, Louisiana, to play fast and loose with its creditors. While still under Reconstruction rule Louisiana had encountered difficulties in paying the interest on its outstanding bonds. In 1870, debt service exceeded $1,000,000 and the next year rose above $1,300,000; by 1872 almost one-third of the state's total revenue went to its creditors.[19] In 1874, the legislature responded by creating the Board of Liquidation to fund the state debt.[20] The Board was to issue new bonds, called "consolidated bonds," and offer them in exchange for old bonds at the rate of sixty cents on the dollar. To induce bondholders to make this trade the new bonds were to yield the then high return of 7 percent. A contemporaneous amendment to the Louisiana constitution declared that the consolidated bonds were valid contracts with the state and imposed a tax to service the bonds, which was to be levied and collected annually without the need for legislation[21]—a further inducement for the bondholders.

Only one year later, however, the legislature enacted another statute that directed the Board to exchange consolidated bonds for the outstanding debt of the powerful Louisiana Levee Company at par, not at the reduced rate of exchange offered other creditors.[22] Henry S. McComb, a bondholder who had accepted consolidated bonds, sued the Board in federal court to keep his security from being diluted and won an order against the exchange with the Levee Company. Affirming the decision for a unanimous Court, Justice Joseph P. Bradley ruled that the Eleventh Amendment did not insulate a public officer from judicial compulsion in the performance of his nondiscretionary duty: "[I]t has been well settled, that, when a plain official duty, requiring no exercise of discretion, is to be performed, and performance is refused, any person who will sustain personal injury by such refusal may have a *mandamus* to compel its performance; and when such duty is threatened to be violated by some positive official act, any person who will sustain personal injury thereby, for which adequate compensation cannot be had at law, may have an injunction to prevent it. In such cases, the writs of *mandamus* and injunction* are somewhat correlative to each other."[23]

---

* An injunction was a remedy developed by the equity courts. Although in general an injunction may be used to order a person to do or refrain

Whether or not the officer was acting pursuant to state law was immaterial if the Court found the law unconstitutional. Chief Justice Marshall's Federalist faith in the rights of property and the power of the national courts seemed to be alive and well. Northern creditors of Southern states seemed to be well protected. Shortly after Justice Bradley announced the Court's decision in *McComb,* however, the election of 1876 precipitated the crisis that resulted in the end of Reconstruction.

In the Louisiana gubernatorial contest that year the Republicans ran Stephen B. Packard, and the Democrats ran "what was left of Francis T. Nicholls," a one-armed, one-legged Confederate war hero.[24] Both won. That is, Nicholls received a majority of the votes and was sworn in as governor, and Packard received a majority of the votes accepted as valid by the Republican-dominated Returning Board and was also sworn in. Each attempted to act as governor while awaiting the outcome of the political crisis in Washington. The federal government was paralyzed by the dispute over certification of presidential electors. To settle this dispute Congress created the Electoral Commission described in the preceding chapter. Justice Bradley, the "fifth judge" on the Electoral Commission, voted to count Louisiana's Republican electors, as well as all other contested Republican electors, thus making Rutherford B. Hayes President of the United States. Although Hayes depended for his election on the Louisiana electors certified by the same Returning Board that had certified Packard as governor, Hayes promptly abandoned the unhappy Packard and recognized the Democrat Nicholls. The loser was consoled with the lucrative American consulship in Liverpool, while fifty relatives and friends of the members

---

from doing something, when public officers are involved the affirmative duty to act is usually enforced by the legal writ of mandamus—as sought, for example, by the plaintiffs in *Marbury v. Madison.* See Chapter III.

of the Returning Board got jobs in the U.S. Customhouse.[25] Nor did the Pelican State suffer: during the next fiscal year Louisiana received more federal money for public works than any other state.[26]

By 1879 the Bourbons were in the saddle in Louisiana and a constitutional convention was called to replace the state's Reconstruction Constitution. So determined were the Bourbons to reduce taxes that the convention added to the Constitution of 1879 an extraordinary provision known as the Debt Ordinance,[27] ending the tax imposed by constitutional amendment in 1874 and reducing the rate of interest on the consolidated bonds from 7 to 2 percent for the first five years, 3 percent for the next fifteen years, and 4 percent thereafter. If the bondholders preferred, they were permitted to exchange their consolidated bonds for still other bonds bearing 4 percent interest immediately but available at only seventy-five cents on the dollar. In addition the Debt Ordinance provided that interest due on the consolidated bonds in January 1880 would not be paid at all.

Needless to say, bondholders who had already surrendered 40 percent of their claims were loath to accept lower rates of interest or to surrender a further quarter of their principal. Several immediately brought suit in federal court claiming that the Debt Ordinance violated the Contracts Clause. In *Louisiana ex rel.* Elliott v. Jumel*[28] a bondholder sought to compel Louisiana to order the state auditor, Allen Jumel, to pay the interest on the consolidated bonds in accordance with the terms agreed earlier. In 1883—the year of the *Civil Rights Cases*—by a vote of seven to two the Supreme Court denied relief. The Court's opinion, written by Chief Justice Morrison R. Waite, did little more than note that Louisiana law prohibited suit against the state in its own courts and

---

* *"Ex rel.,"* short for *"ex relatione"* ("on the information of"), is used to describe a legal action instituted in the name of a state but on the information of a private person with an interest in the matter.

that the Eleventh Amendment foreclosed federal courts. Since the state could not be sued neither could its officers. This was the maxim "The king can do no wrong" with a vengeance. *McComb* was distinguished on the specious ground that the Board of Liquidation had been the trustee of the consolidated bonds in that case. What really troubled the justices was the difficulty of enforcing a judgment for the bondholder: "The remedy sought, in order to be complete, would require the court to assume all the executive authority of the State, so far as it related to the enforcement of this law, and to supervise the conduct of all persons charged with any official duty in respect to the levy, collection, and disbursement of the tax in question until the bonds, principal and interest, were paid in full, and that, too, in a proceeding in which the State, as a State, was not and could not be made a party. It needs no argument to show that the political power cannot be thus ousted of its jurisdiction and the judiciary set in its place."[29] Among the majority incidentally were Justice Bradley, the author of *McComb,* and Justice Miller, who had joined in that decision. These two justices who changed their minds on the Eleventh Amendment were the only surviving Republicans to have served on the Electoral Commission of 1877.

The only surviving Democratic justice from the Commission was Stephen J. Field, brother of the brilliant codifier David Dudley Field and the famous entrepreneur Cyrus W. Field. In *Jumel* Field filed a vigorous dissent. Rhetorically asking if the Contracts Clause was of any efficacy he replied: "The majority of the court answer No. I answer, adhering to the doctrines taught by a long line of illustrious judges preceding me, 'Yes, it is;' and though now denied, I feel confident that at no distant day its power will be reasserted and maintained."[30] The theory Field would have relied on, had he been writing for a majority, was simple: "When a State enters into the markets of the world as a borrower, she, for the time, lays aside her sovereignty and becomes responsible as a civil corporation, and although suits against her even then may not be allowed, her officers can be compelled to do what she then contracts that they shall do."[31] In defense of his position Field invoked one of the most powerful concepts of late nineteenth-century jurisprudence: property. "If contracts are not observed," he said, "no property will in the end be respected; and all history shows that rights of persons are unsafe when property is insecure."[32] The other dissenter in *Jumel,* Justice John Marshall Harlan, shared Field's conviction that the decision was an unfortunate break with precedent: "[T]he opinion of the court is in conflict with the spirit and tenor of our former decisions, subversive of long-established doctrines, and dangerous to the national supremacy as defined and limited by the Constitution. . . ."[33] Ironically this threat to national supremacy emerged within twenty years of Appomattox.

The stakes were high and the bondholders evidently men with excellent legal advice and considerable political influence. Shortly after Louisiana's constitutional convention—about the time, in other words, that the *Jumel* litigation was commenced—the legislatures of New Hampshire and New York passed extraordinary legislation.[34] Adopting a domestic version of the strategy advocated by Benjamin R. Curtis at the time of Mississippi's default forty years earlier, these two states offered their names and legal advisers to citizens who stood to lose if Louisiana were permitted to readjust its debt. The attorneys general of the two Northern states were authorized to accept assignments of Louisiana bonds and to pay any money collected, less expenses, to the assignors. The bondholders' legal advisers obviously feared that Justice Field's views on the Eleventh Amendment would not prevail in the post-Reconstruction Supreme Court. So they attempted an end run around the Amendment. Whatever its effect on the Court's jurisdiction, the Eleventh Amendment did not touch the Supreme Court's original jurisdiction over "controversies between two or more states."[35] The justices could not dodge their responsibility under the Contracts Clause on jurisdictional grounds—or so the litigators supposed. In fact they did just that. In *New Hampshire v. Louisiana*,[36] decided at the same time as *Jumel,* the Court held in another opinion by Chief Justice Waite that the Eleventh Amendment prevented it from hearing cases in which a state acting as a "mere collecting agent"[37] for its citizens seeks relief against another state.

New Hampshire and New York had each appeared as a sort of artificial *parens patriae,* successor of the British monarch as "father of his country" and protector of those unable to protect themselves. Specifically the states had asserted their rights as sovereigns to collect from another sovereign debts owed their citizens. "Such power is well recognized as an incident of national sovereignty," Chief Justice Waite admitted, "but it involves also the national powers of levying war and making treaties."[38] The Chief Justice may well have had in mind the vigorous actions of European nations on behalf of their citizens holding unpaid Egyptian bonds—actions that had culminated barely a year earlier in the bombardment of Alexandria by the British Navy. American states lacked such power to enforce their citizens' claims; they had surrendered it on joining the Union. In proof of this the Chief Justice relied on the holding in *Chisholm v. Georgia* that a citizen of one state could sue another state in federal court. From this holding the Chief Justice inferred that the Constitution as originally understood did not permit a state to sue on behalf of its citizens, there being no reason to allow two remedies. Ergo when the Eleventh Amendment superseded *Chisholm,* the citizen was left remediless. Implicitly, of course, the Chief Justice was conceding the correctness of *Chisholm*. If that case had been wrong, then there would be no reason to suppose that states had surrendered their sovereign rights to sue on behalf of their citizens. Accepting the correctness of *Chisholm* the Waite Court was maintaining unbroken the judicial tradition that extended back to the days of the Founding Fathers. Within a few short years, however, the Court would jettison this venerable tradition and rewrite the history of the Eleventh Amendment.

In response to the decisions in 1883, legal commentators were loud in their wail. The New Hampshire and New York strategy had apparently been long in preparation and law reviews had staked out Northern and Southern positions on the issue.[39] But *Jumel* was the bombshell. One of the leading legal scholars of the day, John Norton Pomeroy, was left almost speechless: "In combating the reasoning and conclusions of the court, we feel ourselves to be in the position of one called upon to substantiate an axiom, or to sustain a truism."[40] But as the bondholders learned to their cost the United States Constitution is not a set of axioms or truisms; it is what the Supreme Court says it is. Reminiscent of the response to *Chisholm* a resolution had been introduced in Congress to amend the Constitution by repealing the Eleventh Amendment. The proposal would have given Congress power to provide "by appropriate legislation for the legal enforcement of the obligation of contracts entered into by any of the States of the Union."[41] But the North was sick of trying to coerce the South and the moneylenders lacked popular sympathy.

The decisions in *Jumel* and *New Hampshire* indicated that the Louisiana adjustment of 1879 was going to last. Coincidentally North Carolina also adjusted its debt in 1879.[42] Antebellum bonds were scaled down to 40 percent of face value; bonds issued for internal improvements during and after the war were scaled down to 25 percent; and bonds to fund unpaid interest in 1866 and 1868 were scaled down to 15 percent. As accrued interest was not provided for and as interest on the new bonds was lower than on the old, the settlement overall equalled less than 13 percent of the claim.[43] The special tax bonds were not included at all; they were repudiated outright. By constitutional amendment overwhelmingly ratified in 1880, the legislature was deprived of the power to pay anything on the special tax bonds; any proposal to pay them had to be approved by a majority of all the qualified voters of the state.[44] By this means bonds with a face value of more than twelve million dollars and accrued interest of seven million dollars were relegated to the dustbin of history.[45]

The only remaining question was whether the bondholders could get into federal court to complain about the state's impairment of the obligation of contracts. Litigation began with what seemed the strongest case. Among the bonds converted at forty cents on the dollar were some authorized in 1855 to aid the Atlantic and North Carolina Railroad.[46] Like the construction bonds involved in *Swasey,* these bonds were secured by a lien on stock owned by the state. In 1890 in *Christian v. Atlantic & North Carolina Railroad,*[47] bondholders sued the company, its president and directors, the holder of the state's proxy, and the state treasurer. The bondholders asked the federal court to enjoin the railroad from paying dividends to the state, to appoint a receiver to collect the dividends for the bondholders, and to order the sale of stock if the dividends proved insufficient. *Christian* was in other words the identical twin of *Swasey.* The only difference was that in *Christian* the state already held the stock certificates while in *Swasey* no certificates had been issued. Of course in *Swasey* the lower court had promptly ordered the issuance of certificates to the receiver. But Justice Bradley writing for the Court refused to countenance a comparable order in *Christian.* Although the state had admittedly mortgaged the stock, it had retained possession of it. The mortgagees were out of possession and the mortgagor in possession was a sovereign state immune from suit. The decision in *Swasey* by Chief Justice Waite, who had died two years earlier, was reread in light of his later opinion in *Jumel.*

We are referred to a decision made at the circuit by Chief Justice Waite in the case of *Swasey v. North Carolina Railroad Company* . . . in which, in a case similar to the present, it was held that, inasmuch as the shares of stock belonging to the State were pledged for the payment of the complainants' bonds, they were held by the railroad company as trustee for the bondholders as well as the State; and that if the trustee was a party to the suit, it was not necessary that the State should be a party. We are not certain that we are fully in possession of the facts of that case; but if they were the same as in the present case, with the highest respect for the opinions of the lamented Chief Justice, we cannot assent to the conclusions to which he arrived. In the general principles, that a State cannot be sued; that its property, in the possession of its own officers and agents, cannot be reached by its creditors by means of judicial process; and that in any such proceeding the State is an indispensable party; Chief Justice Waite certainly did express his emphatic concurrence, in the able opinion delivered by him on behalf of the court, in the case of *Louisiana v. Jumel*. . . . His views in the Swasey case seem to have been based on the notion that the stock of the State was lodged in the hands of the railroad company as a trustee for the parties concerned, and was not in the hands of the State itself, or of its immediate officers and agents. But if the facts in that case were as he supposed them to be, the facts in the present case are certainly different from that. No stockholder of any company ever had more perfect possession and ownership of his stock than the State of North Carolina has of the stock in question. There may be contract claims against it; but they are claims against the State, because based solely on the contract of the State, and not on possession.[48]

North Carolina's failure to secure for itself the certificates in *Swasey* had, in other words, cost it many years' worth of dividends—estimated at two and a half million dollars.[49] The litigators in that case were early birds who got the worm.

The Court's unwillingness to interfere in the post-Reconstruction financial readjustment was obvious. But too much money was at stake to leave any loophole unexplored. By its terms the Eleventh Amendment did not apply to suits brought against one of the United States by citizens of the same state. If in-state plaintiffs could recover in federal court, Southern bonds would regain their value. In the archaic language of Law French, a legacy of the Norman Conquest, bonds are *choses in action*, that is, things enforceable by legal action, as opposed to *choses in possession,* things susceptible to physical possession. Since it had been established a century earlier that commercial *choses in action* were transferable, bonds were freely enforceable by subsequent purchasers. If legal action was maintainable in any jurisdiction, a market for bonds would naturally develop there.

It was a simple matter for a North Carolina citizen to sue his state and its officer in federal court for payment of the long-overdue interest on the special tax bonds. His argument was obvious: the act authorizing the bonds and imposing a special tax to service them was a contract, the obligation of which subsequent statutes had impaired. In *North Carolina v. Temple*[50] this argument was made by a North Carolinian in federal circuit court. The two judges who heard the suit disagreed on the key question of the suability of the state. Judge Hugh L. Bond, perhaps recalling his sitting with Chief Justice Waite more than a dozen years earlier in the Swasey case, believed the action maintainable but his colleague Judge Augustus S. Seymour disagreed. On appeal Justice Bradley of the Supreme Court quickly disposed of the matter. Sovereign immunity, constitutionally recognized by the Eleventh Amendment, protected the state. As for the suit against the officer it was "virtually" a suit against the state and as such impermissible under *Louisiana v. Jumel.* Justice John Marshall Harlan dissented, as he had in *Jumel,* in defense of suits against officers:

73

I dissent from so much of the judgment in this case as holds that this suit cannot be maintained against the auditor of the State of North Carolina. The legislation of which complaint is here made impaired the obligation of the State's contract, and was therefore unconstitutional and void. It did not, in law, affect the existence or operation of the previous statutes out of which the contract in question arose. So that the court was at liberty to compel the officer of the State to perform the duties which the statutes, constituting the contract, imposed upon him. A suit against him for such a purpose is not, in my judgment, one against the State. It is a suit to compel the performance of ministerial duties, from the performance of which the state's officer was not, and could not be, relieved by unconstitutional and void legislative enactments.[51]

In *Hans v. Louisiana*,[52] a similar suit decided the same day as *Temple,* Justice Bradley rewrote the history of the Eleventh Amendment. Looking backward a hundred years he saw sovereign immunity writ large in the Constitution. The decision in *Chisholm* created such a "shock of surprise,"[53] he said, that a constitutional amendment was adopted to restate the original understanding. Of course this history lesson contradicted that in the earlier New Hampshire case. Only half a dozen years before, in the opinion written by Chief Justice Waite and joined by Justice Bradley, the Court had accepted *Chisholm* as a correct interpretation of the Constitution as it then stood. Indeed it had reasoned that states on adopting the Constitution had surrendered their rights as sovereigns to collect debts from other sovereigns on behalf of their citizens because the Constitution provided a forum in which citizens could sue states on their own behalf. Despite the inconsistent rationales *New Hampshire* and *Hans* together were effective to cut off the bondholders' remedies.

How did Justice Bradley suddenly attain such unhedged certitude about the original understanding and the Eleventh

Amendment? No surprising discoveries about the historical record had been made in the decade of the 1880s. The Justice himself merely rehashed the familiar quotations from Madison, Marshall, and Hamilton. With regard to *Chisholm* Bradley declaimed: "In view of the manner in which that decision was received by the country, the adoption of the Eleventh Amendment, the light of history and the reason of the thing, we think we are at liberty to prefer Justice Iredell's views. . . ."[54] Yet Iredell's dissent was manhandled; although it clearly rested on the Judiciary Act of 1789—an act which incidentally had been repealed and replaced in 1875—Bradley treated it as a constitutional opinion. For the key concept of sovereign immunity, nowhere mentioned in the Constitution, he dipped into a dissenting opinion in an 1882 suit against federal officers brought by the son of Robert E. Lee, challenging the government's title to the former Lee estate that had become Arlington National Cemetery.[55] Although the majority had upheld suit against the officers, the dissenters had argued that the federal government's sovereign immunity extended to them as well. Attributing sovereign immunity to the states, Bradley began the confusion that still prevails between federal and state sovereignty.

Nothing had arisen since the decision of the New Hampshire case to change Bradley's view of the past—except the pressing need for a new rationale to justify a new result. If sovereign immunity had not existed, the Justice would have had to invent it. As it was, all that was required was to rewrite a little history. A distinguished constitutional historian has labeled the practice—which didn't cease in 1890—"law-office history."[56] As such it is only a specific instance of a larger phenomenon. During the next decade New York theatergoers would applaud George Bernard Shaw's witty dramatization of another instance. In the *Devil's Disciple*, British General John Burgoyne is portrayed receiving a prediction of his inevitable defeat by the American Revolutionaries at

75

Saratoga; when asked what history would say about it, the General coolly replied: "History, sir, will tell lies, as usual."[57] History's propensity to prevaricate is sometimes a harmless peccadillo, but when the Supreme Court lies about the past it does so to justify its decisions in the present. In *Hans* its history lesson translated directly into dollars and cents. "[T]he obligations of a State rest for their performance upon its honor and good faith," said Justice Bradley, "and cannot be made the subjects of judicial cognizance unless the State consents to be sued, or comes itself into court. . . ."[58] That is to say: the creditors are at the mercy of the debtor. But if that was the rule, there was an exception: "Whilst the State cannot be compelled by suit to perform its contracts, any attempt on its part to violate property or rights acquired under its contracts, may be judicially resisted. . . ."[59] The rule applied to the creditors of Louisiana and North Carolina as well as to the creditors of other Southern states; the exception, as will appear in the next chapter, applied to Virginia.

Although lawyers and judges continue to treat *Hans* for convenience as an interpretation of the Eleventh Amendment, it is really nothing of the sort. The Amendment is completely silent on the subject of suits against one of the United States by citizens of the same state; it can hardly be read to prohibit them. Instead *Hans* is an interpretation of Article III of the Constitution, which the Eleventh Amendment altered in other respects. According to *Hans,* despite the words extending the judicial power to "all cases . . . arising under"[60] the Constitution, laws, and treaties of the United States, the meaning is limited to cases not against states. Such a reading would have produced a shock of surprise among earlier lawyers and judges. In the fourth edition (1864) of his respected treatise on federal courts Alfred Conkling had reiterated the widespread view that the Eleventh Amendment applied only to diversity jurisdiction: "if the case arises under the constitution, &c., or if it is of admiralty or maritime jurisdiction, it matters not who may be the parties."[61] Benjamin R. Curtis had told Harvard Law School students the same thing in 1872.[62]

By virtue of Justice Bradley's expansive reading of the Eleventh Amendment only one of North Carolina's creditors was able to collect in full. The United States of America as trustee of funds held for Indian tribes owned almost two hundred thousand dollars' worth of construction bonds. Although other holders of this issue had compromised with the state in 1882 and accepted new bonds par for par with remission of some interest, the federal government had stood out, insisting on the contract debt. In 1889, North Carolina tendered the full principal and interest due on the bonds which had matured in 1884 and 1885. Not content with its pound of flesh, the national government demanded interest for the time after maturity. The state refused and the United States invoked the jurisdiction of the Supreme Court. Untouched by the Eleventh Amendment, the Constitution extends judicial power to "controversies to which the United States shall be a party."[63] In 1890 in *United States v. North Carolina*[64] the Court accepted jurisdiction. In the realms of legal logic perhaps there was enough to justify the argument that sovereign immunity protected a state as much from suits of the federal government as from suits of picayune individuals. But *raison d'état* dictated a different conclusion. The federal government needs the power to call states to account; there is nothing in the language of the Constitution that expressly prohibits it; so the Court ignored sovereign immunity. It also ignored the fact that the United States is itself immune from suit by anyone, including states, without its consent.[65] In terms of *Realpolitik* the conclusion is impeccable. The fears of rendering unenforceable judgments that haunted the Court in its earlier decisions on Southern bonds disappeared when the Attorney General of the United States filed suit. If judgment were rendered on behalf of the plaintiff, the Court could safely trust the executive branch to see to its collection. An 1870 statute provided that money owed the United States by a state would be deducted from federal appropriations for that state.[66] Jurisdiction was assured; ironically the Court denied the federal government the extra interest it claimed.

By 1890, the war was over. Most of the states of the Old Confederacy had repudiated some of their obligations and the Supreme Court, taking refuge in its claimed lack of jurisdiction, washed its hands of the matter. The important precedents were set in cases coming from Louisiana and North Carolina. Two other Southern states also appeared briefly at the bar during this period but their cases only confirmed the general trend. In 1883, the year Louisiana repulsed attacks on its officers by citizens of another state and on itself by states on behalf of their citizens, Georgia was vicariously haled before the Court to answer a charge of violating the Contracts Clause. The case arose out of Georgia's repudiation, after Reconstruction ended in that state, of an issue of railroad bonds endorsed during the governorship of Rufus B. Bullock, a hated Carpetbagger. Attempting to circumvent the Eleventh Amendment, the plaintiff sued state officers and the state-owned railroad in *Cunningham v. Macon & Brunswick Railroad*.[67] Although Georgia challenged the legality of its endorsement, the question of jurisdiction was paramount. *Davis v. Gray* was directly in point, but the Court in an opinion by Justice Miller, who had voted with the majority in that case, explicitly questioned its correctness and implicitly overruled it. Holding that the state was not only an indispensable party but the "only proper defendant in the case,"[68] the Court dismissed the suit for want of jurisdiction. Again it was the inability to fashion a remedy that led the Court to refuse to entertain the right: "If any branch of the State government has power to give plaintiff relief it is the legislative."[69] Why not sue the legislature? Miller asked rhetorically. His answer: "The absurdity of this proposition shows the impossibility of compelling a State to pay its debts by judicial process."[70] In 1886, South Carolina officers had their turn in the dock. In *Hagood v. Southern*[71] plaintiffs sued state officers to compel receipt of scrip that the state had once promised to accept in payment of state taxes. Here too the Court countenanced the violation of the Contracts Clause by denying jurisdiction. As will appear in the next chapter, however, a resourceful lawyer representing holders of similar promissory paper issued by Virginia was more successful on behalf of his clients; working with the realities of judicial power William L. Royall was able to transmute scraps of paper into gold.

By 1890, the hundredth anniversary of the Supreme Court, Southern bonds were mostly dead. They had died on the courthouse doorstep in the 1880s. If any one justice signed the death certificate it was Justice Joseph P. Bradley. Although in 1873 in *Davis v. Gray* he had joined in the uncompromising reaffirmation of *Osborn* and in 1876 he had authored the opinion in *McComb* that relied on *Davis,* Bradley voted against the creditors of Louisiana in *Jumel* and *New Hampshire* in 1883 and wrote the opinions in 1890 that put paid to the North Carolina and Louisiana litigation: *Christian, Temple,* and *Hans.* A policy-making judge is often hard to spot: he camouflages himself with legal arguments and blends into the background like a chameleon. Like a chameleon he is visible only when he moves. With respect to the Eleventh Amendment Justice Bradley was caught in the act of moving. His views changed in response to the great events leading to the end of Reconstruction; before 1877 the Amendment posed no serious impediment to the exercise of federal jurisdiction, but between 1877 and 1890—or, to be exact, between 1883 when the first Louisiana cases reached the Court and 1890 when the last one did—the Amendment was in the ascendant. This was not, as one distinguished authority would have it, because the Eleventh Amendment was "an insuperable obstacle" to enforcement of the Contracts Clause.[72]

Any judge who could think his way out of a paper bag could think his way around the Eleventh Amendment. Judges like Bradley had done it before 1877 and judges after 1890 would do it again. That it was not done in the 1880s was because the Court did not want to do it. After the troops were ordered back to barracks in 1877, there were no means by which to enforce unpopular policies in the South. In Louisiana, for example, once President Hayes had accepted Governor Nicholls, the parallel administration of "Governor" Packard crumbled. No constitutional court worth its salt would have attempted to put it back together again without all the horses and all the men. For the same reason, the Supreme Court refused to invalidate the Louisiana Debt Ordinance of 1879. Like the Marshall Court in *Marbury v. Madison* the Court in the Gilded Age did not want to issue an unenforceable order. In the earlier case a strained reading of the Judiciary Act of 1789 did the trick; in the 1880s it was the Eleventh Amendment.

No more than an introductory course in the realities of judicial power was required to teach Justice Bradley this lesson. A humorist of the next generation summed it up well. The Irish-American barman Mr. Dooley, creation of Chicago journalist Finley Peter Dunne, put it this way: "A coort's all r-right enough, but no coort's anny good onless it is backed up be a continted constabulary, its counthry's pride, as th' pote says."[73] Without the constables contracts are unenforceable; without the prospect of enforcement court orders are not worth the paper they are written on—and Bradley knew it. Although he was a staunch defender of national rights and federal power and although repudiation stank in his nostrils,[74] he was ready, as in the *Legal Tender* and *Civil Rights Cases,* to do what had to be done. But the true measure of Bradley's greatness will appear in the next chapter, which covers the parallel cases involving Virginia. In those cases

80

the Justice showed that he had mastered the advanced course in judicial power as well.

Although the war was over by 1890, the bondholders in the best tradition of vanquished minorities continued to mount guerrilla attacks. In 1896, holders of North Carolina special tax bonds sued the state, claiming that the amendment to the state constitution that prohibited payment was an impairment of their contracts. The United States Supreme Court rejected the argument on the ground that under North Carolina law before the amendment the state supreme court had had no power to issue a binding judgment against the state. As there had never been a remedy under state law the constitutional amendment worked no impairment.[75] No consideration was given to the loss of a federal remedy. Once this state of affairs was reached, would-be purchasers of state bonds could have no illusions about enforceability. As North Carolina's feisty jurist Walter Clark expressed it: "Whether a sovereign State will perform its contract and pay out money under it, must ever be left solely to the sense of right and justice in the sovereign. This is inherent in sovereignty, and every one, who makes any contract of any kind with a State, does so with the knowledge that this right is safeguarded and reserved to each State by the Eleventh Amendment to the United States Constitution, and by express provision in the State Constitution."[76] In the ancient language of the common law: *"Caveat emptor."*[77] ("Let the buyer beware.") Curiously, as will appear in a later chapter, purchasers of city and county bonds did not have to be quite so wary.

Although the federal judiciary was unwilling to upset the fiscal applecart, political conditions in North Carolina late in the nineteenth century created the possibility that the state supreme court would itself come to the aid of the creditors. In that case the Eleventh Amendment would be, of course, irrelevant: it applied only to suits in federal court. Agrarian discontent had produced a short-lived but vigorous Populist Party in the state. Pursuing a policy of limited cooperation with the dwindling Republican Party, a policy stigmatized by Democrats as the "fusion" of the two parties, the Populists had broken the post-Reconstruction Democratic stranglehold on state politics. The fusion ticket had captured the legislature in 1894, and in 1896 in a three-way race among Republicans, Populists, and Democrats, the Republican Daniel L. Russell was elected governor. Under the banner of "white supremacy" the Democrats counterattacked, recapturing the legislature in 1898 and the governorhip in 1900. Once in power they laid the foundation for long-term domination by amending the state constitution to disfranchise the Negroes, the Republican's mainstay. A literacy test was imposed for voting, but to preserve the franchise of illiterate whites the notorious grandfather clause was appended. It exempted from the test anyone who had been eligible to vote on January 1, 1867, that is, before black North Carolinians were enfranchised, or anyone who was the "lineal descendant" of a person who had then been eligible.[78] *

Temporarily, however, the white supremacists had lost control of the state supreme court: at the turn of the century three of its five members were Republicans. Under the circumstances it is hardly surprising that the chief event of the 1901 legislative session was the impeachment of Republican justices.[79] Mortality had already eliminated one of the fusion judges, so the targets were Chief Justice Daniel M. Furches and Associate Justice Robert M. Douglas—the latter, incidentally, the son of Stephen A. Douglas, Lincoln's

---

* In 1915, the U.S. Supreme Court invalidated grandfather clauses in *Guinn v. United States,* the first case to rely on the Fifteenth Amendment in striking down state law. By then the North Carolina clause had done its work; in 1900 the new white supremacist governor had launched a literacy drive.

debating partner half a century earlier. In addition to seeking a clean sweep of state offices the Democrats feared specifically that the state court would invalidate the recently adopted grandfather clause. With frank racism this was called the "nigger in the woodpile."[80] There was also fear that the court would validate the repudiated state bonds. Whatever may be true of academics, politicians have never ignored the link between the composition of the bench and the obligation of contracts. Although the Democrats failed to cleanse the court because of defections from their own ranks, the message nonetheless got through: bondholders had no realistic hopes of recovery through state courts.

The beleaguered Governor Russell's term expired in 1901. Without a job and in need of funds he spent the last years of his life in pursuit of the vast legal fees that would belong to anyone who could collect the hundred million dollars owed by Southern states. Russell devised an ingenious legal stratagem, his secret "scheme," to tap the pot of gold.[81] In 1904, he arranged a test case in the United States Supreme Court. In *South Dakota v. North Carolina*[82] a plaintiff at last won a judgment on state bonds. South Dakota had acquired its bonds the easy way: by gift. A closely divided Court distinguished *New Hampshire v. Louisiana* on the ground that South Dakota was suing on its own behalf, rather than as "a mere collecting agent" for its citizens. The economic impact of this decision was very great. Once bondholders learned that there existed a plaintiff that could successfully invoke the judicial power of the United States, their spirits rose—and so did the value of their bonds. By threatening to donate bonds to states which could collect at par, the bondholders had a powerful weapon to compel settlement with them at anything less than par. As the donor candidly admitted in his letter to South Dakota: "If your State should succeed in collecting these bonds it would be the inclination of the owners of a majority of the total issue now outstanding to make additional donations to such governments as may be able to collect from the repudiating State, rather than accept the small pittance offered in settlement."[83]

What about the problem of enforcement, the bogey that had haunted earlier cases concerning Southern bonds? This time the Court had an answer. The bonds in question were secured by a mortgage on stock owned by the state,[84] so the Court devised a simple foreclosure proceeding: "[I]n default of . . . payment an order of sale [shall] be issued to the Marshal of this court, directing him to sell at public auction all the interest of the State of North Carolina in and to one hundred shares of the capital stock of the North Carolina Railroad Company, such sale to be made at the east front door of the Capitol Building in this city, public notice to be given of such sale by advertisements once a week for six weeks in some daily paper published in the city of Raleigh, North Carolina, and also in some daily paper published in the city of Washington."[85] It is worth noting that the sale was to proceed without certificates of the stock to be sold. No certificates had ever been issued to the state, although it was recognized on all sides that North Carolina owned the stock. The marshal was simply to auction off "all the interest" the state owned. Never before had a marshal been ordered to execute such an order. As the wags observed, a federal statute prohibited the sale of "goods or wares of any description by itinerants, peddlers or others" in or near the Capitol.[86] Unwilling to test the resolve of President Theodore Roosevelt to enforce court orders against a recalcitrant state, North Carolina reluctantly negotiated a compromise with its creditors.[87]

Governor Russell's strategy for collecting Southern debts by tactical donations proved only partially successful despite his famous victory in the South Dakota case. Northerners were increasingly uncomfortable about accepting gifts of what they were being told was tainted money. Reconstruction, once viewed in the North as a generally advisable and idealistic policy that had foundered on Southern intransigence and racism, was being reconsidered. Professor William A. Dunning of Columbia University, dean of American Southern historians, began a new tradition of academic treatment of the topic with his influential book on Reconstruction,[88] published in 1907. On the popular level Thomas Dixon, a North Carolina native, dramatized the same subject in his once widely read novel, *The Clansman,* published in 1905. Crudely racist, Dixon's book included an enthusiastic portrayal of the Ku Klux Klan's night-riding in South Carolina. Blacks had had a majority in that state's House of Representatives—the only legislative body in which that was the case—so it was easy to blame corruption on the ex-slaves. Dunning exaggeratedly described South Carolina as "thoroughly Africanized" and depicted the "small body of decent white men who were still striving to maintain their rights and their property against the flood of barbarism."[89] In his fictional account of official extravagance and waste, Dixon incorporated sections of a post-Reconstruction South Carolina legislative report,[90] a report prepared to create sympathy for the state's debt repudiation at issue in *Hagood v. Southern.* The details of Dixon's now forgotten novel, including its scenes of Negro misgovernment, were made vivid for millions of Americans by the genius of D. W. Griffith, America's first major film director, who immortalized the tawdry story in 1915 as *The Birth of a Nation.* Endowed with these mephitic associations Southern bonds became unwelcome gifts. South Dakota refused a second offer of North Carolina bonds. Oblivious to facts, the public failed to appreciate that the proffered bonds had not been issued by ignorant and corrupt ex-slaves but had instead been sold by upstanding white gentlemen whose white successors had subsequently refused to honor them.

In despair the litigators for the bondholders tried their final gamble. While the Eleventh Amendment barred federal jurisdiction over suits "against one of the United States . . . by citizens or subjects of any foreign state," it did not, as Benjamin R. Curtis had long ago pointed out, preclude suits by foreign sovereigns. Plans were made to give North Carolina obligations to Venezuela and Colombia, and in 1916 bonds were actually donated to Cuba. This gift led to the filing of suit against the Tar Heel State,[91] but diplomatic pressure was exerted and the complaint was withdrawn. The idea was, however, to reappear later. In the meantime America's allies in World War I developed an interest in the matter. Struggling to repay their mountainous war debts to the United States, the allies sought an offset in the amount of unpaid Southern bonds owned by their citizens. Questions were asked repeatedly in the British houses of Parliament.[92] Although in the upper chamber their lordships conscientiously puzzled over the intricacies of the Eleventh Amendment,[93] in the House of Commons Austen Chamberlain, the Foreign Secretary, silenced a critic by telling him tartly to "give a little study to the Constitution of the United States."[94] Like the French Bourbons, it seems, the creditors never forgot anything; nor, like the Bourbons, did they ever get anything. In 1934, the Principality of Monaco finally forced the Supreme Court to decide the issue.[95] Involved were thousands of dollars' worth of antebellum Mississippi bonds, but an affirmative ruling would have affected millions of dollars' worth of repudiated Reconstruction obligations. Like South Dakota thirty years earlier, Monaco was the recipient of a completed gift. Like South Dakota's donor, Monaco's was moved not by altruism but by a desire to induce a settlement. That desire was frustrated, however, by the Supreme Court's decision that federal courts lack jurisdiction over such suits, absent consent by the state. As in *Hans* the Eleventh Amendment was relied on as constitutional recognition of sovereign immunity.*

Soon after *Monaco* was decided, another popular Southern

* For further details see Chapter IX.

novelist provided the reading public with another fictional-
ized account of Reconstruction, including a plea on behalf of
repudiation. In her 1936 Pulitzer-Prize-winning novel *Gone
with the Wind,* Margaret Mitchell penned a vivid description
of the miseries of life in post-Civil-War Georgia under the Yan-
kee heel. Her opportunistic heroine Scarlett O'Hara adapted
to the situation by collaborating with Carpetbaggers; her will-
ingness to receive the hated Governor Bullock caused even
the long-suffering Melanie Wilkes to desert her. Corruption
was largely attributed to the unhappy race of ex-slaves: "These
negroes sat in the legislature where they spent most of their
time eating goobers and easing their unaccustomed feet into
and out of new shoes. Few of them could read or write. They
were fresh from cotton patch and canebrake, but it was within
their power to vote taxes and bonds as well as enormous expense accounts to themselves and their Republican friends.
And they voted them. . . . Bonds were issued running into
the millions."[96] Lest it be thought that the issues were enforceable obligations, the author quickly added: "Most of
them were illegal and fraudulent but they were issued just
the same. The state treasurer, a Republican but an honest
man, protested against the illegal issues and refused to sign
them. . . ."[97] Describing the Macon and Brunswick Railroad, a defendant in the *Cunningham* case in 1883, the novelist justified repudiation:

> The state-owned railroad had once been an asset to the
> state but now it was a liability and its debts had piled up to
> the million mark. It was no longer a railroad. It was an
> enormous bottomless trough in which the hogs could swill
> and wallow. Many of its officials were appointed for politi-
> cal reasons, regardless of their knowledge of the operation
> of railroads, there were three times as many people em-
> ployed as were necessary, Republicans rode free on passes,
> carloads of negroes rode free on their happy jaunts about
> the state to vote and revote in the same elections.

The mismanagement of the state road especially infuriated the taxpayers for, out of the earnings of the road, was to come the money for free schools. But there were no earnings, there were only debts, and so there were no free schools.[98]

The Southern case against the bonds is typified by *Gone with the Wind:* whatever the technical legal arguments against them (and legal ingenuity could be counted on to find some), the emotional case rested on racism. But racism pure and simple, however potent an ingredient in popular fiction, is an unsatisfactory *ratio decidendi* in light of the Reconstruction Amendments. Although Justice Bradley proclaimed the end of the necessity for the Negro to be the "special favorite of the laws," he added that the freedmen's civil rights were "to be protected in the ordinary modes by which other men's rights are protected."[99] And in *Plessy v. Ferguson*[100] the Court squared Jim Crow with the Fourteenth Amendment by linking "separate" with "equal."

The bond cases were cases about contracts; the technicalities were therefore arguments about the validity of contracts. At bottom they were not worth very much. In the late nineteenth and early twentieth century American law was dominated by the concept of "freedom of contract"; the unmistakable trend was to eliminate obstacles to creating binding legal agreements and to enforce rigorously obligations once undertaken. *"Pacta sunt servanda"* ("Contracts are to be kept")[101] was a Roman maxim[102] that found favor with American judges. Whatever their personal feelings about the Negro, the nine elderly men making up the Supreme Court were unwilling to unsettle the law of contracts. At that time it was viewed as impracticable to screen contracts for fairness. Nor was there any feasible way to scale them down judicially. It was an all-or-nothing proposition: a contract is a contract is a contract. Federal jurisdiction was another matter. Expanding the Eleventh Amendment and sovereign immunity benefited only states. "Dismissed for want of jurisdiction" said nothing about the validity of the underlying obligations— indeed, it was not inconsistent with dicta underscoring their validity. Woe to the state that had to rest its case on arguments against its own contracts.

VI

An Exception: Virginia

The Civil War determined the nature of the federal Union but when the arms fell silent many questions remained unanswered. Reconstruction marked but did not remake Southern society. The compromise that gained Southern acquiescence in the decision of the Electoral Commission altered the balance of power within the nation. In due course it altered the bondholders' balance sheets as well. Resolving disputes between bondholders and debtor states the Supreme Court recognized the new realities of power and found in the Eleventh Amendment a reason for not issuing orders that could not be enforced. Lacking a remedy the bondholders' right to millions of dollars disappeared. But Virginia was fated to be an exception to the rule that states south of the Mason-Dixon line could not be made to pay. For half a century the Commonwealth of Virginia litigated its obligations—first with its bondholders, then with West Virginia, the state "made from its rib." The reason the Old Dominion could not slough off its creditors was that it had made the coupons that represented the interest on its bonds receivable in payment of state taxes. The reason the Mountain State could not continue to deny its obligations was that it was not a beneficiary of the historic Compromise of 1877. Between them these reasons speak volumes about the judicial power of the United States.

When the firing began at Fort Sumter in 1861, Virginia was carrying a large public debt, as befit an old and prosperous state. War brought the usual rapid increase of indebtedness but defeat relieved the debtor of liability on this score. During hostilities, however, the state had suspended payment on antebellum debts, still recognized as legitimate in 1865. Compounding the unpaid interest added subtantially to the total. By the end of the struggle the Commonwealth's obligations, excluding its war debt, amounted to approximately forty-one million dollars.[1] And Virginia, more than any other state in or out of the Union, had been ravaged by war. An extraordinary amount of the actual fighting, concentrated between the rival capitals of Washington and Richmond, had taken place on Virginia soil. An unhealthy percentage of the young white male population had been killed or maimed. Livestock and farm implements had been stolen or destroyed. The slaves had, of course, been emancipated without compensation. The body politic itself had been dismembered: one-third of the Old Dominion had been officially recognized as the separate state of West Virginia.[2] In the calculations of the tax collector all these developments added up to a shorter tax roll.

Reconstruction ended early in Virginia: by 1869, self-government had been restored. The Redeemers were self-proclaimed Conservatives, dedicated to good government and sound money. Among their first acts the Conservatives authorized the creation of a statewide system of free elementary schools.[3] Public education is a costly business, however, and the fate of the public schools for two decades was linked to the state of the public debt. Under the leadership of Governor Gilbert C. Walker, a Northern businessman trying to attract Northern capital, the Conservatives enacted the fateful Funding Act of 1871.[4] By then the state debt had risen to $47,090,867.[5] The Commonwealth denied its liability on one-third of the total, attributing it to the new government in Wheeling. As to that share, the bondholders were offered certificates, to be paid "in accordance with such settlement as shall hereafter be had between the states of Virginia and

West Virginia."[6] As to the balance, however, the Commonwealth offered the bondholders an attractive deal: they could exchange their old bonds for new ones called consolidated bonds, "consols" for short, payable in thirty-four years and yielding 6 percent interest. As was customary the interest was represented by coupons attached to the bonds, each coupon maturing at a given date in the future. As a further inducement to the bondholders to make the exchange the coupons were declared "receivable at and after maturity for all taxes, debts, dues, and demands due the state."[7] In other words, the coupons were made legal tender for obligations that were as certain to occur as death itself. It is well to dwell on the importance of these coupons to the capitalists. What every lender fears, of course, is default, and the coupons were an earnest of repayment. There would always be a market for coupons clipped from the bonds and prices in that market would always be buoyant. The slightest discount from face value would make it in the economic interest of taxpayers to buy.

Given these inducements the bondholders responded with alacrity. By December 1871, they had exchanged $32,416,-036 of old obligations for consols worth $21,610,691.[8] The carrying charges on this debt, even excluding the share assigned to West Virginia, soon became a hot political issue. The coupons, denounced as the "cut-worms of the Treasury,"[9] sapped the Commonwealth's income. Between January 1, 1873, and October 1, 1878, the state received coupons worth almost a million dollars per year in lieu of taxes.[10] In political terms the issue was often whether to pay the capitalists or the schoolteachers. The monied interest was not without its defenders. In the uncompromising words of one governor: "Free schools are not a necessity. . . . They are a luxury . . . to be paid for, like any other luxury, by the people who wish their benefits."[11] It was reported that a prominent debt payer declared publicly that it would be better to burn the schoolhouses than to default on the debt.[12] But public education had its own constituency and political pressure in favor of default built rapidly. Until the end of the 1870s the debate was contained within the Conservative Party, although the powerful faction in favor of readjustment often had its way. In 1872, the legislature overrode a gubernatorial veto and repealed the section of the Funding Act that made the coupons receivable for state taxes.[13] The judges of the Virginia Supreme Court of Appeals, however, represented the earlier tendency in Conservatism. In *Antoni v. Wright*[14] they held the new statute unconstitutional. The state's bond was its contract; the federal Constitution, once more recognized as supreme in Richmond, denied to the state the power to pass any "law impairing the obligation of contracts"[15]; the repealer, impairing the bondholders' contract, was therefore void. The remedy was a writ of mandamus ordering the tax collector to accept coupons.

The Commonwealth did, of course, stop the issuance of consols. Those bondholders unlucky enough to have failed to make the switch in time went remediless. As to them the state had withdrawn its generous offer before acceptance so no contract had been consummated. In place of consols the latecomers were offered bonds known as "peelers" that lacked tax-receivable coupons. In the ensuing controversy little interest was taken in the peelers and little interest was paid on them. Lacking the leverage of the consols' coupons the peelers had a claim of low order on the impecunious debtor.

All attention focused on whether the state could legally default on the tax-receivable coupons. Then as now there were more ways than one to skin a creditor. In 1873 the legislature, with the blessing of the newly elected Conservative governor, Gen. James Lawson Kemper C.S.A., imposed a tax on the coupons and ordered the tax collectors to deduct it from the coupons as they were tendered.[16] The effect was, of course, to reduce the rate of interest on the bonds. By this time the state judiciary had come to terms with the new political tendency and upheld the tax. But the Old Dominion was not an island entire of itself, it was a piece of the continental Union. Federal judges might have something to say on the matter. Sure enough, in 1881 in *Hartman v. Greenhow*,[17] a suit brought by a taxpayer against the treasurer of Richmond, the tax was challenged in the Supreme Court of the United States. In an opinion by Justice Stephen J. Field, in which Justice Bradley joined, the tax was held to be a violation of the Contracts Clause and the Virginia court was instructed that the proper remedy was a writ of mandamus. No mention was made of the Eleventh Amendment. Before legal proceedings were over, however, the state attempted to readjust its debt by agreement with its creditors. In 1879, the legislature had passed the McCulloch Act,[18] named in honor of Hugh McCulloch, Secretary of the Treasury in the Lincoln and Johnson administrations and subsequently agent for the bondholders. The McCulloch Act provided for funding the debt into bonds yielding 3 percent interest for ten years, 4 percent for twenty years, and 5 percent for ten years. In the shorthand of the day the new bonds were known as "ten-forties." Some bondholders made the exchange but many awaited further legal and political developments in hopes of more favorable terms.

In 1879 the political system that had governed Virginia since Reconstruction broke down. Unable any longer to contain the raging debate on fiscal policy the Conservative Party split into warring factions. Funders, known for their attachment to the Funding Act of 1871, were filled with zeal for the good name of Virginia or were simply convinced that it was impossible to default on the coupons. Their opponents, dedicated to the cause of repudiation, politely styled themselves Readjusters. That year the Readjusters won control of the legislature; two years later they captured the governorship. In short order they elected to the U.S. Senate two arch-

Readjusters, William Mahone and H. H. Riddleberger.* With all the instrumentalities of state government at their command the Readjusters set about killing the coupons if they were indeed mortal.

At the same time that their counterparts in Louisiana and North Carolina implemented programs of repudiation, the Virginia Readjusters set their own plans in motion. Since the direct route of outright repudiation had been closed by earlier state judicial decision and since the somewhat more circuitous route relying on the taxing power had been blocked by the Supreme Court in *Hartman,* legal ingenuity was called for. Two statutes of 1882[19] known by the cognomen "coupon killers" were designed to do away with their victims by interfering with the manner of their receipt. Ostensibly aimed at suppressing forged, stolen, and invalid coupons the new legislation prohibited tax collectors from accepting any coupons whatsoever except "for the purpose of identification and verification."[20] Taxpayers tendering coupons were required to pay their taxes in cash and then sue the state to compel acceptance of the coupons. The burden of proving the validity of the coupons was placed on the plaintiffs. In case they prevailed in one court the state's attorney was authorized—and in 1884 required[21]—to appeal from court to court. Before taxpayers could demand refunds they would bear the law's proverbial delay not to mention expense. The remedy described was made exclusive and the Virginia courts were stripped of the power to issue any writs whatsoever interfering with the collection of taxes.[22]

The coupon killers were designed to induce bondholders to exchange their consols for other bonds, popularly known as "Riddlebergers" in honor of the Readjuster Senator. The laws' prohibitions and requirements were necessary because

* From the adoption of the federal Constitution until the ratification of the Seventeenth Amendment in 1913, U.S. Senators had been chosen by state legislatures.

95

the Riddlebergers yielded only 3 percent, half the return on the older obligations, and Riddleberger coupons were not receivable for state taxes.[23] Although the new bonds were not to mature for fifty years, the state was empowered to redeem them at face value at any time after eighteen years. Not surprisingly, owners of consols did not queue up to make the exchange; instead, they haled Virginia officers into federal court, seeking to compel them to accept coupons as promised. On March 5, 1883, the date of Louisiana's sweeping victories, Virginia also won: the Supreme Court upheld the coupon killers in *Antoni v. Greenhow*.[24] Five justices joined in the opinion of Chief Justice Morrison R. Waite that the statutes left the owners of coupons with "an adequate and efficacious remedy"[25] and that they were not, therefore, unconstitutional impairments of the obligation of contracts. Such a holding was in marked contrast with earlier interpretations of the Contracts Clause; it had once been said that "[i]f the remedy afforded be qualified and restrained by conditions of any kind, the right of the owner . . . is impaired. . . ."[26] Waite, on the contrary, reached his conclusion despite frank admission that "the commercial value of the bonds and coupons has been impaired by the hostile legislation of the State."[27]

Although the Chief Justice did not find the Eleventh Amendment an impediment to a decision on the merits, Justice Stanley Matthews offered an alternative rationale that denied jurisdiction on that basis and that attracted the support of three of the five who had joined Waite, including Justice Bradley. "[F]or a breach of its contract by a State no remedy is provided by the Constitution of the United States against the State itself," Matthews said, "and a suit to compel the officers of a State to do the acts which constitute a performance of its contract by the State is a suit against the State itself."[28] As Matthews expressly recognized, the logical consequence of this position was that Virginia could repeal all remedies for the wrong of refusing to receive the coupons as promised. Whatever the rationale, the Readjusters had won. The Court had concluded that Southern state debts were not collectible and had been shown as yet no reason to single out the Old Dominion's for special treatment. Virginia was not yet an exception to the general rule.

The Readjusters seemed to have discovered a route out of the labyrinth of debt in which the Funders had wandered. Although the Readjusters (properly so-called) lost the legislative elections in 1883, the victorious Funder-Conservatives (newly reorganized as Democrats) showed little of their former zeal for paying Virginia's pound of flesh. In fact the Democratic solons passed a joint resolution advising creditors that "any expectation that any settlement of the debt of this state upon any other basis [than the Riddleberger Act] . . . is absolutely illusory and hopeless."[29] They quickly followed up their legal victory in *Antoni* with still more statutes designed to kill the coupons. Taxpayers who tendered coupons and refused to pay their taxes in money were deprived of the right to bring an action of trespass or trespass on the case* against tax collectors who levied on their property.[30] The Tax Act declared state license fees payable only in "lawful money of the United States."[31] The same act imposed a license fee of $1000 on sellers of coupons, as well as a tax of 20 percent of the face value of all coupons sold.[32] Further, the act required lawyers who sued the Commonwealth on coupons to buy a special license which cost $250, ten times the fee for ordinary law practice.[33] The Democrats also stole the Readjusters' thunder on another issue by providing that the school tax could not be paid in coupons, but only in "lawful money of the United States."[34]

To a less imaginative generation it might appear that all

---

* Trespass was the common-law form of action used to remedy direct injuries. Trespass on the case (or "case" as it was generally called) was used to remedy indirect injuries.

legal ingenuity was now spent and that the coupons were dead. Burial would, however, be premature. The credit for resurrecting the bondholders' hopes belongs to the tireless Funder, William L. Royall, a collateral kinsman of Chief Justice Marshall.[35] Although he was of a slave-owning family and was a Confederate veteran, Royall devoted his talents to the cause of the coupon clippers. On their behalf he appeared before the Supreme Court almost every term from 1881 to 1890,[36] twice challenging his own imprisonment by his home state.[37] In 1885, Royall discovered the key to success. Unlike the bondholders of other Southern states the creditors of Virginia did not need to ask for a court order requiring politicians to raise taxes and pay interest. They did not even need an order compelling tax collectors to accept their coupons. That was the fallacy in *Antoni* and it was to be repeated by South Carolina's creditors in 1886 in *Hagood v. Southern* (discussed in the previous chapter). All the bondholders really needed was an order discharging their liability for taxes.[38] Royall's legal strategy was simple. A taxpayer would tender coupons; when they were refused the taxpayer would seek no legal remedy; when in due course the tax collector levied on his goods for delinquent taxes, the taxpayer would bring an action of detinue* against the tax collector. The rightfulness of the levy would turn, of course, on whether the taxes were in law delinquent.

In eight cases in 1885 known collectively as the *Virginia Coupon Cases*[39] the Supreme Court divided five to four but found no delinquency. The honors of explaining this result were left to Justice Matthews, the author of the more extreme rationale in *Antoni*. His analysis of the plaintiff's rights was commonplace enough. The Funding Act of 1871 was characterized as "not only a law, but a contract."[40] The statute pro-

---

* Detinue was the common-law form of action for the return of personal property wrongfully withheld or detained.

hibiting the tax collector from receiving coupons in lieu of money was unconstitutional.

> That, it is true, is a legislative act of the government of Virginia, but it is not the law of the State of Virginia. The State has passed no such law, for it cannot; and what it cannot do, it certainly, in contemplation of law, has not done. The Constitution of the United States, and its own contract, both irrepealable by any act on its part, are the law of Virginia; and that law made it the duty of the defendant to receive the coupons tendered in payment of taxes, and declared every step to enforce the tax, thereafter taken, to be without warrant of law, and therefore a wrong. He stands, then, stripped of his official character; and, confessing a personal violation of the plaintiff's rights for which he must personally answer, he is without defence.[41]

Matthews was, of course, echoing Marshall who in turn had echoed English constitutional theory. The legal irresponsibility of the king, transferred to the state, was interpreted to make it incapable of authorizing an illegal act. If the state— the "artificial person" Justice Wilson had described in *Chisholm*—was blameless, then one of those persons who think, speak, and act on its behalf was blamable.

Turning to the remedy, Matthews recognized that the tax collector was immunized by statute from actions of trespass or case brought by taxpayers who had tendered coupons. To be sure, the action of detinue had been left untouched. As if suspecting that detinue would be the next to go if he rested the decision on that nicety, Matthews went on to assume that every action against the tax collector was forbidden by some statute or other. All would be in vain; all would be unconstitutional. "The contract with Virginia was not only that the coupons should be received in payment of taxes, but, by necessary implication, that the tax-payer making such a tender should not be molested further, as though he were a delin-

quent, and that for every illegal attempt subsequently to enforce the collection of the tax, by the seizure of property, he
should have the remedies of the law in force when the contract was made, for redress, or others equally effective."[42] To
preserve the obligation of contracts, the Supreme Court
would reverse adverse judgments in the state courts.[43] In appropriate cases it would also sanction the issuance of a federal writ of injunction prohibiting the seizure of property.[44]
The Court was saying in effect: "No, Virginia, there is no
Santa Claus."[45]

As if in disbelief the readjusting Democrats redoubled their
efforts to kill the coupons. Using their control over the state
law of evidence, they cast obstacles in the way of collection.
Although the state had made the genuineness of coupons the
ostensible issue, they prohibited expert testimony on the question.[46] To close the market for coupons they required taxpayers tendering coupons to produce the bonds from which
they had been cut.[47] State criminal law was also brought into
play. The Readjusters expanded the ancient offense of champerty* to include soliciting or inducing suit against the state.[48]
They expanded the equally ancient offense of barratry** to
include the solicitation or inducement of suit against the state
by a licensed attorney; any practitioner found guilty of this
newly defined crime would be perpetually disbarred.[49] Turning to the law of procedure, the Readjusters reduced to one
year the period in the statute of limitations for proving the
genuineness of coupons,[50] a move clearly aimed at cutting off
forever the large number of coupons that had not been received because of the preceding hostile legislation. Finally in
an attempt to counter the decision in the *Virginia Coupon*

---

* Champerty was the common-law crime committed by a person who
assisted a plaintiff in a lawsuit in return for a share in anything eventually
awarded by the court.

** Closely related to champerty, barratry was the common-law crime of
provoking and maintaining lawsuits.

100

Cases, a special proceeding was created to deal with the tax-payer who tendered coupons in payment of taxes. Instead of the usual levy he would be proceeded against in the name of the state, not in the name of the tax collector.[51] A precedent for this stratagem had actually been set by the federal government. Fifty years earlier in a struggle with South Carolina over enforcement of an unpopular tariff, Congress had countered the state's seizure of goods from federal customs agents by enacting that "all property taken or detained by an officer or other person under authority of any revenue law of the United States, shall be irrepleviable,* and shall be deemed to be in the custody of the law," not of the revenue officer.[52] The Virginians' object, of course, was to deprive the taxpayer of anyone to sue; they hopefully christened their latest statute the "coupon crusher."

Made bold by his victory in the *Virginia Coupon Cases,* William Royall took the offensive on behalf of his clients. In 1887, he successfully petitioned the federal circuit court in Richmond for a temporary injunction prohibiting Rufus A. Ayers, the Virginia attorney general, and other state officers from suing taxpayers who tendered coupons. When Ayers defied the order, he was imprisoned for contempt of court. To Royall's chagrin, however, the Supreme Court in *In re** Ayers*[53] ordered his release. Citing the Eleventh Amendment, the Court disclaimed jurisdiction and refused to be drawn into a struggle with the politicians. *In re Ayers* did not mean that Royall's underlying strategy was flawed, it only meant that he could not force the pace. When Virginia finally moved against those who had tendered coupons, Royall

---

* Property is irrepleviable if the common-law action of replevin was not available. If it was available, replevin was the common-law form of action by which an owner could reclaim goods wrongfully taken from him.

** *"In re,"* literally "in the matter of" or "concerning," is sometimes used in the caption of a legal proceeding in which a party makes an application on his own behalf. Such proceedings are more often captioned *"Ex parte"* ("on behalf of").

would have a strong defense. Despite more legislation and litigation the handwriting was on the wall: the days of readjustment were numbered; the Commonwealth's balances would be found wanting.

In the climacteric year 1890, when Louisiana and North Carolina won their final victories in the Supreme Court, Virginia suffered its final defeat. In *McGahey v. Virginia*[54] the Court vindicated Royall's strategy and ordered the Old Dominion to live up to the terms of its bonds. Explaining this result for a unanimous Court, Justice Joseph P. Bradley rehearsed the twenty-year history of the Virginia coupons. While noting that the justices had not always been unanimous, Bradley laid down four propositions on which all now agreed: (1) that Virginia had entered into binding contracts with the holders of the bonds and coupons issued under the Funding Act of 1871; (2) that the Virginia legislature had passed various statutes that unconstitutionally impaired the obligation of those contracts; (3) that Virginia could not be sued by the holders of the bonds and coupons because of the Eleventh Amendment; but (4) that Virginia's officers could not molest taxpayers who had tendered coupons in payment of state taxes. Cataloging the taxpayer's remedies, Bradley declared that he could proceed "by suit to recover his property, by suit against the officer to recover damages for taking it, by injunction to prevent such taking where it would be attended with irremediable injury, or by a defence to a suit brought against him for his taxes or the other claims standing against him."[55] In what appears to be a concession to the school supporters, however, the Court upheld the act prohibiting the receipt of coupons in payment of the school tax. Public education and public credit were finally uncoupled. Concluding his opinion the Justice sententiously observed: "It is certainly to be wished that some arrangement may be adopted which will be satisfactory to all the parties concerned, and relieve the courts as well as the Commonwealth

of Virginia, whose name and history recall so many interesting associations, from all further exhibitions of a controversy
that has become a vexation and a regret."[56] The state began
at once to treat in earnest with the bondholders and a settlement was reached at last.[57] New bonds, known as "century
bonds" because they matured in a hundred years, were exchanged for consols, peelers, ten-forties, and Riddlebergers
at the rate of about two for three. The state was left with a
debt of $31,469,054.[58] Interest on the centuries was 2 per-
cent for the first ten years and 3 percent thereafter. The war
with the capitalists was over at last. With the immodesty be-
fitting a successful advocate, William Royall pronounced
himself "very proud of the result, for, single-handed and
alone, I had forced this settlement, with the legislative, executive, and judicial departments of the government, and an
overwhelming majority of the people of the State against
me."[59] Like all such long drawn-out contests it left its mark
on the loser. Its debt experience led Virginia to adopt a pay-
as-you-go policy that endured well into the second half of
the twentieth century.

Virginia was different, the Funding Act had made it so.
Whereas lenders to other states had put their trust in prom-
ises, albeit of the most solemn constitutional kind, Virginia's
creditors had relied on a simple statute. Because of the realities of the federal system, it was harder for the Commonwealth to renege. For this reason it is unrealistic to suggest,
as one scholar does, that Virginia Conservatives like their
counterparts elsewhere "could easily have maintained their
position by stealing the Readjusters' thunder, defying the
courts, and forcibly reducing the interest burden."[60] After
1871, nothing could be as easy for Virginia as for its Southern neighbors. Plaintiffs suing on other bonds had to ask the
Supreme Court to order state politicians to do the very acts
they had been elected not to do. To enforce such orders the
political branches of the federal government would have had

to violate the cardinal principle of the Compromise of 1877 and send the troops back to the South. As an excuse not to issue these orders the Court dusted off the Eleventh Amendment. But as Chief Justice Marshall had demonstrated in *Marbury v. Madison,* it makes a difference whether the judicial power is exercised offensively or defensively. The plaintiffs' case against Virginia did not require orders compelling the Commonwealth's officers to act, only to refrain from acting. The economic effect was, to be sure, the same: the Old Dominion was just as poor if its income fell or its expenditures rose. But the difference in terms of judicial power was substantial. Under the federal system the last word on whether taxes have been paid or not belongs to the judges. It is so if they say so.

Of course, it is possible for a state to defy such pronouncements. It might proceed to levy on the taxpayer's property precisely as if taxes had not been paid. But this does not necessarily mean that federal troops would be required to enforce the judgment. Without the strong arm of the executive the Court could not prevent the physical taking of goods, but by its say-so alone it could deprive the taker of *title,* the legal abstraction describing the relationship between persons and property. Title may sound insubstantial but it translates directly into prices in the marketplace. Buyers are understandably reluctant to purchase goods when there is a controversy concerning ownership. Lawyers describe it, in picturesque phrase, as a "cloud on title." Without coercion the Court may be unable to award actual possession but it can certainly determine title. Unable to hurl thunderbolts it can at least summon up clouds.

Justice Bradley was the theorist who finally mastered the complexities of power both real and judicial. Although before 1877 he had been an upholder of the Marshallian tradition respecting the Eleventh Amendment, and in 1881 he had voted in favor of the creditors of Virginia, he switched in

1883 and came out against the creditors of Southern states. In 1890, he finally got it straight: after the Compromise of 1877 the Southland could not be coerced, but Virginia was different. In that term he wrote the opinions of the Court that explained it all: the general rule of nonliability applied to Southern states like Louisiana and North Carolina, but an exception to the general rule existed in favor of the creditors of Virginia. As will appear in the next chapter, in the same term he also joined in the opinion in favor of the creditors of cities and counties. High politics did not necessitate any weakening in the Court's resolve to make municipal corporations do their duty.

An unusual glimpse at the inner workings of the Supreme Court in 1890 and at the mastermind himself was provided by a newcomer to the Court, Justice David J. Brewer. In an after-dinner speech to a group of young lawyers, the justice described the conference room where court decisions were made: "There is a long table, and we all sit down at the side except Justice Bradley, who takes the end because his legs are too long to sit sideways. He looks all dried up, but there is more vinegar and hard fight in him than in 20 of you boys. When they all get settled the tug of war commences. They are all strong men, and do not waste a word. They lock horns and the fight is stubborn; arguments are hurled against each other, the discussion grows animated and continues so for hours."[61] Out of those animated discussions came the fateful decisions on public debts and the Eleventh Amendment. Appointed in 1870, because of his grasp of political and economic realities, the "fifth judge" on the notorious Electoral Commission of 1877, Bradley was uniquely prepared to sort out the complex issues raised by the end of Reconstruction. Seasoned with his vinegar, the opinions of the Court laid down the law for the Republic's second century. His mastery of the advanced course in judicial power was the true measure of his greatness.

105

In 1890, Virginia's struggle with its burden of debt was only two-thirds over. Nineteen years earlier, in 1871, Virginia had disclaimed liability on one-third of the antebellum debt and issued certificates attributable to West Virginia. Although the West Virginia Constitution of 1862 had bound the new state to assume an "equitable proportion" of the public debt of the Old Dominion and had directed the legislature in Wheeling to provide for its payment "as soon as may be practicable,"[62] the Mountain State had never paid a cent. During the two decades in which Virginia struggled with its self-assessed share of indebtedness it paid little attention to the share putatively owed by the state "made from its rib." Once the Commonwealth had settled with the bondholders, however, it took up the matter with its neighbor. In 1894, the Virginia General Assembly created a Debt Commission to treat with West Virginia.[63] After half a dozen years of fruitless negotiations it empowered the Commission to accept the deposit of certificates that represented the share attributed to West Virginia and to bring suit if necessary on behalf of the bondholders.[64] Holders of the overwhelming majority of certificates promptly deposited them with the Virginians; of the $15,481,692 of certificates outstanding, $13,173,435 was deposited.[65]

But West Virginia was in no hurry to settle. Over the decades it had grown accustomed to think that it had come into existence with a clean slate. Perhaps it believed that loyalty in the Civil War earned it credit in its accounting with the secessionists. Whatever its motive the Mountain State was unyielding in negotiations. Relying on an act passed by the unionist rump of the Virginia legislature,[66] a sort of government-in-exile during the Civil War, West Virginia claimed that its fair share equaled the amount of borrowed money that had actually been spent within the western counties plus "a just proportion" of the ordinary expenses of state government minus taxes paid during the same period. Calculations on this basis varied widely, sometimes showing that West Virginia owed Virginia four million dollars and sometimes showing that Virginia actually owed West Virginia three million dollars![67]

Negotiators on behalf of the Old Dominion must have thought their hand strengthened by the decision in 1904 in *South Dakota v. North Carolina,* in which the Supreme Court demonstrated that its writ still ran against states. In 1906, Virginia filed papers opening a legal battle with West Virginia that raged for a dozen years.[08] Virginia asked the Court to determine West Virginia's portion of the state debt and to issue a writ of mandamus compelling payment.[69] West Virginia predictably challenged the Court's jurisdiction. Since the Court had, it argued, no power to enforce a judgment against a state, there was no jurisdiction to issue one. Without a remedy there is no right. In a second challenge to the jurisdiction West Virginia argued that Virginia had an insufficient interest in the controversy because the debt, if any, was owing not to the Commonwealth but to the owners of the certificates. With respect to the Louisiana state debt, New Hampshire had not been permitted to sue on behalf of its citizens despite its well-recognized role as *parens patriae.* Why then could Virginia sue on behalf of the bondholders, many of whom were not even Virginia citizens? While finding many precedents opposed to West Virginia's first argument the justices dismissed the second with an ipsedixitism: "We are satisfied that . . . we have jurisdiction. . . ."[70] The matter was then referred to an officer of the Court known as a "master" for ascertainment of the facts necessary for decision. In 1911 the Court, using the master's figures, apportioned the antebellum debt on the basis of property values exclusive of slaves. On this reckoning West Virginia owed 23.5 percent of the total.[71] Although the certificates represented one-third of the debt, West Virginia was held accountable for only one-quarter; the bondholders simply lost the difference. At this stage no coercion was applied to the Mountain State. As Justice Oliver Wendell Holmes observed for the Court: "Great States have a temper superior to that of private litigants, and it is to be hoped that enough has been decided for patriotism, the fraternity of the Union, and mutual consideration to bring it to an end."[72]

West Virginia showed itself unaccommodating, however, and took exception to the calculations. It convinced the Court in 1915 to reduce its liability by attributing to it a proportional share of those assets pledged for the retirement of the debt held by Virginia at the outbreak of the war.[73] While that setoff lessened the defendant's liability, the Court in the same action greatly increased it by holding the state liable for interest compounded since 1861. As of July 1, 1915, the West Virginia debt was calculated to be $12,393,929, of which $4,215,622 was principal and $8,178,307 interest.[74] In vain West Virginia urged that it had a claim against the United States derived from Virginia arising out of the cession of the Northwest Territory in 1783 and that its share would discharge the judgment.[75]

Fraternal feelings proved insufficient to move the Mountain State to appropriate the necessary sum, so in 1918 Virginia asked the Court to consider ways and means of enforcing its judgment.[76] Invoking federal judicial power against a state gave pause to staunch states' righters in Virginia, but only briefly.[77] In reply the Court confidently opined that its orders were federal orders, sustainable "by every authority of the federal government, judicial, legislative, or executive."[78] Judicial power included, the Court hinted, the power to issue a writ of mandamus to the West Virginia legislature requiring it to levy a tax, and even the power to levy the tax itself. Before exercising this awesome power the Court announced its intention to give Congress an opportunity to bring legislative power to bear. Although proceeding with all deliberate speed, the Court made clear that West Virginia would eventually be

108

compelled to pay. Any other result, the Court said, would "overthrow the doctrines irrevocably settled by the great controversy of the Civil War."[79] In 1919, West Virginia conceded defeat and paid the certificates, outstanding since 1871.[80]

There are tactics and strategies in law as in war and the justices of the Supreme Court are constrained by circumstances no less than are generals in the field. After the end of Reconstruction the justices, whatever their personal feelings about private property, countenanced the repudiation of millions of dollars' worth of Southern state bonds. But during the same years, the Virginia coupon killers failed in their mission. The provision in the Funding Act of 1871 making the coupons receivable for state taxes put the creditors of Virginia in position to take advantage of federal judicial power. Although the Court in the 1880s was unwilling to try to make its writ run in the newly restored Southern states, it had fewer misgivings when the lone state of West Virginia was in the dock a generation later. While moving cautiously it nonetheless moved inexorably to judgment. The chances of making this defendant do justice to its creditors were much better. Compared to investors in other Southern obligations the investors in Virginia securities did well, although their recovery was a long time coming. Throughout the decades-long controversy the Eleventh Amendment and sovereign immunity played noticeably minor roles.

VII

Another Exception: Cities and Counties

In 1890, the year Louisiana and North Carolina won but Virginia lost, the Supreme Court also faced the issue of the liability of cities and counties on their bonds. A county out West had defaulted. Perhaps with an eye to the success most Southern states had had with the Eleventh Amendment, the lawyer for the county challenged the Court's jurisdiction. Cities and counties are parts of states; technically they are municipal corporations, created by state law to administer local government. If a state is immune from suit, the argument ran, then cities and counties are also immune. In *Lincoln County* [*Nevada*] *v. Luning*[1] the justices unanimously rejected this reasoning. Writing the opinion of the Court, Justice David J. Brewer, the nephew of that doughty debt-payer, Justice Stephen J. Field, observed that "the records of this court for the last thirty years are full of suits against counties, and it would seem as though by general consent the jurisdiction of the Federal courts in such suits had become established."[2] Of course thirty years earlier, at the outbreak of the Civil War, the purest Marshallian tradition on the Eleventh Amendment was still being upheld. The unsettling of that tradition, which made this particular argument plausible, had occurred within the past decade.

With unconscious irony Brewer cited none other than the great Chief Justice. In *Osborn v. The Bank of the United States,* John Marshall had laid down the law on the Eleventh Amendment: it applies only when a state is "a party on the record"[3]—to be precise, when it is named as defendant. A county is not a state, said Brewer, so it is not protected by the Eleventh Amendment. *Quod erat demonstrandum!* Of course, Brewer was forced to admit, such simple reasoning was not consistent with *In re Ayers,* the case of the Virginia attorney general decided only three years earlier. For the matter of that, it was not consistent with *North Carolina v. Temple,* decided the same day. Those cases established that the Eleventh Amendment was applicable whenever a state is the real, even if not the nominal, defendant. But cities and counties, Brewer said, are parts of the state in only a "remote sense."[4] To this day the law remains as Justice Brewer stated it in 1890: cities and counties may not shelter behind the Eleventh Amendment although whatever power they have is derived from the parent state. In this regard, at least, the Marshallian tradition remains unbroken. To those who insist on logical symmetry in the law—most noticeably law students—this places an "unjustifiable strain" on the logic of federalism.[5] To Chief Justice Marshall, perhaps, the immunity of the states had seemed an intolerable strain on nationalism. To the judges of the Gilded Age, however, logic was not everything. It just so happened that counties had tended to issue bonds in the West, while in the South, states had usually done the job. Property in the form of bonds could be defended in the mid-West and West, but similar property in the South had to be sacrificed to the higher politics of the Compromise of 1877.

In *Luning* the lawyer for the county also advanced one technical argument worth noting. The state of Nevada, when it empowered its counties to issue bonds, had made express provision for suits against them, but only in the county courts.[6] The reason for providing for suits at all may have been to reassure purchasers of the bonds that in the event of dispute or default they would get their day in court. But suit in the court of the debtor county was unappealing to dissatis-

111

fied bondholders: judge and jury were too likely to be influenced by the consequences for county taxpayers. So plaintiffs like Luning preferred to resort to federal court where life-tenured judges and less provincial juries might take a dimmer view of default. But did federal courts have jurisdiction when state law limited suit to courts of the state? The county's attorney insisted they did not. The Supreme Court held they did. The question, as Brewer observed, had been answered more than twenty years before in *Cowles v. Mercer County* [*Illinois*].[7] That case had involved a similar statute[8] which the Court had struck down with the words: "The power to contract with citizens of other States implies liability to suit by citizens of other States, and no statute limitation of suability can defeat a jurisdiction given by the Constitution."[9]

For thirty years, as Justice Brewer pointed out, counties had tried in vain to escape their obligations. Disputes centered particularly around so-called railroad-aid bonds. To the eastern part of the United States settlers had come before the age of the railroad; when railroads were built they linked established communities. But in the West, railroads were pioneer roads; towns grew up along the lines, and metropolises at the railheads. Where the rails ran was a matter of economic life and death. As fast as western counties were organized they began to compete for railroad connections. All they had to offer was their credit and they pledged it in aid of railroads with the abandon of speculators. During the frenzied bidding, opportunities for graft and fraud abounded. If railroads never reached completion or if they charged extortionate rates when they did, zeal in repayment predictably waned. The effect was proportionately greater as counties were filled with newcomers lacking any involvement in the earlier financing.

The shady side of municipal finance from 1860 to 1890 generated a plethora of cases for the high court and revealed the extent of judicial power to coerce reluctant cities and counties to pay their lawful debts. The leading case of *Board of Commissioners [of Knox County, Indiana] v. Aspinwall,*[10] decided while Roger Taney was still Chief Justice, set the tone for the Gilded Age and after. State law authorized the county to aid railroad construction but required that bond issues be approved by voters at special elections.[11] Although an election had indeed been held, it was later claimed that inadequate notice had been given. In 1859, the Supreme Court refused even to examine the evidence; it was enough that the county board of commissioners had certified that prescribed forms had been followed and that the present holders of bonds were bona fide purchasers, that is, good faith buyers who had bought without notice of any irregularity. What made the Knox County case famous was its sequel. The board of commissioners refused to levy the tax necessary to satisfy the judgment. In 1861, the bondholders, now judgment creditors of the county, asked the federal circuit court to compel the levy by writ of mandamus. The writ was issued and the Supreme Court affirmed the order.[12] A few years later a disgruntled justice was to call this "the first instance in which a Federal court ever issued a writ of mandamus to a State officer in the history of this government."[13] As it turned out, this concern was voiced too soon: although orders to municipal officers continued to be issued at a great rate, orders to state officers properly so-called fell off markedly after 1877.

In early 1864, during the last months of Taney's life, the Supreme Court decided the notorious case of *Gelpcke v. City of Dubuque [Iowa].*[14] Pursuant to state law[15] the city had issued railroad-aid bonds but had soon defaulted. Its principal defense was that after it had issued the bonds the state supreme court had overruled an earlier decision and declared the law authorizing them invalid under the state constitution.[16] A bondholder sued the city in federal court, relying for jurisdiction on diversity of citizenship. In such cases the rule was—and is—that federal courts accept state court interpretations of the state constitution. In *Gelpcke,* however, the Supreme Court applied state law as it had been when the bonds were issued, not as it then was. In consequence it ruled in favor of the plaintiff. In ringing words Justice Noah H. Swayne declared: "We shall never immolate truth, justice, and the law, because a State tribunal has erected the altar and decreed the sacrifice."[17] The result, of course, was that the law of Iowa was one thing in state court and another in federal court.

In *Riggs v. Johnson County [Iowa]*[18] in 1868, the inevitable collision occurred. After holders of defaulted bonds had obtained a federal writ of mandamus ordering municipal officers to levy the necessary tax, the officers were enjoined by a state court from obeying. The Supreme Court upheld its version of Iowa law. A year later the Court explained how it expected to make its writ run. In *Supervisors [of Lee County, Iowa] v. Rogers*[19] it authorized the local federal court to appoint a United States marshal to levy and collect the tax. If there was any doubt about whether the strong arm of the executive would uphold the Court, it was dispelled by a public expression from the White House. In a letter to Gen. John A. Dix, Civil War veteran and president of one of the railroads involved, from another general and president, the word went forth:

> Executive Mansion,
> Washington, D.C., June 20, 1870.
>
> To Gen. J. A. Dix:
> Dear Sir:—Yours of the 11th inst., stating that the report had been circulated in Iowa, that I had stated that I would not enforce the laws for the collection of taxes to pay railroad bonds, if resisted by the citizens, is received. It is hardly necessary for me to deny such a statement. I would hardly invite a community to resist the laws which I am sworn to execute. I do, however, emphatically deny the re-

port, and state further that if it becomes my duty to use force to execute the laws of Iowa, or any other State, I shall do so without hesitation.

Very respectfully, your obedient servant.

U. S. Grant.[20]

The letter was duly published in Iowa newspapers. Barely five years after Appomattox, the threat of force by the war hero-President could not be shrugged off. As if more were needed to compel compliance, the Supreme Court ruled in 1871 in *Amy v. Supervisors* [*of Des Moines County, Iowa*][21] that county officers could be held liable out of their own pockets for damages resulting from their refusal to obey a mandamus to levy a tax.

Since bondholders were invoking diversity jurisdiction a nice question of federal law arose. The bonds and any coupons cut therefrom were freely bought and sold in the marketplace. The present owner of any given bond might well not be the original purchaser. Yet a clause of the Judiciary Act of 1789, known as the Assignee Clause, excluded from the diversity jurisdiction of lower federal courts "any suit to recover the contents of any promissory note or other chose in action in favour of an assignee, unless a suit might have been prosecuted in such courts to recover the said contents if no assignment had been made."[22] This seemed to mean that unless the original purchaser had not been a citizen of the state whose law was to be applied, his assignee could not invoke diversity jurisdiction. Of course this would make some bonds of the same issue enforceable in federal courts while others were not, and would wreak havoc in the bond market. As always the Court was equal to its task: "Bonds with coupons, payable to bearer, are negotiable securities and pass by delivery. . . ."[23]—by delivery, that is, not by assignment. Without a formal assignment the Assignee Clause is not implicated; its effect is limited to excluding only those cases in which the assignment was merely collusive, to get federal

115

court jurisdiction when it would not otherwise be available.

The Court was resolved that counties would pay their railroad-aid bonds and troops were ready to enforce the orders. In 1876, a distinguished federal judge late of the Iowa Supreme Court, John F. Dillon, observed that the Court had "set a face of flint against repudiation, even when made on legal grounds deemed solid by the State courts, by municipalities which had been deceived and defrauded."[24] Two years later a justice usually in the minority on municipal bond cases confided to a private correspondent: "Our court or a majority of it are, if not monomaniacs, as much bigots and fanatics on that subject as is the most unhesitating Mahemodan [sic] in regard to his religion."[25] Of course, a new dispensation was soon to be revealed in behalf of Southern state bonds.

In 1881, the admission of Dakota Territory to statehood foundered in part on Eastern resentment at repudiation of railroad-aid bonds by one of the Territory's counties.[26] Although the Supreme Court had as usual ruled in favor of the bondholders,[27] the county refused to pay. In its recalcitrance the municipal corporation was aided and abetted by the territorial legislature, which repealed a prior law authorizing a levy upon the property of counties for the satisfaction of judgments.[28] The purpose of this repeal was to disable federal courts from levying on county property, since by federal law their power to order collection in diversity suits was measured by what state law provided for state courts.[29] If this were not enough, the territorial legislature also passed an act enabling county commissioners to terminate their offices by filing resignations with the county clerk.[30] The purpose was to frustrate federal writs of mandamus and to protect county officers from the consequences of disobedience. Whenever writs were issued, the officers immediately resigned. In other states municipal officers became so adept at resigning that federal orders were stymied for years.[31] This loophole in national judicial power was not closed until 1961, when the Federal Rules of Civil Procedure were amended to provide for the automatic substitution of the resigning officer's successor.[32] In the case of Dakota Territory the penalty was political: statehood was postponed almost a decade.[33]

With regard to municipal bonds the Compromise of 1877 was a point on which nothing turned. In 1874 a treatise writer had confidently stated: "while doubts have been expressed as to the power of the circuit courts of the United States to issue the writ of mandamus to municipal officers, commanding them to levy a tax in payment of judgments recovered in those courts upon municipal obligations, the right is now clearly established, both upon principle and authority."[34] In succeeding editions in 1884 and 1896 the author repeated the statement verbatim.[35] Throughout the decade in which Southern states (except Virginia) were vindicating their right to repudiate, Western counties were being held to the highest standards of fiscal probity. In 1891 a scholarly article in the *Harvard Law Review* could congratulate the Court for displaying "firm moral fibre" in the county bond cases.[36]

"Moral fibre" always comes at a cost. For three decades, as Justice Brewer observed in 1890, the Supreme Court had wrestled with defaulting counties. A modern authority on this period reckons that "cases on municipal bonds bulked larger than any other category of the Court's business."[37] Frequent experience with this line of work had taught the justices by 1876 that public bodies determined to renege were redoubtable opponents. Orders to pay would have to be backed up by force. So long as the President and Congress were willing, the Court could insure the obligation of contracts. Up to the inauguration of Rutherford B. Hayes the support of the elected branches could be relied upon. States as well as counties could be held to the mark. Thereafter the politicians were unwilling any longer to coerce the South. With respect to

117

state bonds, the Court faced a resolute and united Southland determined to have its way. A hasty revival of the Eleventh Amendment saved it from humiliation. With respect to municipal obligations, however, the balance of power was different. Sparsely settled counties in politically insignificant states could not command the sympathies of the highest powers in the nation. Seizing on the elusive distinction between states and their political subdivisions, the Court could maintain the Marshallian tradition respecting municipalities. That it made the justices look like bullyboys, imperiously commanding hapless counties but impotently deferring to the virile states of the Old Confederacy, could not be helped.

The payoff for this display of "moral fibre" came on the financial markets. In 1889, Wall Streeters ranked municipal bonds second only to federal securities.[38] Because cities and counties could be compelled to pay up if necessary, they enjoyed a high credit rating. The historic process of importing capital to develop the mid-West and West continued unabated. After the Eleventh Amendment decisions in the 1880s, of course, state bonds ranked lower on Wall Street. States were less credit-worthy than their creatures. By then, however, the Southland had happily relapsed to its former role in the American economy: exporting cash crops and importing finished goods. Foreign investment in internal improvements was not a high priority in the region. Southerners were grateful to be relieved of so much debt and anxious to restore insofar as possible the antebellum social and racial arrangements.

The special status of cities and counties in American law has continued up to the present. States are protected by the Eleventh Amendment but municipal corporations are not. As intermediate bodies proliferate in state government, problems of definition arise. A state department of banking has been held to be protected by the Amendment,[39] but a state

118

board of education has not.[40] A bridge and tunnel district has been held to be protected,[41] but a bridge and tunnel authority has not.[42] A state university construction fund has been held to be protected,[43] but the board of trustees of an internal improvement fund has not.[44] The test is said to be whether a monetary judgment against the body in question would be satisfied out of the state treasury;[45] sometimes the question is asked whether the body is the state's "alter ego." In 1977, the Supreme Court held that "a local school board . . . is more like a county or city than it is like an arm of the State"[46] and is therefore unable to avail itself of the Eleventh Amendment. In consequence a private citizen could call the school board to account for violating his constitutional rights. Because local governmental units are not considered parts of states for Eleventh Amendment purposes, federal law may bear on them in ways not possible with respect to states. For example, in 1978 the Supreme Court held that the civil rights provision of the Ku Klux Klan Act[47] applies to municipal corporations despite the Eleventh Amendment.[48] Cities and counties that deprive a citizen of civil rights are therefore answerable "in an action at law, suit in equity, or other proper proceeding for redress."[49] States, on the contrary, are immune from all such proceedings.

The distinction in Eleventh Amendment law between cities and counties on the one hand and states on the other produces bizarre results. If a state provides for suits against municipal corporations, it may not limit the suits to state courts only; that is, if a state tries to limit such suits, the limitation is invalid and the suit may be brought in federal as well as in state court. This was the rule laid down in 1869 in *Cowles v. Mercer County* [*Illinois*], cited by Justice Brewer in 1890, and is still the law today.[50] But in 1900 in *Smith v. Reeves*[51] the Supreme Court held that a state may limit suits against itself to state courts; that is, a limitation on suits against a state to courts of the state is effective and the local federal court may not hear the case. So zealous has the Supreme Court been to prevent extensions of federal jurisdiction that it has refused to permit suit against a state in federal court despite the fact that state law permitted the action "in any court of competent jurisdiction."[52] Such apparently general permission was not construed to include federal courts when monetary claims against the state were involved.[53] In 1985, the Court reaffirmed that "[t]he test for determining whether a State has waived its immunity from federal court jurisdiction is a stringent one": there must be "an unequivocal waiver specifically applicable to federal court jurisdiction."[54] Unlike the hapless cities and counties—and state bodies sufficiently like them—states can decide not only whether they will be sued but where.

VIII

From 1890 to 1908

The principal speaker at the annual meeting of the New York Bar Association on January 25, 1908, was the prominent New York lawyer William D. Guthrie. His topic was the Eleventh Amendment.[1] What interested lawyers who represented America's largest corporations in this aspect of constitutional law was the current political unrest about the issuance of injunctions by lower federal courts against state officers. Only three months earlier a convention of state attorneys general had called for limitations on the power of federal judges to issue such orders.[2] President Theodore Roosevelt had referred to the problem in his State of the Union message,[3] and in Congress, bills[4] and even a constitutional amendment[5] had been offered to curtail federal jurisdiction. The question was expected to figure in the upcoming presidential campaign.

Reviewing for his audience the history of the Eleventh Amendment Guthrie noted that Chief Justice Marshall's reasoning in *Osborn v. The Bank of the United States* had been expressly "reaffirmed by the Supreme Court as late as 1873 in the case of *Davis v. Gray,* which was a suit against the governor of the state of Texas"; but, Guthrie lamented, "it has since been repudiated in later cases."[6] What Guthrie had in mind, of course, was the line of cases from the 1880s dealing with Southern state bonds. The Amendment, it had been held, barred relief not only against states but also against state officers in fiscal matters. It prevented suits against a

121

state by other states suing on behalf of their citizens. It even influenced the decision to refuse to hear suits by a citizen against his own state or its officers. But the abnegation of federal judicial power had never been complete. Virginia had not been permitted to renege on its coupons, and cities and counties had not been permitted to shelter their defaults behind the Eleventh Amendment. Indeed as the politicians in 1908 were well aware, the Amendment had not prevented issuance by lower federal courts of injunctions prohibiting state officers from enforcing state regulatory laws.

The reassertion of federal judicial power had begun soon after the Southern bond cases. Benefiting from a perspective that Guthrie was denied, a twentieth-century scholar who reviewed the Court's work from 1890 to 1920 described "sophistry" as "the common coin of the Court in coping both with sovereign immunity and the bar of the Eleventh Amendment."[7] Some such development was inevitable. As Chief Justice Marshall had long before observed, the federal Union would be ungovernable without power to call constituent states to account. Marshall had squared the Eleventh Amendment with federalism by sanctioning in America the English practice of suits against officers. The Louisiana and North Carolina bond cases, however, discredited that approach, at least for the time being.

But the English bag of tricks was not empty. Since the Middle Ages Englishmen had been able to test the rightfulness of the king's possession of disputed property by means of the "petition of right"—or, in Law French, *"petition de droit."*[8] Since a subject could not sue the king in his own courts without permission, the petitioner appealed directly to the sovereign. Once the petition was endorsed with the words, also in Law French, *"Soit droit fait al partie"* ("Let right be done to the party"),[9] the judges could take jurisdiction and decide the case as if between ordinary litigants. In time the granting of the petition became routine and formed an important element in constitutional monarchy. In the American Republic the significance of this bit of ancient history lay in the fact that a sovereign could consent to be sued. Once the Supreme Court had linked the Eleventh Amendment with sovereign immunity in *Hans v. Louisiana,* it was possible to argue that a state could consent to be sued in federal court despite the Eleventh Amendment; or, in other words, that the state could waive the immunity conferred by the Eleventh Amendment.

Such an argument would be attractive; after all, what harm could it do? If a state consented to suit, the problem of enforcing an adverse judgment would be lessened. And the argument seemed analogous to one advanced so long ago in *Chisholm.* Chief Justice Jay had worried aloud in that case about suits against the United States: How could judgments be enforced? But if the government consented to suit the problem would disappear. Suits against consenting states seemed equally safe. Only a technicality remained: the Constitution extends the judicial power to "controversies to which the United States shall be a party."[10] If the Court took jurisdiction over a suit to which the federal government had consented, it could point to that grant of power. But the Eleventh Amendment forbids the Court to construe the judicial power to extend to suits "against one of the United States by citizens of another state, or by citizens or subjects of any foreign state." How could the Court exercise jurisdiction, with or without consent, in an area forbidden to it by the Eleventh Amendment? The question worried Guthrie in his address to the New York Bar Association. As he understood it, it was a "fundamental principle that a federal court cannot exercise jurisdiction in any case to which the judicial power of the United States, as delegated and defined in the Constitution, does not extend."[11]

But this technicality never troubled the Court. In 1906 in *Gunter v. Atlantic Coast Line Railroad,* the Court treated as "elementary" the proposition that a state can waive its Eleventh Amendment immunity.[12] The idea had indeed been gaining ground for decades—ever since, in fact, the Court had given the Amendment an expansive reading in the Southern bond cases. In *New Hampshire v. Louisiana* in 1883, the Court had opined that the "evident purpose of the amendment . . . was to prohibit all suits against a State by or for citizens of other States, or aliens, *without the consent of the State to be sued. . . .*"[13] Within weeks of uttering that dictum the Court provided an example: in *Clark v. Barnard,* Rhode Island was permitted to intervene as a defendant in an ongoing lawsuit; the state's Eleventh Amendment immunity, said the Court, is "a personal privilege which it may waive at pleasure."[14] In *Hans v. Louisiana* in 1890, a sweeping discharge of state liability was coupled with the notion that jurisdiction could be exercised if the state waived its immunity: "the obligations of a State rest for their performance upon its honor and good faith," intoned Justice Bradley, "and cannot be made the subjects of judicial cognizance *unless the State consents to be sued, or comes itself into court.*"[15] In *Hans* the Eleventh Amendment had been linked with sovereign immunity; at common law the sovereign could consent to suit; so too under American law—despite the words of the Amendment.

In *Gunter* consent (or waiver) was used to solve a problem from the past, a legacy (if you will) of the Compromise of 1877. Early in the twentieth century South Carolina challenged an exemption from state taxes claimed by the Atlantic Coast Line Railroad, an exemption dating from the days of state sponsorship of railroad building, before the Civil War. South Carolina's problem was that the exemption had been challenged once before—and upheld by the Supreme Court. In 1868 the state had assessed taxes on the line despite the exemption. Two years later Thomas E. B. Pegues, a shareholder in the railroad, had sued to enjoin the company from paying the taxes, and the state tax collectors from collecting them. The shareholder won in federal circuit court and in *Humphrey v. Pegues*[16] the Supreme Court affirmed the decision. In the high court the attorney for the South Carolina officers made no mention of the Eleventh Amendment. *Humphrey* was argued and decided in early 1873, while the Court had under consideration *Davis v. Gray*, the case against the Texas governor that elicited the Court's ringing affirmation of *Osborn*. The Eleventh Amendment was simply not a winning argument in those days, and the state's attorney wasted no words on it. A few years later, after the Compromise of 1877, the situation changed dramatically.

In *Gunter* in 1906, the state's attorney relied volubly on the Eleventh Amendment. The jurisdictional argument was, after all, his only hope. In the changed circumstances of the Populist and Progressive eras the justices were astute to defend corporate privileges against state spoliation. But how could the Court uphold its 1873 decision in light of the Eleventh Amendment? Consent (or waiver) was the answer. "Although a State may not be sued without its consent," said the Court, "such immunity is a privilege which may be waived, and hence where a State voluntarily becomes a party to a cause and submits its rights for judicial determination, it will be bound thereby and cannot escape the result of its own voluntary act by invoking the prohibitions of the Eleventh Amendment."[17] A stickler like Guthrie might be troubled about how the Court could take jurisdiction—even with the consent of the state—when the judicial power by virtue of the Eleventh Amendment cannot be construed to reach such a case.[18] The argument he would have preferred was technically more precise: "It does not follow that, because a State cannot be sued, it may not authorize its agent to defend without pleading the absence of the real party in interest, and the denial of jurisdiction over the State as principal does not necessarily imply a denial of jurisdiction over the officer when doing or attempting to do an illegal act as its agent or repre-

125

sentative."[19] This was close to the argument advanced by Justice Field dissenting in *Jumel* twenty-five years earlier. Perhaps the Court was unwilling to resurrect a viewpoint that would cast doubt on the Southern bond cases. In any event, consent, whatever its theoretical drawbacks, entered Eleventh Amendment law.

The theory was sufficient to sustain the particular corporate privilege at issue in *Gunter,* but unless greatly expanded it would not solve all the problems of corporate capitalism. While the law concerning consent would expand (and contract) in later years, the pressing problems of state interference with business needed an already mature theory. Suits against officers—the old standby of the common law and Chief Justice Marshall's preferred approach—offered a more attractive alternative. As the fictional Mr. Dooley observed: "I care not who makes th' laws iv a nation if I can get out an injunction."[20] Although lower federal courts had been getting out injunctions with alacrity, the practice as Guthrie was acutely aware had not been finally rehabilitated by the Supreme Court. Indeed the decision in *In re Ayers,* the case concerning the Virginia attorney general, had erected formidable obstacles. No sooner were the Southern bonds disposed of than the Supreme Court began the process of removing the new impediments. In 1891 in *Pennoyer v. McConnaughy*[21] the Court upheld an injunction prohibiting state officers from enforcing an unconstitutional state statute that interfered with contractual rights acquired earlier from the state.

From then on, at least in cases challenging state regulation of railroads, a new spirit was evident. Relying on the Due Process and Equal Protection Clauses of the Fourteenth Amendment, the Supreme Court regularly upheld injunctions against state officers. In one of the cruellest ironies of American constitutional history, the central Reconstruction Amendment was converted to the use of business. Following the Negro's short span in the sun, the corporation enjoyed a long season as the "special favorite of the laws." In 1894 in *Reagan v. Farmers' Loan & Trust Co.*[22] the Court upheld an injunction that prohibited the Texas attorney general and members of the state railroad commission from enforcing freight and passenger rates found by the Court to be unreasonably low. In 1898 in *Smyth v. Ames*[23] the Court upheld an injunction restraining the Nebraska board of transportation from proceeding against railroads that violated prescribed rate schedules. But the ghost of *In re Ayers* had not yet been laid; in 1899, it revived and inspired the Court to overturn an injunction that prohibited the Alabama attorney general and other law officers of the state from enforcing an allegedly unconstitutional statute fixing tolls on a railway bridge and from prosecuting agents of the railroad for charging illegal rates.[24]

Since most plaintiffs suing states in the 1890s alleged violations of the Fourteenth Amendment, it was open to the justices to have held that that Amendment superseded the Eleventh Amendment. In 1903 in *Prout v. Starr*[25] they approached such a holding. Opining that the Eleventh Amendment cannot prevent federal courts from inquiring "whether the salutary provisions of the Fourtenth Amendment have been disregarded by state enactment,"[26] the Court enjoined Nebraska's attorney general from enforcing the railroad rate schedules litigated earlier in *Smyth v. Ames*. As Guthrie made clear in his address to the New York Bar Association, the corporate bar was alert to the possibilities of this argument. With characteristic virtuosity he pointed to a possible refinement: since each of the Reconstruction Amendments gives Congress enforcement power,[27] it could be argued that the national legislature can "confer on the courts of the United States jurisdiction of suits against States or state officers as an appropriate means of enforcing the later amendments."[28] Although not adopted at the time, the idea was to be read into American constitutional law in the last quarter of the twentieth century.[29]

127

By the time Guthrie spoke, the problem of repudiated Southern bonds was clearly a specter from an increasingly distant past. The present was dominated by the grander issue of government power to regulate the economy. In 1895 in *Pollock v. Farmers' Loan & Trust Co.*[30] the Court construed legislative power not to extend to the enactment of a national income tax. The Constitution requires that "direct taxes" must be apportioned among the states on the basis of population.[31] Although there was authority that only head taxes and property taxes were "direct" within the meaning of the Constitution,[32] the Supreme Court held that an income tax was as well. As the fiscal needs of the national government grew more pressing, the Sixteenth Amendment was adopted, empowering Congress to "lay and collect taxes on incomes . . . without apportionment. . . ."[33] Not since *Chisholm v. Georgia* had a court case led so directly to constitutional amendment. *Pollock* ranked, in the eyes of Charles Evans Hughes, as a "self-inflicted wound"[34] of the magnitude of *Dred Scott*[35] and the *Legal Tender Cases*.[36] State regulation of the economy was no more welcome to the justices. In 1905 in *Lochner v. New York*[37] they held that a state law prohibiting employment of bakers for more than ten hours a day or more than sixty hours a week violated the Due Process Clause of the Fourteenth Amendment.

Whether states could shelter their regulatory acts behind the Eleventh Amendment was finally answered in the landmark case of *Ex parte* Young*[38] on March 23, 1908—not two months after Guthrie's somber address. Test cases[39] had been filed before Guthrie spoke, challenging regulatory legislation in Minnesota[40] and North Carolina.[41] Both states had attempted to preclude judicial review by imposing enormous

---

* *"Ex parte"*—in English, "on behalf of"—is the usual caption of a legal proceeding in which one party makes an application on his own behalf, as to be released from prison. Such proceedings are occasionally captioned *"In re,"* as in *In re Ayers* discussed in Chapter VI.

penalties for violation on railroads and their agents. The normal legal route for testing the validity of a law is to violate it and then in a subsequent prosecution, to offer in defense the alleged defect. But civil disobedience can be discouraged by the imposition of Draconian penalties. North Carolina's railroad statute, Guthrie observed, imposed fines that would amount to $2,500,000 a day, and Minnesota's set fines that in one month might aggregate several hundred million dollars. Both statutes also included severe punishments for railroad employees who violated their provisions. "If Congress or a state legislature," Guthrie declaimed, "can compel any class to submit to an unconstitutional statute by imposing ruinous fines and penalties, or other provisions intended to operate *in terrorem* . . . then the constitutional limitations imposed by the people can be readily circumvented and nullified, and our supposed rights and liberties will exist only in the grace or self-restraint of legislatures."[42]

In the Minnesota case, stockholders in the railroads sought a federal injunction against the state attorney general, Edward T. Young, prohibiting his enforcement of the rates. Young defended on the ground that as an agent of the state he was immune from suit by virtue of the Eleventh Amendment. Pending decision on that point, the circuit court judge issued a preliminary order enjoining Young from enforcing the law. When the attorney general promptly violated the injunction by suing one of the railroads in state court, the judge jailed him for contempt of court. Young's petition for habeas corpus, like Ayers's before it, brought the matter to the Supreme Court. This time, however, the Court refused to issue the writ, distinguishing *In re Ayers* and rehabilitating the Marshallian tradition concerning suits against state officers. *Young* is in fact *Osborn* redivivus. When a state officer seeks to enforce an unconstitutional statute, "he is in that case stripped of his official or representative character and is subjected in his person to the consequences of his individual conduct."[43] In other words, a state is conclusively presumed to be incapable of authorizing an unconstitutional act; therefore any such act attempted by a state officer must be his own; acting on his own, the officer is *a fortiori* unable to avail himself of the Eleventh Amendment, which protects states alone. In republican garb this is the old maxim of constitutional monarchy: "The king can do no wrong." The act challenged as unconstitutional in *Ex parte Young* was the taking of corporate property without due process, contrary to the Fourteenth Amendment. Ironically the Court had held in the *Civil Rights Cases* a quarter-century earlier that that Amendment applies only to actions taken by states.[44] Young was thus deemed to threaten state action for purposes of the Fourteenth Amendment, at the same time he was held unprotected by the state immunity conferred by the Eleventh Amendment.

The North Carolina case, *Hunter v. Wood*,[45] was decided the same day as *Ex parte Young* and along the same lines. James H. Wood was a ticket agent for the Southern Railway in Asheville, North Carolina. His employer had challenged the state's railroad law in federal circuit court and had won an injunction against state officers. In defiance of the injunction Wood was arrested and tried for violating state law. On conviction he was sentenced to thirty days on the road gang. Like his better, Attorney General Young, Wood applied for a federal writ of habeas corpus, which was granted. Hunter, the sheriff of Buncombe County, was ordered to release him. The Supreme Court disposed of the case summarily on the strength of *Ex parte Young*. Both decisions were bitterly unpopular. As Senator Lee S. Overman of North Carolina reported: "Whenever one judge stands up in a State and enjoins the governor and the attorney-general, the people resent it, and public sentiment is stirred, as it was in my State, when there was almost a rebellion. . . . let one little judge stand up against the whole State, and you find the people of the State rising up in rebellion."[46] At bottom the issue was whether persons, of the corporate variety or otherwise, could have their federal rights determined in the first instance in federal court. That they could, outraged the people of North Carolina not because federal judges were littler than state judges but because, protected by life tenure and vested with the judicial power of the United States, they were less responsive to popular sentiment.

The legal community, like the public at large, displayed little love for *Ex parte Young*. To be sure, corporate counsel like Guthrie welcomed the decision for its guarantee that federal courts would be open to their clients. But among legal commentators, especially in later years, the case is barely tolerated. It rests, so the pundits say, on a legal fiction and that in itself is enough to damn it in analytical minds. One authority has written a learned article entitled "Suing the Government by Falsely Pretending to Sue an Officer."[47] In fact there is no falsity about it: the officer *is* sued. What the author has in mind is that the officer is sued instead of the state. Another authority puts it simply: "The decision in Ex parte Young rests on purest fiction. It is illogical. It is only doubtfully in accord with the prior decisions."[48] But the same author concludes with grudging praise: "in perspective the doctrine of Ex parte Young seems indispensable to the establishment of constitutional government and the rule of law."[49] Yet another scholar says the same thing in other words: "if sovereign immunity were a bar to all injunctions against government officers, the Supreme Court has feared there would be no effective way to enforce the Constitution. Consequently, when a state officer was alleged to have acted unconstitutionally or beyond his statutory authority, the Court invoked the fiction that he was not acting for the state and therefore was not protected by its immunity."[50] This is how the case stands: precariously balanced—a fiction tolerated because of its seeming indispensability to the attainment of higher goals.

The fictitiousness of *Ex parte Young,* while accepted on all sides, merits closer inspection. Legal fiction is part of the common-law tradition. It means a court's acceptance of an allegation by one party that the opposing party is not permitted to disprove. Examples abound. In sixteenth-century England, courts assumed jurisdiction over acts that took place overseas by simply permitting plaintiffs to allege that the foreign location was "in the parish of St. Mary-le-Bow in the ward of Cheap," that is, in mid-London.[51] In 1774, on the eve of the American Revolution, an English court took jurisdiction over a case concerning an assault that allegedly occurred on the Spanish island of Minorca.[52] The defendant was not permitted to prove that Minorca is not in fact within the sound of Bow Bells. Chief Justice Lord Mansfield rejected the proffered geographical evidence with the words: "Cheapside is named as a venue; which is saying no more, than that the party prays the action may be tried in London."[53] At first blush legal fiction seems an outrage to commonsense and justice. The court acts *as if* A is B when everyone knows A is not B. The practice has been under constant criticism since the days of the English reformer Jeremy Bentham in the late eighteenth century.[54] Dickens ridiculed it in a famous passage: when the henpecked Mr. Bumble was informed of the law's supposition that a wife acts at the direction of her husband, he spluttered: "If the law supposes that . . . , the law is a ass—a idiot."[55] It is important to note, however, that even in its heyday legal fiction was not a means of avoiding important issues; it actually facilitated their decision. Lord Mansfield would never have denied defendant's right to disprove the alleged assault.

In *Ex parte Young* plaintiffs were really and truly suing Edward T. Young. Young was, as alleged, the attorney general of Minnesota. He proposed to—and did in fact—sue the railroads to enforce a law of Minnesota. Like the legal fiction of pretending Minorca is in London, the so-called fiction of suing the state by suing an officer is a means of getting at the real issue: whether a wrong has been done. But *Ex parte Young* was nonfictional in that Young was really and truly about to damage the interest of plaintiffs. Whether what he was about to do amounted to a legal injury depended on the authority of his employer, the state. If the state could constitutionally authorize the act then the loss suffered by plaintiffs was not a wrong for which the law provided a remedy. *"Damnum sine injuria"*—not every loss (*damnum*) amounts to a legal injury.[56] If the state could not constitutionally authorize the act then Young was not acting by its authority. By the same token an officer of a private corporation performing acts that the corporation cannot legally authorize is not acting on its behalf. He is said to be acting *"ultra vires"* or "beyond the powers" conferred on the corporation. By the same terms, an agent who exceeds the authority given him by his principal is not acting pursuant to his agency. There is nothing fictitious about it.

Absent the Eleventh Amendment, plaintiffs could have sued either Minnesota or Young. There is no legal fiction involved in choosing the latter. But the state can act only through officers. The state is an *"artificial* person," as Justice Wilson pointed out in *Chisholm;* "those, who think and speak, and act, are *men."*[57] How can the state's immunity be conceded, it is asked, if it can be so easily circumvented? The question may be unfair to the Framers. It is possible that the original understanding of Federalists who supported the Amendment was that some degree of state sovereign immunity was tolerable because the sovereign immunity known to common law did not immunize the sovereign's officers. Perhaps it is a mistake to look only at the state's immunity and ask: why not its officers? Perhaps one should look at the officers' suability and ask: why not the state? The answer to the last question seems obvious: because of the Eleventh Amendment. The Eleventh Amendment prohibits suits by certain plaintiffs against "one of the United States." This answer too may be unfair to the Framers. The original understanding—indeed the unbroken understanding of bench and bar for the first century of the Republic—seems to have been that the Amendment touched only diversity jurisdiction, not federal question jurisdiction. In the latter, of course, the all-important question is whether the state has attempted to violate the federal Constitution. "Attempted" is the right word because the artificial person known as a state can only act constitutionally. Were its statute constitutional, its officers would share its immunity. If an unconstitutional statute is involved, then the state, properly so-called, has not acted at all. It is hardly too much to say that a state acting in violation of the federal Constitution, if such a thing could be imagined, is not a "state" within the meaning of the Constitution.

Taking the matter a step further, one might ask: who is the state? There is, of course, a famous answer: *"L'état c'est moi!"* ("I am the state"), attributed to *Le Grand Monarque* Louis XIV.[58] But in a republic there is no reason other than common usage to confuse the state with the government of the day. The better answer in political theory would seem to be that the state is the people. At about the time *Ex parte Young* was decided, the proper relationship between government and people occupied the private speculations of Samuel Clemens (Mark Twain), one of America's great writers. His conclusion, expressed with characteristic vigor, was not published until long after his death.

> [I]n a republic, who is "the Country?" Is it the Government which is for the moment in the saddle? Why, the Government is merely a *servant*—merely a temporary servant. . . . Its function is to obey orders, not originate them. Who, then, is "the Country?" Is it the newspaper? is it the pulpit? is it the school superintendent? Why, these are mere parts of the country, not the whole of it; they have not command, they have only their little share in the command. They are

but one in the thousand; it is in the thousand that command is lodged. . . .

Who are the thousand—that is to say, who are "the Country." In a monarchy, the king and his family are the country; in a republic it is the common voice of the people.[59]

The people in their sovereign capacity may be immune from suit. But it does not follow that the government of politicians and bureaucrats should share this aspect of sovereignty except, of course, when they do what they are supposed to do.

IX

After Ex Parte Young:

The Eleventh Amendment in the

Twentieth Century

With *Ex parte Young* the fundamental corpus of modern Eleventh Amendment law was complete. State officers can be enjoined from enforcing unconstitutional state laws. The only exception to this general rule was laid down in the Virginia bond cases: an injunction will not issue, as held in *In re Ayers,* if the effect would be to require a state to pay its debts. In other regards, too, the modern law of the Eleventh Amendment had emerged by 1908. Since the immunity conferred by the Amendment had been assimilated by the judges to the sovereign immunity known to common law, a state can consent to suit—in other words, it can waive its immunity—both in cases within the terms of the Amendment and in those outside it. No immunity exists, however, to suits by the United States or by another American state. The Eleventh Amendment says nothing about such suits and in this regard means exactly what it does not say. But again there is an exception, this time established in the Louisiana bond cases: as held in *New Hampshire v. Louisiana* a state may not collect debts owed to individual citizens rather than to the public fisc. Even this exception, however, did not prevent the Court the year before *Ex parte Young* from holding that Virginia could sue West Virginia on behalf of holders of its bonds regardless of their citizenship.

Although the United States and American states may in general sue a state, the same is not true of citizens suing their own state. As held in *Hans v. Louisiana,* another bond case, the judicial power of the United States does not extend so far. In this regard the Eleventh Amendment means (or implies) much more than it says. Viewed as a constitutional example of sovereign immunity, the Amendment bolstered a finding of such immunity in the apparently unqualified language of the Constitution. Although in 1908 it was still in the bosom of time, the question of suits against American states by foreign countries was also answered in the context of a bond case. In 1934 in *Monaco v. Mississippi* the judicial power was again found wanting. Here too the Eleventh Amendment means more than it says. On the other hand, cities and counties, municipal corporations generally, are not eligible for the protection accorded their parent states. As the Court said in *Lincoln County v. Luning,* the Amendment says states and means it.

Although the basic body of Eleventh Amendment law had evolved by the early twentieth century, legal evolution did not stop then. The perennial judicial task of refining, defining, and distinguishing continued unabated. But in the twentieth century the trend became harder to spot. During the age of Marshall and Taney, that is to say, during the nineteenth century up to the Civil War, the Amendment had not been favored. The consistent judicial view was that *Chisholm v. Georgia* had been correctly decided. By overruling *Chisholm,* the Amendment had introduced an innovation, but one rendered tolerable by recourse to the common-law practice of suits against officers. The era of Reconstruction after the Civil War was hospitable to this view, but the end of Reconstruction necessitated accommodation. Suits against officers were curtailed in 1883, and in 1890 the original understanding of *Chisholm* was abandoned. The case was now viewed as a bad mistake, corrected if not erased altogether by the Eleventh Amendment. During this decade the Amendment enjoyed a brief popularity with the judges. Thereafter it again fell out of favor. Suits against officers were possible once more and the state's consent to suit emerged as another route around the Amendment. The trend away from a sympathetic view of state immunity was clear.

After *Ex parte Young,* however, the trend has not been clearly one way or the other. The grab bag of precedents was full. In many cases one result or another could be adequately supported. Unlike Chief Justice Marshall and the *tabula rasa* or Justice Bradley and *raison d'état,* the justices in the twentieth century were free to pick and choose among competing policies. In consequence a pattern of increasing complexity emerged. The Amendment expanded in some directions and contracted in others. Suits against officers remained the principal means of avoiding the Eleventh Amendment but they survived under accumulating disabilities. In the words of one eminent scholar: "For half a century [after *Ex parte Young*] Congress and the Court have vied in placing restrictions on the doctrine there announced."[1] Stigmatized as legal fiction, the law of *Ex parte Young* labors under a heavy conceptual handicap, often falling victim to concepts whose fictitiousness is better masked. Consent to suit or waiver of immunity—the other prime means of avoiding the Eleventh Amendment— has also had its ups and downs. Express waiver first gave way to implied waiver, a theory that could have vastly curtailed the Amendment; but then the threshold of implication was raised. With regard to the liability of cities and counties the old line has also more or less held. But amid the complexities of modern local government it has proved difficult in some cases to distinguish municipal corporations from the state. (See Chapter VII.)

While the old lines wavered but held, victories and defeats occurred on other fronts. The Eleventh Amendment invaded admiralty jurisdiction, and sovereign immunity was turned against foreign countries. But in the last quarter of the twentieth century new inroads were made or threatened. The argument that Congress is empowered by the Reconstruction Amendments to lift Eleventh Amendment and sovereign immunity, mooted by William Guthrie early in the century,[2] was accepted by the Court at last. Scholars and dissenting justices proposed to revert to Chief Justice Marshall's suggestion that the Amendment applies only to diversity jurisdiction. And the peculiar notion that state courts have a duty to hear suits barred from federal courts by the Eleventh Amendment has begun to be discussed.

The search for logical consistency probably explains the expansion of Eleventh Amendment immunity that occurred in the first third of the twentieth century. In 1921 in *Ex parte New York*[3] the Court held that the Amendment, limited by its terms to suits in "law or equity," barred federal jurisdiction over admiralty proceedings against a state without its consent. Belatedly overruling Justice Washington's decision in *United States v. Bright* in 1809,* the Court claimed that doubt had long existed about the Amendment's effect on admiralty but concluded that "the doubt was based upon considerations that were set aside in the reasoning adopted by this court in *Hans v. Louisiana*."[4] In other words, once the Eleventh Amendment had been reconceptualized in the bond cases after the Civil War, the new understanding would be followed at the expense of the original understanding. Purism could be afforded in the twentieth century; by then admiralty was a relatively small part of federal jurisdiction. It is impossible to believe, however, that the constitutional draftsmen in the late eighteenth century, when the American economy was decidedly mercantilist and when a dispute at sea could easily become a *casus belli,* understood that state vessels were beyond the reach of the judicial power of the United States.

* See Chapter III.

The effect of the decision in *Ex parte New York* is, of course, that states are placed above the law, not accountable in federal court for wrongs done to private citizens. Over the years exceptions to this unattractive rule have perforce been recognized. State-owned vessels not used for governmental purposes have been denied immunity; in such cases the state is treated like any other proprietor liable for its wrongs.[5] Sometimes a fictitious consent to suit is discovered: by offering dockyard cranes for rent, for example, a state was held to have waived its immunity.[6] Or a state may be held to have consented to suit in federal court by engaging in commercial activity regulated by the federal government.[7] These developments led one recent commentator to assert that if *Ex parte New York* arose today "a federal court would probably take jurisdiction of the case based on one of several exceptions to the amendment."[8]

In 1934, the last of the Southern bond cases, *Monaco v. Mississippi,*[9] reached the Supreme Court. Unpaid Mississippi bonds issued a century earlier had been donated to the Principality of Monaco. Although the face value was $100,000, compounding the unpaid interest made the total claim $574,300.[10] Invoking the Supreme Court's original jurisdiction over "all cases . . . in which a state shall be party,"[11] Monaco attempted to execute the strategy advocated by Benjamin R. Curtis shortly after repudiation. The Principality argued that since the Eleventh Amendment made no mention of suits against a state by a foreign country, these were still within the judicial power of the United States. Rejecting this argument, the Court again succumbed to conceptualism: "Behind the words of the constitutional provisions," it said, "are postulates which limit and control."[12] Chief among them is the postulate that "States of the Union, still possessing attributes of sovereignty, shall be immune from suits, without their consent. . . ."[13] *Hans v. Louisiana* had applied the principle to suits against a state by its own citizens; *Ex parte New York* applied it to cases in admiralty; and *Monaco* held that "the same principle applies to suits against a State by a foreign State."[14] To reach this result the Court had to discard a dictum of Chief Justice Marshall uttered in 1821: the Eleventh Amendment "does not comprehend controversies between . . . a State and a foreign State. The jurisdiction of the Court still extends to these cases: and in these a State may still be sued."[15] * For its revelation of the Founders' true intentions the Court preferred Justice Bradley's version in 1890.

Behind the postulate of state sovereignty, of course, may have lain more practical considerations. Southern bonds were dead. The United States had just outfaced its European allies who sought to offset their war debt with unpaid Southern debts to their citizens. Certainly the Great Depression was an inauspicious time to revive the hopes of the coupon clippers. Yet thirty years earlier, in *South Dakota v. North Carolina,* the Court had refused an Eleventh Amendment plea and had forced a recalcitrant state to pay. In *Monaco* the Court distinguished the South Dakota case on grounds of reciprocity: states of the Union are susceptible to suits by one another. In colloquial terms, what's sauce for the goose is sauce for the gander. But, said the Court, foreign states by virtue of sovereignty are immune from suits by states in American courts; ergo they should not be allowed to sue states either.[16] Oddly enough, in 1976, Congress legislated to make foreign states liable to suits in federal courts, including suits in admiralty.[17] It remains to be seen whether states of the Union will be able to avail themselves of this right.[18]

Although it had to garble the original understanding, the Court drew one clear lesson from the history of the Southern bond cases: federal courts should not in general order states to pay money. Inevitably, because a lawcourt was involved,

---

* See *Cohens v. Virginia,* discussed in Chapter III.

141

this lesson was restated as a rule. Born of the necessities of post-Reconstruction politics, it was fathered upon the Eleventh Amendment: "[T]he rule has evolved," the Court said in 1974, "that a suit by private parties seeking to impose a liability which must be paid from public funds in the state treasury is barred by the Eleventh Amendment."[19] A learned federal judge has recently pointed out the possible consequences of such a rule: "If the older industrial states of the Northeast, faced with shrinking revenues, decided to balance their budgets not by curtailing support for services such as higher education and welfare, but by eliminating debt service, the shock to the nation's banking system, and thus to the nation's money supply, would be profound. Yet under current eleventh amendment doctrine, federal courts would not be able to hear suits by bondholders against the states."[20] *Caveat emptor.*

In the mid-twentieth century the Supreme Court erected obstacles in the tried and true common-law routes around sovereign immunity: consent to suit and suits against officers. Consent to suit, or waiver of immunity from suit, had first appeared in American constitutional law immediately after Eleventh Amendment immunity had been expanded in the late nineteenth century. Its appearance at that time confirms that enforcement was the Court's principal concern: consent or waiver cannot alter the extent of judicial power under the Constitution but it can alter the realities of the exercise of that power. Consent to suit can be expressly given; a state by its constitution or law can permit itself to be sued, or its law officer may be empowered to put in an appearance on its behalf in a lawsuit. As a general rule, whatever can be done expressly can also be done by implication. Consent can therefore be express or implied. Legal fiction is not necessarily involved in the process; consent may be so plain in the circumstances that it may reasonably be implied; in a term once fashionable it may be "implied in fact." Of course once facts are scrutinized for implied consent, the possibility arises that consent will be found where it never truly existed. The fact-finder may simply have erred, or may have indulged in fiction. In the latter case, consent will be "implied in law." This is legal fiction: the court acts *as if* A had consented without regard to whether A had in fact consented.

Implied consent entered Eleventh Amendment law in 1959 in *Petty v. Tennessee-Missouri Bridge Commission*.[21] Two states had formed a commission to build a bridge.[22] The Constitution requires that such interstate compacts have congressional approval,[23] which was duly obtained.[24] The compact itself conferred on the commission the power, usual in corporate charters, "to sue and be sued in its own name"[25] and the congressional approval provided that nothing in it should "affect, impair, or diminish any right, power, or jurisdiction of the United States."[26] Interpreting the compact, the Court found implied waiver of Eleventh Amendment immunity. Under the circumstances consent was seemingly implied in fact. In 1964 in *Parden v. Terminal Railway*[27] consent was found in more exiguous facts. The question was whether Alabama could be sued under the Federal Employers' Liability Act (FELA)[28] by employees of a state-owned railroad. The answer was that it could because it had consented: "By adopting and ratifying the Commerce Clause, the States empowered Congress to create such a right of action against interstate railroads; by enacting the FELA in the exercise of this power, Congress conditioned the right to operate a railroad in interstate commerce upon amenability to suit in federal court as provided by the Act; by thereafter operating a railroad in interstate commerce, Alabama must be taken to have accepted that condition and thus to have consented to suit."[29] Passing over the fact that railroads had not yet been invented when Alabama joined the Union, one may nonetheless observe that consent in this case was fictitious, implied in law. The fathers had consented and the children were being

143

sued. The route seemed open to find implied consent under any valid federal law. Chief Justice Marshall had long ago opined that adoption of the federal Constitution amounted to consent to be sued in any case involving a federal question.[30]

In 1973, however, obstacles were cast in the path of implied consent in a case cumbersomely captioned *Employees of the Department of Public Health & Welfare v. Department of Public Health & Welfare*.[31] The issue was whether a state had consented to suit by its own employees under the federal Fair Labor Standards Act[32] by continuing to operate a state hospital after the Act had been amended to cover state employees. The answer was no and *Parden* was distinguished. Since the statute empowered the United States to sue on behalf of employees, the Court saw no reason to imply consent to suit by employees on their own behalf. The case clearly signaled that implied consent is not the foolproof argument it had earlier seemed.[33]

In 1974 in *Edelman v. Jordan*[34] a closely divided Supreme Court further weakened the theory of consent. State officers had been sued for violating federal law. In their defense they made no mention of the Eleventh Amendment or sovereign immunity. After losing in the federal trial court, these officers appealed and at that stage raised the issue for the first time. Reaffirming a 1945 decision, the Supreme Court permitted the belated challenge: "the Eleventh Amendment defense sufficiently partakes of the nature of a jurisdictional bar so that it need not be raised in the trial court. . . ."[35] Since the officers won on this point, the plaintiffs had put on their case for nothing. The analytical difficulty with this result lies in reconciling it with the theory of consent. If the Eleventh Amendment were a true jurisdictional bar, no amount of consent could vest the court with judicial power. If consent may not be conclusively presumed from appearance and defense on the merits, then a state and its officers can play cat and mouse with plaintiffs. Since a judge is duty bound to notice defects in jurisdiction *sua sponte* ("on his own"), he may be in the unseemly position of repeatedly asking defendants if the court is still empowered to decide the case.

Despite the drawbacks, suits against officers remain the principal means of avoiding the Eleventh Amendment. *Ex parte Young* has been limited but never overruled. Only a few months after it was decided in 1908, the Court acted to limit its effects. In *Prentis v. Atlantic Coast Line Railroad*[36] it ruled that federal courts should not enjoin state officers until the state system had had a chance to operate. The practical effect of this rule is to require would-be plaintiffs to exhaust state administrative appeals before making a federal case of the matter. The Court was careful to note, however, that this rule was merely an exercise of discretion on its part; it did not suggest a deficiency of jurisdiction. The judicial power of the United States could reach the case; the Court merely stayed its hand.

Dissatisfaction with federal injunctions against state officers had appeared before *Ex parte Young*. As William Guthrie had balefully observed in 1908, bills were then pending in Congress to curtail the power of federal courts to issue injunctions in suits against officers.[37] *Ex parte Young* only fed the dissatisfaction and led directly to one unfortunate innovation in federal jurisdiction: the Three-Judge Court Act[38] of 1910. Senator Overman of North Carolina had emphasized the resentment engendered when "one little [federal] judge" stands up against a state,[39] so Congress created a court composed of three judges and provided for direct appeal from this court to the Supreme Court. In practice the Three-Judge Court Act strained the limited personnel of the federal judiciary and created endless complications concerning what could and could not be done by a single judge. In 1976, long after it had outlived its usefulness, the Act was repealed.[40]

Far more significant than congressional restrictions on the

doctrine announced in *Ex parte Young,* however, were other restrictions imposed by the Court itself. These may be summarized under two headings—"Abstention" and "Our Federalism"—and traced to two leading cases: *Railroad Commission v. Pullman Co.*[41] in 1941 and *Younger v. Harris*[42] in 1971. In the first case Pullman was seeking to enjoin enforcement of an order of the Texas Railroad Commission, claiming that the order violated the Fourteenth Amendment and that it also violated state law. The order in question forbade the operation of sleeping cars by porters and required their operation by conductors. Since porters were black and conductors white the effect was segregationist. Rather than decide the case, the Supreme Court in a decision by Justice Felix Frankfurter ordered the trial court to abstain until state courts had decided the issue of state law. It has been astutely suggested that the Justice led the Court to order abstention so as to postpone decision of the portentous civil rights claim until after the then-impending world war.[43] Whatever its genesis the effect of the doctrine is to hold up federal adjudication of a federal question for an indefinite period.

Younger v. Harris, thirty years later, was a suit by a state criminal defendant against the state's attorney, seeking to enjoin prosecution on the ground that the state law was unconstitutional. The Court denied the injunction because it preferred to permit state courts to decide such issues first. A special application of abstention, this decision was rested by its author Justice Hugo Black on what he called "Our Federalism": "a system in which there is sensitivity to the legitimate interests of both State and National Governments, and in which the National Government, anxious though it may be to vindicate and protect federal rights and federal interests, always endeavors to do so in ways that will not unduly interfere with the legitimate activities of the States."[44] It has been observed that *Younger* represents a backsliding on the great issues of the Civil War; it amounts, in short, to "reconstructing Reconstruction."[45]

Neither Abstention nor Our Federalism is a jurisdictional doctrine, although both undoubtedly restrict access to federal court. Lately, however, the Supreme Court has announced genuine restrictions on its power to remedy wrongs done by states. In 1974 in *Edelman v. Jordan*[46] the remedy available in suits against officers in federal courts was actually cut back. In that case it was proved that state officers administering a federal-state welfare program had violated federal law by denying payments to certain claimants. The Court ordered the officers to obey the law in future but refused to order payments to make up for past violations. While in the Southern bond cases the Court had merely held that states may not be made to pay their debts, in *Edelman* the rule was extended to prohibit ordering a state to pay for losses incurred by its breach of federal law. Although the defendants were state officers and the plaintiffs citizens of the state, the Court found the remedy "barred by the Eleventh Amendment."[47]

In 1984 in *Pennhurst State School & Hospital v. Halderman*[48] a closely divided Court further limited the right to sue state officers. The plaintiff, a resident in a state institution for the mentally retarded, sued the hospital and state and county officers, alleging violation of both federal and state law. Although the federal claim had been rejected at an earlier stage in the proceedings,[49] the lower federal court adjudicated the claimed violation of state law. In technical terms jurisdiction to decide the question of state law was "pendent"; that is, it hung on the fact that a federal court with jurisdiction over federal claims may decide related state claims, even if the federal claims are ultimately rejected. Pendent jurisdiction saves judges and litigants the time and trouble of two separate lawsuits based on the same facts. Reasoning that

147

state officers acting in violation of state law are not acting by authority of the state, the court issued a judgment against defendants. On appeal it was reversed by the Supreme Court. Although *Ex parte Young* apparently supported the lower court decision, the Supreme Court cut back on that landmark case. It was, the majority confidently asserted, a "fiction" necessary to preserve the supremacy of federal law.[50] Once federal interests were safe, its reasoning no longer applied. Pendent jurisdiction, despite undoubted advantages, could not be exercised in suits against states. To permit as much, the Court said, would conflict with "the principles of federalism that underlie the Eleventh Amendment."[51]

When officers are sued for damages payable out of their own pockets or criminally prosecuted for violations of law, the Eleventh Amendment is not implicated at all. But the Court in the twentieth century has developed a new immunity which may be available in such cases: "official immunity," that is, immunity for state officers. Not prescribed by the Constitution, this immunity has been read into the civil rights section of the Ku Klux Klan Act of 1871, still the principal authorization for private suits against state officers. Although the statute provides a cause of action against "every person" who under color of state law deprives the plaintiff of civil rights,[52] the Court has exempted state legislators,[53] judges,[54] prosecutors,[55] policemen,[56] and governors.[57]

Although sovereign immunity and the Eleventh Amendment have generally fared well in the twentieth century, they have not proved to be invincible arguments. During the New Deal in the 1930s the Court abandoned its role, evident since 1890, as champion of the rights of property and found for itself a new role as defender of civil rights.[58] Most dramatically displayed in the school desegregation case in 1954,[59] the new departure marked the end of the judiciary's long adherence to the Compromise of 1877. Encouraged by the Court, Congress, too, departed from its long-time commitment to give the South a free hand on race. In 1957, it passed the first civil rights act[60] since 1875, and in the 1960s it enacted epoch-making legislation.[61] To vindicate congressional power in this field the Court discovered exceptions to the Eleventh Amendment. In 1976 in *Fitzpatrick v. Bitzer*[62] it held that Congress, when it acts to enforce the Fourteenth Amendment,[63] can abrogate (or waive) a state's Eleventh Amendment immunity.[64] In 1980 in *City of Rome v. United States*[65] it implied that the same result would obtain with respect to federal legislation under the Fifteenth Amendment.[66] These exceptions, of course, were the ones claimed by William D. Guthrie in his address in 1908.[67]

Still more daring theories have been proposed by scholars and judges dissatisfied with the recent expansion of the Eleventh Amendment. Harking back to Chief Justice Marshall's suggestion that the Amendment applies only to diversity jurisdiction, not to federal question jurisdiction, Justice William J. Brennan has argued repeatedly that in suits outside the literal scope of the Amendment, state sovereign immunity exists only by virtue of common law.[68] In consequence, in cases arising under federal law Congress has power to eliminate the immunity. Emphasis is placed on the fact that Justice Iredell's dissent in *Chisholm* rested on the absence of a statutory remedy, not on the lack of constitutional power. As to *Hans:* "The opinion can . . . sensibly be read to have dismissed the suit before it on the ground that no federal cause of action supported the plaintiff's suit and that state-law causes of action would of course be subject to the ancient common-law doctrine of sovereign immunity."[69] Starting from similar premises one scholar has gone so far as to maintain that sovereign immunity is "altogether a common law doctrine";[70] that is, that Congress—and perhaps even the courts themselves—can lift the immunity in *all* cases, even those literally covered by the Amendment. Insofar as these theories depend on congressional action, Justice Bradley

149

might well have welcomed them. If Congress had wanted Southern states to pay their debts, the Court need have had no fears about enforcement.

Finally it has been suggested that Congress may make states suable in their own courts on federal causes of action even when the Eleventh Amendment closes federal courts.[71] Although this theory is the *dernier cri,* it faintly echoes an ancient dictum of Spencer Roane, judge of the Virginia Court of Appeals and Thomas Jefferson's candidate to replace John Marshall as Chief Justice. In 1814, Roane explained the underlying logic of the recent suggestion: "It is also to be borne in mind, that one of the last amendments to the constitution, which declares, that the judicial power of the United States, shall not be construed to extend to suits brought against a state, by citizens of another state, or of a foreign state, is confined to the Federal Courts, in exclusion of those of the states: for, if the State Courts were also inhibited from this jurisdiction, the parties last mentioned would be left without any redress whatever, when aggrieved by a state!"[72] At the time it was cause for exclamation even by the premier states' rights judge that states might be above the law. The modern suggestion is more modest than Judge Roane's, being limited to cases in which Congress affirmatively directs state courts to do right to the parties. The suggestion has been roundly criticized by scholars and certainly seems impracticable. If a citizen has a complaint against his own state, it is strange to send him for help to courts of the state. To be sure, state judges are duty bound to uphold the Constitution of the United States no less than are federal judges,[73] but in few cases would the appearance of partiality be more likely than in cases against the state. And the history of the Virginia coupons shows that state legislatures have ample opportunity to erect procedural barriers to recovery in state courts. In light of the history of the Eleventh Amendment it is odd, however, to hear the following criticism by a leading legal analyst: "If this theory is sound, one wonders why state courts were never required to grant relief on state-issued bonds in the wave of 19th-century defaults. . . ."[74] Why, indeed!

In 1983, a talented law student wrote in a reputable law review: "The eleventh amendment generally provides that a private citizen may not sue a state in federal court without the state's consent."[75] The accompanying footnote merely quoted the Amendment: "The judicial power of the United States shall not be construed to extend to any suit in law or equity commenced or prosecuted against one of the United States by citizens of another state, or by citizens or subjects of any foreign state." The careful reader with no legal training notices at once that the footnote provides inadequate support for the statement. The Eleventh Amendment says nothing at all about suit by "a private citizen"; it refers only to suit by "citizens of another state" and, of course, by foreigners. The Amendment does not say comprehensively that a citizen "may not sue a state" in federal court; it excludes only suits "in law or equity." Nor does the Amendment say a word about "the state's consent." Nonetheless the sentence correctly sums up the modern law of the Eleventh Amendment, eked out by sovereign immunity. Citizens whether of the state sued or of another state are not permitted to sue a state; sovereign immunity prohibits it when the Eleventh Amendment does not. The prohibition applies to admiralty and maritime jurisdiction as well as to law and equity; the Amendment has been read expansively. Consent by the state to be sued does lift the bar as well of sovereign immunity as of the Amendment. And finally although not comprehended by the student's comment, the ban on jurisdiction applies to foreign states, not only to their citizens or subjects; sovereign immunity is the rationale. Thus has judicial construction filled the gaps left by the Framers.

So thick has the crust of legal tradition grown that the lawyer or law teacher who reads the student's summary is apt to overlook the discrepancy between statement and footnote. A century ago the Eleventh Amendment was reconceptualized as a recognition of sovereign immunity. Thereafter the concept, part of the United States's unwritten constitution, rather than the language of the Amendment has been predominant. Sovereign immunity cannot, however, be accorded the constituent parts of a federal Union without jeopardizing the sovereignty of the Union itself. Nor can a vigorous doctrine of sovereign immunity be reconciled with the rule of law. If English judges had been as solicitous for the maxim "The king can do no wrong" as American judges have been for state sovereign immunity, constitutional government would never have evolved in England—or America for that matter. Exceptions had perforce to be recognized: suits against officers, consent by the sovereign, and limitation by later amendments. So pressing is the need to limit sovereign immunity that much talent has been devoted to discovering further exceptions. The result of all this pulling and hauling has naturally been distorted doctrine, what the latest scholars call "the theoretical incoherence of eleventh amendment jurisprudence."[76]

X

An Epilogue on the
Rule of Law and Legal History

Public debts existed from time immemorial. The Lord's command to ancient Israel was: "[T]hou shalt lend unto many nations, but thou shalt not borrow"[1]—a commandment which incidentally the modern state of Israel has not kept. In actuality the problem is not so much borrowing as repaying. The fathers have taken the money and the children even unto the third and fourth generation are left to repay it. Whatever the moral obligation, the legal one is dependent upon the power of courts to enforce repayment. In the context of the federal Union the legal obligation of states to pay their debts—or respect other parts of the Constitution—ultimately depends on the reach of the judicial power of the United States. Without judicial power behind it a right may become worthless—or, to use the metaphor Scrooge uses in *A Christmas Carol,* may become "a mere United States' security."[2]

Because public debts depend on law, judicial decisions denying the enforceability of state bonds raise questions about the rule of law. Although commonly agreed to be worth having, there is no consensus on exactly what the phrase means; according to the *Oxford Companion to Law,* the rule of law is "a concept of the utmost importance but having no defined, nor readily definable, content."[3] In general it connotes a "government of laws and not of men,"[4] that is, a system in which power is wielded in an orderly and

153

principled way, without fear or favor. The term was first popularized a century ago by A. V. Dicey in an important book on English constitutional law.[5] Although always supposedly beyond political dispute, the rule of law has occasionally been bandied about by politicians on both sides of the Atlantic.[6] One American legal scholar recalls its use as a slogan in the anti-Communist rhetoric of the 1950s, although he recognizes as well a "respectable academic version" with an emphasis on "procedural regularity and the following of precedents."[7] Lately a self-proclaimed Marxist historian has incongruously hailed the rule of law as an "unqualified human good,"[8] while a Harvard Law School professor has, even more incongruously, questioned its value.[9]

With respect to the rule of law, the history of the Eleventh Amendment prompts reflections that are somber. By exempting states from accountability for wrongs to certain individuals the Amendment itself is a breach of the rule of law. Unlike constitutional monarchs, American states are in some cases able to shelter official wrongdoers. When the Supreme Court's interpretation of the Amendment is examined, the record is hardly more encouraging. To the extent that the rule of law is bound up with following precedents, decisions on the Eleventh Amendment breach it as often as they observe it. In 1883 the Court broke with a half-century of precedents; after 1890 it undercut or evaded its most recent decisions. Since 1908, precedents permit one thing or another and provide no clear guide. The Southern bond cases which produced the distortions in the first place are more explicable in political than in legal terms. The Court proved itself a respecter of persons, albeit persons of the artificial variety.

To contemplate the Court's alternative, however, is to recognize the fragility of the rule of law. To have upheld the Marshallian tradition in the 1880s would have meant certain disaster for an institution already convalescent from self-inflicted wounds in the *Dred Scott* and *Legal Tender Cases*.

Avoiding further injury was perhaps all that was possible at the time. Having once recovered its élan the Court embarked on a glorious career defending rights—first property rights and eventually civil rights. Cold comfort may be taken in the fact that it had earlier sacrificed the interests of the capitalists as readily as the rights of black Americans to the demands of the higher politics.

Drawing lessons from history is risky business, especially in legal history. "Quoting History is not speaking like a Lawyer," declaimed counsel for state officers in the *Writs of Assistance Case*,[10] a *cause célèbre* before the American Revolution. At the heart of the matter is the perpetual tension between legal history and more conventional legal analysis. The goal of analysis is to discern significant relationships among persons within the relevant jurisdiction and to correlate those relationships one with another in a logical manner. As it is practiced today, legal analysis depends on concepts of apparently timeless significance that aid in discerning and correlating these personal relations. Legal history, on the other hand, by tracing the emergence and manipulation of concepts may raise doubts about the validity and meaning of legal analysis. Analysis is supposedly not contingent on time and place, while history is inevitably preoccupied with such particularities. In the eyes of the legal historian the legal analyst may occasionally appear guilty of hopeless anachronism. Witness the recent criticism of the theory that state courts could be made to hear claims against states: it is objected to on the ground that, if true, state courts would have been ordered to adjudicate post-Reconstruction bond cases. More likely, if the political will had been present after the Compromise of 1877, the Supreme Court would have done the dirty work itself. To the analyst, on the contrary, the legal historian often seems engaged in the irrelevant chronicling of the blunders of earlier lawyers. If the right answer was finally arrived at, of what interest is the process of trial and error leading

155

to it? After *Hans v. Louisiana,* doubts that had persisted for a century could be confidently laid aside.

If legal history were indeed no more than the accumulation of details concerning the inevitable emergence of legal concepts—and some legal historians themselves act as if it were[11]—then the criticism of it by legal analysts would be well founded. If a legal concept, like murder, will "out" sooner or later, then when and how it outs matters less than what it essentially is. With respect to some legal concepts this is very likely so. Yet even in such cases legal history may be more than the careful dressing up of an idea in period garb. Retracing the trail of a concept may disclose an inestimable but strangely neglected mental accomplishment: legal imagination. The ingenious process by which English judges transmuted "The king can do no wrong" from the dross of despotism into the precious metal of constitutionalism is an heroic exploit of the mind. Chief Justice Marshall's brilliant decision in *Marbury v. Madison,* turning weakness into strength, secured American constitutionalism. And the much disparaged "fiction" in *Ex parte Young* maintains the supremacy of federal law. Practitioners may be inspired by the efforts of the indefatigable lawyers for the bondholders, and state attorneys may be instructed, if not edified, by Virginia's resourceful obstructionism.

Sometimes legal history can do even more than recount feats of legal imagination. Legal concepts are always invented for a purpose; no more than ideas in any other discipline do they emerge in a process of self-actualization. Sovereign immunity, for example, was a rationalization of the fact that the king was not subject to compulsion by courts of his own creation. Consent to suit or waiver of immunity squared that fact with the need to do justice. Moreover legal analysis is itself a product of legal imagination—just as much as the concepts it employs. As practiced today, legal analysis depends on concepts, but an older analytical tradition focused on texts.

A century ago, for example, lecturers on federal jurisdiction rehearsed the relevant parts of the federal Constitution—the judicial power of the United States extends "to all cases, in law and equity, arising under this Constitution . . . ; to all cases of admiralty and maritime jurisdiction . . . ; to controversies between two or more states; between a state and citizens of another state . . . and between a state, . . . and foreign states, citizens or subjects"[12]—and then pointed out the Eleventh Amendment as modifying those grants of power to which it refers.[13] After 1890, however, the analysts switched their *modus operandi*. The Eleventh Amendment as reconceptualized by Justice Bradley in *Hans v. Louisiana* was no more than a specimen of sovereign immunity. Thereafter the concept became the starting point: the texts, both of the original Constitution and of the Eleventh Amendment, were reread in light of it.[14]

By coincidence, legal education was just then being refashioned in the image of the Harvard Law School and new forms of pedagogy were displacing the lectures of the past. The case system—embodied in a new academic genre, the casebook—directed attention away from texts and toward judicial opinions; the dialogue method of instruction, associated with the great name of Socrates, explored the meaning of general concepts, not the nice particularities of legal documents. Scientific models of inquiry were all the mode. The concept of sovereign immunity promptly entered the jurisprudence of concepts, known to the erudite by its German name *Begriffsjurisprudenz*. Legal logicians quickly observed that sovereign immunity attaches to the national government as well as to the states and that it protects sovereigns from more than the limited classes of plaintiffs listed in the Eleventh Amendment. The problem with legal concepts—as, more obviously, with legal fictions—is that they may achieve a life of their own. Of course, the result-oriented Court of 1890–1908 was simultaneously carving out large exceptions to sovereign immunity in terms of other concepts: consent to suit and suits against officers. But the rule in *Hans* remained to prompt the decisions in *Ex parte New York* in 1921, extending the Eleventh Amendment to admiralty cases, and in *Monaco v. Mississippi* in 1934, recognizing the defense of sovereign immunity in suits by foreign countries. The way was open to the logical stalemate and sterilities of today.

Out of this maze legal history offers a clue. The fallacy of legal analysis is that it assumes its own completeness. Lacking time sense it projects its values and deductions backward and forward indiscriminately. Universalizing its conclusions throughout the legal system it labels all other data as alien: usually "politics," sometimes "history." For this reason legal analysts exclude insofar as possible events external to their narrowly defined system. The Compromise of 1877 is ignored, the Civil War barely mentioned. The grand tradition of English constitutionalism is *terra incognita*. The only relevant history, in fact, is that leading up to the adoption of the federal Constitution and its amendments or the so-called legislative history of a statute. The idea that history ends with ratification or enactment explains the fascination and preoccupation of legal scholars with that other concept: the "original understanding."[15] Forensic legal history becomes a battle over the bones of a long-dead past. But putting skeletons to work in the present inevitably disrupts the continuity of authentic history. Reasserting an original understanding or even maintaining it unbroken over time preserves it only *ceteris paribus,* if all other things remain equal—something they never do. Had state officers continued the practice exemplified by Rittenhouse of holding state funds in their own names, it would have been more difficult to assert the bar of the Eleventh Amendment. Until foreign states were made suable in federal court, it was possible to argue the unfairness of permitting them to sue in the same forum. Before states began running schools and hospitals, before they began regulating and participating actively in the economy, before they began legislating against discrimination and providing welfare services—in short, back when the Eleventh Amendment was adopted—the chances of citizens having legal claims against a state were largely limited to people like bondholders who had voluntarily entered into legal relations with a state.

Precisely because legal analysis assumes its own completeness it is often driven to its version of legal history whenever in need of a new—not an old—concept. When Justice Bradley had to support the decision in *Hans* he ransacked eighteenth-century debates on the adoption of the federal Constitution and misconstrued Justice Iredell's dissent in *Chisholm*. Dissenting justices today would rewrite a hundred years of constitutional history. But judges in search of a *ratio decidendi* do not make reliable historians; as witness the inconsistent views of *Chisholm* avouched in *Hans* and in the New Hampshire case only a few years earlier. What genuine legal history can offer, on the contrary, is a candid account of the past and an invaluable perspective on the present; it can, in other words, by explaining how we got where we are, explain more comprehensively where we are. What the past cannot do is answer the problems of the present. That is the task of each generation in its turn. Enlightened and perhaps inspired by its understanding of the past, each generation creates the present. The success of the American Constitution in its third century depends on the judges' continuing ability to reconcile our traditions, institutions, and aspirations.

Notes

I. Introduction

1. Charles Dickens, *A Christmas Carol* (1843), stave 2.
2. Letter from Duff Green to John C. Calhoun (Jan. 24, 1842), reprinted in *American Historical Association Report* (1899), vol. 2, pp. 841, 842; see also *Report of the Commissioner Sent to Europe to Negotiate a Loan*, H.R. Doc. No. 197, 27th Cong., 3d Sess. (1843).
3. U.S. Const. art. I, §10, cl. 1.
4. Id. art. III, §1.
5. Id. §2, cl. 1.
6. Id. art. II, §1, cl. 1.
7. Id. cl. 8.
8. Id. §3.
9. Herbert Broom, *A Selection of Legal Maxims* (1845), p. 91.
10. *Black's Law Dictionary* (5th ed., 1979), p. 1363; see also William Blackstone, *Commentaries on the Laws of England* (1765–69), vol. 3, pp. 23, 109.
11. W. W. Rostow, *The Stages of Economic Growth* (2d ed., 1971), pp. 38, 59.
12. Howard Fink and Mark V. Tushnet, *Federal Jurisdiction: Policy and Practice* (1984), p. 137.

II. Ratification of the Eleventh Amendment

1. 2 U.S. (2 Dall.) 419 (1793).
2. U.S. Const. art. III, §2, cl. 2.
3. Id. cl. 1.
4. Act of Sept. 24, 1789, ch. 20, 1 Stat. 73.
5. Id., §14, 1 Stat. at 81–82.
6. 2 U.S. (2 Dall.) at 449.
7. Id. at 450.
8. Id.
9. Id. at 453 (emphasis in original).
10. Id. at 455 (emphasis in original).
11. Id. at 456 (emphasis in original).

161

12. Id. at 472 (emphasis in original).
13. 2 U.S. (2 Dall.) 402 (1792); id. at 415 (1793); 3 U.S. (3 Dall.) 1 (1794).
14. 2 U.S. (2 Dall.) at 474.
15. Id. (emphasis in original).
16. Treaty of Paris, Sept. 3, 1783, United States-Great Britain, art. IV, 8 Stat. 80, 82, T.S. No. 104.
17. Id. art. V, 8 Stat. at 82–83.
18. *Journals of the Continental Congress, 1774–1789* (1928), vol. 26, pp. 30–31.
19. Id. (Roscoe R. Hill ed., 1936), vol. 32, pp. 176–84.
20. *Messages and Papers of the Presidents, 1789–1897* (James D. Richardson ed., 1896–99), vol. 1, pp. 153–54.
21. Jay's Treaty, Nov. 19, 1794, United States-Great Britain, arts. II, VI, 8 Stat. 116, 117, 119–20, T.S. No. 105.
22. Convention of Jan. 8, 1802, United States-Great Britain, 8 Stat. 196, T.S. No. 108; Act of May 3, 1802, ch. 49, 2 Stat. 192.
23. U.S. Const. art. III, §2, cl. 1.
24. 2 U.S. (2 Dall.) at 478 (emphasis in original); see also *United States v. McLemore*, 45 U.S. (4 How.) 286 (1846) (held: federal government may not be sued without consent).
25. *Augusta* (Ga.) *Chronicle*, Nov. 23, 1793.
26. 2 *Annals of the Congress of the United States* 1991 (1884).
27. Samuel Eliot Morison, Henry Steele Commager, and William E. Leuchtenburg, *The Growth of the American Republic* (7th ed., 1980), vol. 1, p. 292.
28. U.S. Const. art. V.
29. Julius Goebel, *History of the Supreme Court of the United States: Antecedents and Beginnings to 1801* (1971), p. 734 & n.36.
30. Clyde E. Jacobs, *The Eleventh Amendment and Sovereign Immunity* (1972), pp. 66–67.
31. *Messages and Papers of the Presidents, 1789–1897* (James D. Richardson ed., 1896–99), vol. 1, p. 260.
32. Jacobs, *op. cit.*, p. 67.
33. Herman V. Ames, *The Proposed Amendments to the Constitution of the United States During the First Century of Its History*, H.R. Doc. No. 353, Part 2, 54th Cong., 2d Sess. (1897), p. 322 n.321.
34. But see *Coleman v. Miller*, 307 U.S. 433 (1939) (Congress has ultimate authority over promulgation of the adoption of an amendment).
35. 3 U.S. (3 Dall.) 378 (1798).
36. U.S. Const. art. I, §7, cl. 3.
37. 3 U.S. (3 Dall.) at 381 n.

38. Id. at 382.
39. Goebel, *op. cit.*, pp. 738–41 (referring to the unreported case of *Cutting v. South Carolina,* a suit in which the French Republic claimed an interest).
40. 134 U.S. 1 (1890).
41. Id. at 11.
42. U.S. Const. art. III, §2, cl. 1.
43. Act of Sept. 24, 1789, ch. 20, §8, 1 Stat. 73, 76; U.S. Const. art. VI, cl. 3.
44. *The Debates in the Several State Conventions on the Adoption of the Federal Constitution* (Jonathan Elliot ed., 2d ed., Philadelphia, 1836–45), vol. 2, p. 491.
45. Id., vol. 3, p. 207.
46. E.g., *Penn v. Lord Baltimore,* 1 Ves. Sen. 444, 27 Eng. Rep. 1132 (Ch. 1750).
47. See *Penhallow v. Doane's Adm'rs,* 3 U.S. (3 Dall.) 54, 81 (1795); *United States v. Curtiss-Wright Export Corp.,* 299 U.S. 304, 316 (1936); Joseph Story, *Commentaries on the Constitution of the United States* (1833), vol. 1, pp. 190–202. Contra, *Gibbons v. Ogden,* 22 U.S. (9 Wheat.) 1, 187 (1824) (dictum).
48. *The Debates in the Several State Conventions on the Adoption of the Federal Constitution* (Jonathan Elliot ed., 2d ed., Philadelphia, 1836–45), vol. 3, p. 533.
49. Letter from James Madison to George Washington (April 16, 1787), reprinted in *Documentary History of the Constitution of the United States of America, 1786–1870* (1894–1905), vol. 4, pp. 115, 118 (emphasis added).
50. *The Debates in the Several State Conventions on the Adoption of the Federal Constitution* (Jonathan Elliot ed., 2d ed., Philadelphia, 1836–45), vol. 3, pp. 555–56.
51. *The Federalist,* No. 81, at 511 (A. Hamilton) (B. Wright ed., 1961) (emphasis in original).
52. Id., pp. 511–12.
53. See, e.g., *The Debates in the Several State Conventions on the Adoption of the Federal Constitution* (Jonathan Elliot ed., 2d ed., Philadelphia, 1836–45), vol. 3, pp. 660–61 (amendment proposed by Va. deleting from Art. III jurisdiction over most suits against states); id., vol. 2, p. 409 (amendment proposed by N.Y. denying jurisdiction over suits against states).
54. Act of Sept. 24, 1789, ch. 20, §13, 1 Stat. 73, 80.
55. U.S. Const. art. III, §2, cl. 1.
56. Id. amend. XIV, §4 (emphasis added).
57. Jacobs, *op. cit.*, pp. 72–74.
58. E.g., *Brailsford v. Spalding* (C.C. Ga. 1792) (unreported), see Charles Warren, *The Supreme Court in United States History*

(rev. ed., 1926), vol. 1, p. 66 n.1; *Higginson v. Greenwood* (C.C. S.C. 1793) (unreported), see id.; *Ware v. Hylton,* 3 U.S. (3 Dall.) 199 (1796); *Olney v. Arnold,* 3 U.S. (3 Dall.) 308 (1796).

59. William Blackstone, *Commentaries on the Laws of England* (1765–69), vol. 1, p. 59.
60. *Sturges v. Crowninshield,* 17 U.S. (4 Wheat.) 122, 202–3 (1819).
61. U.S. Const. art. III, §2, cl. 1.
62. 2 U.S. (2 Dall.) at 450.

III. Early Interpretation

1. Letter from John Jay to John Adams (Jan. 2, 1801), quoted in Albert J. Beveridge, *The Life of John Marshall* (1916–19), vol. 3, p. 55.
2. 5 U.S. (1 Cranch) 137 (1803).
3. *Fletcher v. Peck,* 10 U.S. (6 Cranch) 87 (1810); *Ware v. Hylton,* 3 U.S. (3 Dall.) 199 (1796).
4. *Martin v. Hunter's Lessee,* 14 U.S. (1 Wheat.) 304 (1816).
5. U.S. Const. art. VI, cl. 2.
6. E.g., *Dr. Bonham's Case,* 8 Co. Rep. 113b, 77 Eng. Rep. 646 (C.P. 1610).
7. William Blackstone, *Commentaries on the Laws of England* (1765–69), vol. 1, p. 91.
8. E.g., *Commonwealth v. Catron,* 8 Va. 634, 4 Call 5 (1782); *Bayard v. Singleton,* 1 N.C. 5, 1 Mart. 48 (1787); *Trevett v. Weeden* (R.I. 1786), in J. Varnum, *The Case, Trevett Against Weeden* (1787).
9. *Journal of the Senate* (John Adams Administration, 1797–1801), vol. 5, pp. 381–90 (1977).
10. Id. at 387–88.
11. Act of Sept. 24, 1789, ch. 20, §13, 1 Stat. 73, 81.
12. Act of April 29, 1802, ch. 31, §1, 2 Stat. 156, 156.
13. 13 *Annals of the Congress of the United States* 315 ff. (1852) (impeachment of Federal District Judge John Pickering in 1803).
14. Beveridge, *op. cit.,* vol. 3, pp. 112–13.
15. U.S. Const. art. III, §2, cl. 2.
16. 9 U.S. (5 Cranch) 115 (1809).
17. 24 F. Cas. 1232 (C.C.D. Pa. 1809) (No. 14,647).
18. U.S. Const. art III, §2, cl. 1.
19. *Waring v. Clarke,* 46 U.S. (5 How.) 441, 459–60 (1847);

accord, *Parsons v. Bedford*, 28 U.S. (3 Pet.) 433, 446–47 (1830) (dictum).

20. 24 F. Cas. at 1236.
21. See, e.g., *Governor of Georgia v. Madrazo*, 26 U.S. (1 Pet.) 110, 124 (1828) (dictum); Joseph Story, *Commentaries on the Constitution of the United States* (1833), vol. 3, pp. 560–61; Alfred Conkling, *A Treatise on the Organization, Jurisdiction and Practice of the Courts of the United States* (4th ed., 1864), p. 4.
22. *Ex parte New York*, 256 U.S. 490 (1921).
23. 19 U.S. (6 Wheat.) 264 (1821).
24. See also *Worcester v. Georgia*, 31 U.S. (6 Pet.) 515 (1832) (Marshall, C.J.) (rejecting *sub silentio* Eleventh Amendment objection when noncitizen sued state on writ of error).
25. 19 U.S. (6 Wheat.) at 406–07.
26. U.S. Const. art. III, §2, cl. 1.
27. Id.
28. 19 U.S. (6 Wheat.) at 402–03. Marshall had posed the same hypothetical case almost twenty years earlier. *Marbury v. Madison*, 5 U.S. (1 Cranch) 137, 179 (1803).
29. 22 U.S. (9 Wheat.) 738 (1824).
30. Id. at 857.
31. Blackstone, *op. cit.*, vol. 1, p. 238; vol. 3, p. 254.
32. Herbert Broom, *A Selection of Legal Maxims* (1845), p. 43.
33. 26 U.S. (1 Pet.) 110 (1828). For a later case involving the same dispute see *Ex parte Madrazzo* [sic], 32 U.S. (7 Pet.) 627 (1833).
34. 26 U.S. (1 Pet.) at 123–24.
35. *Livingston's Ex'x v. Story*, 36 U.S. (11 Pet.) 351, 397 (1837) (Baldwin, J., dissenting); *Rhode Island v. Massachusetts*, 37 U.S. (12 Pet.) 657, 731 (1838); *McNutt v. Bland*, 43 U.S. (2 How.) 9, 23 (1844) (Daniel, J., dissenting); *Luther v. Borden*, 48 U.S. (7 How.) 1, 55 (1849) (Woodbury, J., dissenting); *Howard v. Ingersoll*, 54 U.S. (13 How.) 381, 409 (1851).
36. *Kentucky v. Dennison*, 65 U.S. (24 How.) 66, 97 (1861).
37. *McNutt v. Bland*, 43 U.S. (2 How.) 9, 23, 27 (1844) (Daniel, J., dissenting); *Florida v. Georgia*, 58 U.S. (17 How.) 478, 500 (1855) (Curtis, J., dissenting).
38. See *Livingston's Ex'x v. Story*, 36 U.S. (11 Pet.) 351, 397 (1837) (Baldwin, J., dissenting); *Luther v. Borden*, 48 U.S. (7 How.) 1, 55 (1849) (Woodbury, J., dissenting).
39. *Scott v. Sandford*, 60 U.S. (19 How.) 393 (1857).
40. Charles Dickens, *A Christmas Carol* (1843), stave 2.

41. *The Times* (London), May 19, 1843, at 5, col. 3.
42. William Wordsworth, "To the Pennsylvanians" (1845), in *The Poetical Works of William Wordsworth* (William Knight ed., 1896), vol. 8, pp. 179–80.
43. William Wordsworth, Additional Note (1850) on "Men of the Western World! In Fate's Dark Book," (1842) id., p. 113.
44. Act of Sept. 24, 1789, ch. 20, §11, 1 Stat. 73, 78.
45. U.S. Const. art. III, §2, cl. 2.
46. Act of Sept. 24, 1789, ch. 20, §25, 1 Stat. at 85.
47. *Beers v. Arkansas,* 61 U.S. (20 How.) 527 (1858); accord *General Oil Co. v. Crain,* 209 U.S. 211 (1908); but see *Georgia R. R. & Banking Co. v. Musgrove,* 335 U.S. 900 (1949) (per curiam), dismissing appeal from 204 Ga. 139, 49 S.E.2d 26 (1948).
48. Letter from Daniel Webster to Baring Bros. & Co. (Oct. 16, 1839), reprinted in *The Papers of Daniel Webster: Correspondence, Vol. 4: 1835–1839* (Charles M. Wiltse and Harold D. Moser eds., 1980), p. 407.
49. Id.; *cf.* U.S. Const. art. I, §10, cl. 1 ("No state shall . . . pass any . . . law impairing the obligation of contracts. . . .").
50. *Trustees of Dartmouth College v. Woodward,* 17 U.S. (4 Wheat.) 518 (1819).
51. *The Papers of Daniel Webster: Correspondence, Vol. 4: 1835–1839* (Charles M. Wiltse and Harold D. Moser eds., 1980), p. 407.
52. *Scott v. Sandford,* 60 U.S. (19 How.) 393 (1857).
53. [Benjamin R. Curtis], "Debts of the States," 58 *North American Review* 109 (1844).
54. U.S. Const. art. III, §2, cl. 1.
55. Id. cl. 2.
56. *Monaco v. Mississippi,* 292 U.S. 313 (1934).
57. Act of Feb. 15, 1833, 1824–38 Miss. Laws 475.
58. *State v. Johnson,* 25 Miss. 625 (1853).
59. Miss. Const. of 1832, art. IV, §2.
60. Joseph G. Baldwin, *The Flush Times of Alabama and Mississippi* (1974), p. 40 (reprint of 1853 sketches).

IV. Reconstruction and American Law

1. U.S. Const. art. I, §8, cls. 1, 2, 11–14, 18.
2. Id. art. II, §2, cl. 1.
3. *Cp.* Cicero, *Pro Milone* (Loeb Classical Library, N.H. Watts trans., 1931) 4.11–12 (*"silent enim leges inter arma"* where self-defense rather than warfare seems to be intended).

4. John Salmond, *Jurisprudence* (7th ed., 1924), p. 142.

5. *Principia,* May 4, 1861, quoted in James M. McPherson, *Ordeal by Fire: The Civil War and Reconstruction* (1982), p. 269; see also Lord Acton, "Political Causes of the American Revolution," 5 *The Rambler* 17 (1861) (describing causes of Civil War), reprinted in Lord Acton, *Essays on Freedom and Power* (Gertrude Himmelfarb ed., 1948), p. 196.

6. U.S. Const. amend. XIII, §1.

7. Id. amend. XIV, §4.

8. Id. amend. XV, §1.

9. Id. amend. XIII, §2; amend. XIV, §5; amend. XV, §2.

10. Act of March 2, 1867, ch. 153, 14 Stat. 428.

11. N.C. Const. of 1868, art. III, §1; art. IV, §16; art. VII, §1.

12. Id. art. X, §6.

13. Id. art. IV, §1.

14. Id. §12.

15. N.C. Code Civ. Pro. 1868.

16. Act of April 9, 1866, ch. 31, 14 Stat. 27.

17. Id. §1, 14 Stat. at 27.

18. Act of May 31, 1870, ch. 114, §16, 16 Stat. 140, 144.

19. Act of May 31, 1870, ch. 114, 16 Stat. 140; Act of Feb. 28, 1871, ch. 99, 16 Stat. 433.

20. Act of May 31, 1870, ch. 114, §1, 16 Stat. 140, 140.

21. Id. §8, 16 Stat. at 142.

22. Act of April 20, 1871, ch. 22, 17 Stat. 13.

23. Id. §1, 17 Stat. at 13 (codified as amended at 42 U.S.C. §1983 (1982)).

24. Act of March 1, 1875, ch. 114, 18 Stat. 335.

25. Act of March 3, 1863, ch. 81, §5, 12 Stat. 755, 756, amended by Act of May 11, 1866, ch. 80, 14 Stat. 46; Act of Feb. 28, 1871, ch. 99, §16, 16 Stat. 433, 438–39; *cf.* Act of July 13, 1866, ch. 184, §67, 14 Stat. 98, 171 (removal of actions against revenue officers).

26. Act of Sept. 24, 1789, ch. 20, §12, 1 Stat. 73, 79; see also Act of Feb. 4, 1815, ch. 31, §8, 3 Stat. 195, 198 (removal of actions against federal officers); Act of March 3, 1815, ch. 94, §6, 3 Stat. 231, 233–34 (same); Act of March 3, 1817, ch. 109, §2, 3 Stat. 396, 396 (same).

27. Act of Sept. 24, 1789, ch. 20, §11, 1 Stat. 73, 78.

28. Act of March 3, 1875, ch. 137, §1, 18 Stat. 470, 470.

29. Act of Feb. 13, 1801, ch. 4, §11, 2 Stat. 89, 92.

30. Act of March 8, 1802, ch. 8, 2 Stat. 132.

31. *Georgia v. Stanton,* 73 U.S. (6 Wall.) 50 (1867).

32. *Mississippi v. Johnson,* 71 U.S. (4 Wall.) 475 (1867).

33. Id. at 500–1.

34. Act of Feb. 25, 1862, ch. 33, §1, 12 Stat. 345, 345.
35. *Hepburn v. Griswold,* 75 U.S. (8 Wall.) 603 (1870).
36. *Knox v. Lee,* 79 U.S. (12 Wall.) 457 (1871).
37. Charles Evans Hughes, *The Supreme Court of the United States* (1928), pp. 50–53.
38. *Scott v. Sandford,* 60 U.S. (19 How.) 393 (1857).
39. Benjamin U. Ratchford, *American State Debts* (1941), p. 183.
40. Act of Jan. 29, 1877, ch. 37, 19 Stat. 227.
41. Letter to the Editor from Joseph P. Bradley, *Newark* (N.J.) *Daily Advertiser,* Sept. 5, 1877, reprinted in *Miscellaneous Writings of the Late Hon. Joseph P. Bradley* (Charles Bradley ed., 1902), pp. 220–21.
42. Act of June 18, 1878, ch. 263, §15, 20 Stat. 145, 152.
43. Act of May 2, 1792, ch. 28, §2, 1 Stat. 264, 264.
44. John J. Gibbons, "The Eleventh Amendment and State Sovereign Immunity: A Reinterpretation," 83 *Columbia Law Review* 1889, 1981 (1983).
45. 109 U.S. 3 (1883).
46. Id. at 24–25.
47. Id. at 25.
48. *Slaughter-House Cases,* 83 U.S. (16 Wall.) 36, 111–24 (1873) (Bradley, J., dissenting).
49. C. Vann Woodward, *Reunion and Reaction: The Compromise of 1877 and the End of Reconstruction* (1951), p. 245.
50. H.R. 10958, 51st Cong., 1st Sess. (1890).
51. 163 U.S. 537 (1896).
52. Id. at 544.
53. Act of July 10, 1890, no. 111, 1890 La. Acts 152.
54. Note, "Limiting the Section 1983 Action in the Wake of *Monroe v. Pape,*" 82 *Harvard Law Review* 1486 n.4 (1969) (citing *United States Code Annotated*).
55. *Brown v. Board of Educ.,* 347 U.S. 483 (1954).
56. Samuel Eliot Morison, Henry Steele Commager, and William E. Leuchtenburg, *The Growth of the American Republic* (7th ed., 1980), vol. 1, p. 787.

V. The Eleventh Amendment and the End of Reconstruction: Louisiana and North Carolina

1. Benjamin U. Ratchford, *American State Debts* (1941), p. 163.
2. Benjamin U. Ratchford, "The North Carolina Public Debt,

1870–1878," 10 *North Carolina Historical Review* 1, 1, 3 (1933).

3. N.C. Const. of 1868, art. V, §5.

4. Letter from the Chevalier de Panat to Jacques Mallet du Pan (Jan. 1796), quoted in *Bartlett's Familiar Quotations* (15th ed., 1980), p. 400.

5. Law of March 8, 1870, ch. 71, 1869–70 N.C. Sess. Laws 119 (repealing special tax acts with regard to bonds issued to railroads).

6. N.C. Const. of 1868, art. 1, §6; art. V, §4.

7. N.C. Const. of 1868, art. 1, §6 (1873), reprinted in 1874 *North Carolina Manual* 57, 58 (N.C. Const. as amended). Law of March 3, 1873, ch. 153, 1872–73 N.C. Sess. Laws 249; Law of Feb. 24, 1873, ch. 85, 1872–73 N.C. Sess. Laws 115; Law of Jan. 19, 1872, ch. 53, 1871–72 N.C. Sess. Laws 81.

8. Law of Nov. 23, 1874, ch. 2, 1874–75 N.C. Sess. Laws 1.

9. Law of Feb. 14, 1855, ch. 32, 1854–55 N.C. Sess. Laws 64; Law of Jan. 27, 1849, ch. 82, §38, 1848–49 N.C. Sess. Laws 138, 154.

10. 23 F. Cas. 518 (C.C.E.D.N.C. 1874) (No. 13,679).

11. Id. at 519 (citation omitted).

12. *Railroad Co. v. Swasey*, 90 U.S. (23 Wall.) 405 (1875).

13. Leon Friedman, "Joseph P. Bradley," in *The Justices of the United States Supreme Court, 1789–1969* (L. Friedman and F. Israel eds., 1969), vol. 2, p. 1190.

14. *Forbes v. Memphis, El Paso & Pac. R.R.*, 9 F. Cas. 408 (C.C.W.D. Tex. 1872) (No. 4,926).

15. Tex. Const. of 1869, art. 10, §7.

16. 83 U.S. (16 Wall.) 203 (1873).

17. Id. at 220.

18. 92 U.S. 531 (1876).

19. J. Mills Thornton, "Fiscal Policy and the Failure of Radical Reconstruction in the Lower South," in *Region, Race, and Reconstruction: Essays in Honor of C. Vann Woodward* (J. Morgan Kousser and James M. McPherson eds., 1982), p. 383.

20. Act of Jan. 24, 1874, no. 3, 1874 La. Acts 39.

21. La. Const. of 1868, amend. I, §1 (1874).

22. Act of March 2, 1875, no. 24, 1875 La. Acts 55.

23. 92 U.S. at 541.

24. Joe Gray Taylor, *Louisiana: A History* (1984), p. 113 (quoting unnamed contemporary source).

25. William Ivy Hair, *Bourbonism and Agrarian Protest: Louisiana Politics, 1877–1900* (1969), p. 20.

26. Id., p. 17.

27. La. Const. of 1879, State Debt Ordinance.
28. 107 U.S. 711 (1883).
29. Id. at 727–28.
30. Id. at 733 (Field, J., dissenting).
31. Id. at 740 (Field, J., dissenting).
32. Id. (Field, J., dissenting) (quoting Sinking-Fund Cases, 99 U.S. 700, 767 (1879) (Field, J., dissenting)).
33. Id. at 746–47 (Harlan, J., dissenting).
34. Law of July 18, 1879, ch. 42, 1879 N.H. Laws 357; Law of May 15, 1880, ch. 298, 1880 N.Y. Laws 440.
35. U.S. Const. art. III, §2, cl. 1.
36. 108 U.S. 76 (1883).
37. Id. at 89.
38. Id. at 90.
39. See Bradley T. Johnson, "Can States Be Compelled to Pay Their Debts?" 12 *American Law Review* 625 (1878) (answering yes); W. H. Burroughs, "Can States Be Compelled to Pay Their Debts?" 3 *Virginia Law Journal* 129 (1879) (answering no).
40. John Norton Pomeroy, "The Supreme Court and State Repudiation—The Virginia and Louisiana Cases," 17 *American Law Review* 684, 702 (1883).
41. H.R. Res. 321, 47th Cong., 2d Sess., 14 *Congressional Record* 1356 (1883).
42. Law of March 4, 1879, ch. 98, 1879 N.C. Sess. Laws 183.
43. Benjamin U. Ratchford, "The Adjustment of the North Carolina Public Debt, 1879–1883," 10 *North Carolina Historical Review* 157, 158–60 (1933).
44. Law of March 14, 1879, ch. 268, 1879 N.C. Sess. Laws 436; *Amendments to the Constitution of North Carolina, 1776–1974* (John L. Sanders comp., 1975), p. 3.
45. Benjamin U. Ratchford, "The Adjustment of the North Carolina Public Dept, 1879–1883," 10 *North Carolina Historical Review* 157, 166 (1933).
46. Law of Feb. 12, 1855, ch. 232, 1854–55 N.C. Sess. Laws 298.
47. 133 U.S. 233 (1890).
48. Id. at 245–46.
49. Benjamin U. Ratchford, "The Conversion of the North Carolina Public Debt After 1879," 10 *North Carolina Historical Review* 251, 257 (1933).
50. 134 U.S. 22 (1890).
51. 134 U.S. at 30–31 (Harlan, J., concurring in part and dissenting in part).
52. 134 U.S. 1 (1890); see also *Louisiana ex rel. New York Guar.*

& *Indem. Co. v. Steele,* 134 U.S. 230 (1890) (state officer cannot be sued by foreign corporation).

53. 134 U.S. at 11.
54. Id. at 18–19.
55. *United States v. Lee,* 106 U.S. 196, 223 (1882) (Gray, J., dissenting in opinion joined by Waite, C. J., and Bradley and Woods, JJ.).
56. Alfred H. Kelly, "Clio and the Court: An Illicit Love Affair," 1965 *Supreme Court Review* 119, 122 & n.13.
57. George Bernard Shaw, *The Devil's Disciple* (1897), act 3.
58. 134 U.S. at 20.
59. Id. at 20–21.
60. U.S. Const. art. III, §2, cl. 1.
61. Alfred Conkling, *A Treatise on the Organization, Jurisdiction and Practice of the Courts of the United States* (4th ed., 1864), p. 4.
62. Benjamin Robbins Curtis, *Jurisdiction, Practice, and Peculiar Jurisprudence of the Courts of the United States* (George Ticknor Curtis & Benjamin R. Curtis eds., 1880), pp. 14, 18.
63. U.S. Const. art. III, §2, cl. 1.
64. 136 U.S. 211 (1890).
65. *Chisholm v. Georgia,* 2 U.S. (2 Dall.) 419, 478 (1793) (Jay, C. J., concurring) (dictum); *United States v. McLemore,* 45 U.S. (4 How.) 286 (1846) (U.S. may not be sued by individual without consent); *Kansas v. United States,* 204 U.S. 331 (1907) (U.S. may not be sued by state without consent).
66. Act of March 25, 1870, ch. 30, 16 Stat. 77.
67. 109 U.S. 446 (1883).
68. Id. at 457.
69. Id.
70. Id.
71. 117 U.S. 52 (1886); see also *Williams v. Hagood,* 98 U.S. 72 (1878).
72. Charles Warren, *The Supreme Court in United States History* (rev. ed., 1928), vol. 2, p. 664.
73. Finley Peter Dunne, *Dissertations by Mr. Dooley* (1906), p. 165.
74. See *Sinking-Fund Cases,* 99 U.S. 700, 750 (1879) (Bradley, J., dissenting).
75. *Baltzer v. North Carolina,* 161 U.S. 240 (1896); see also *Baltzer & Taaks v. North Carolina,* 161 U.S. 246 (1896).
76. *White v. Ayer,* 126 N.C. 570, 614, 36 S.E. 132, 145–46 (1900) (Clark, J., dissenting).
77. Herbert Broom, *A Selection of Legal Maxims* (1845), p. 354.

171

78. Law of Feb. 21, 1899, ch. 218, 1899 N.C. Sess. Laws 341, rewritten by Law of June 13, 1900, ch. 2, 1900 N.C. Sess. Laws 54; *Amendments to the Constitution of North Carolina, 1776–1974* (John L. Sanders comp., 1975), p. 4.

79. *Raleigh* (N.C.) *News & Observer,* Feb. 1 to March 29, 1901.

80. Aubrey L. Brooks, *Walter Clark, Fighting Judge* (1944), p. 127.

81. Robert F. Durden, *Reconstruction Bonds and Twentieth-Century Politics: South Dakota v. North Carolina* (1962), pp. 22, 31–32.

82. 192 U.S. 286 (1904).

83. Id. at 289–90.

84. Law of Dec. 19, 1866, ch. 106, 1866–67 N.C. Sess. Laws 177.

85. 192 U.S. at 321–22.

86. *Raleigh* (N.C.) *Morning Post,* Dec. 13, 1904 at 1, col. 5. See Act of July 1, 1882, ch. 258, §3, 22 Stat. 126, 126 (codified at 40 U.S.C. §193d (1982)).

87. Law of March 6, 1905, ch. 543, 1905 N.C. Sess. Laws 550.

88. William Archibald Dunning, *Reconstruction, Political and Economic, 1865–1877* (1907).

89. Id., pp. 216–17.

90. Compare *Report of the Joint Investigating Committee on Public Frauds and Election of Hon. J. J. Patterson to the United States Senate, Made to the General Assembly of South Carolina at the Regular Session 1877–78* (1878), pp. 7–28 with Thomas Dixon, *The Clansman* (1905), bk. III, chap. 8.

91. *Cuba v. North Carolina,* 242 U.S. 665 (1917) (mem.).

92. E.g., *Parliamentary Debates,* Commons, 5th ser., vol. 161, col. 1775; vol. 172, col. 964; vol. 182, cols. 2205, 2412; vol. 256, col. 1045; vol. 261, cols. 831, 1026, 1820; vol. 278, col. 30.

93. Id., Lords, vol. 76, cols. 862–86.

94. Id., Commons, vol. 182, col. 1287.

95. *Monaco v. Mississippi,* 292 U.S. 313 (1934).

96. Margaret Mitchell, *Gone with the Wind* (1936), chap. 52.

97. Id.

98. Id.

99. Civil Rights Cases, 109 U.S. 3, 25 (1883).

100. 163 U.S. 537 (1896).

101. *Restatement (Second) of Contracts* ch. 11, introductory note (1981). *Cf.* Herbert Broom, *A Selection of Legal Maxims* (7th Am. ed., 1874), p. 698 ("Pacta conventa quae neque contra leges neque dolo malo inita sunt omni modo observanda sunt." "Agreements which are not contrary to the laws nor entered into with a fraudulent design are in all respects to be observed.")

102. *Code of Justinian* 2.3.29.

VI. An Exception: Virginia

1. Benjamin U. Ratchford, *American State Debts* (1941), p. 198.
2. *Messages and Papers of the Presidents, 1789–1897* (James D. Richardson ed., 1896–99), vol. 6, p. 167; Act of Dec. 31, 1862, ch. 6, 12 Stat. 633.
3. Act of July 11, 1870, ch. 259, 1869–70 Va. Acts 402. See Va. Const. of 1870, art. VIII, §3.
4. Act of March 30, 1871, ch. 282, 1870–71 Va. Acts 378.
5. Ratchford, *op. cit.,* p. 201.
6. Act of March 30, 1871, ch. 282, §3, 1870–71 Va. Acts 378, 379.
7. Id. §2, 1870–71 Va. Acts at 379.
8. Ratchford, *op. cit.,* p. 201.
9. James Tice Moore, *Two Paths to the New South: The Virginia Debt Controversy, 1870–1883* (1974), p. 16 (quoting unnamed contemporary source).
10. Ratchford, *op. cit.,* p. 203.
11. Allen W. Moger, *Virginia: Bourbonism to Byrd, 1870–1925* (1968), p. 34 (quoting Gov. F. W. M. Holliday).
12. Charles C. Pearson, *The Readjuster Movement in Virginia* (1917), p. 62.
13. Act of March 7, 1872, ch. 148, 1871–72 Va. Acts 141.
14. 63 Va. 296, 22 Gratt. 833 (1872).
15. U.S. Const. art. 1, §10, cl. 1.
16. Act of March 25, 1873, ch. 231, 1872–73 Va. Acts 207.
17. 102 U.S. 672 (1881).
18. Act of March 28, 1879, ch. 24, 1878–79 Va. Acts 264.
19. Act of Jan. 14, 1882, ch. 7, 1881–82 Va. Acts 10; Act of Jan. 29, 1882, ch. 41, 1881–82 Va. Acts 37.
20. Act of Jan. 14, 1882, ch. 7, §1, 1881–82 Va. Acts 10, 11.
21. Act of March 12, 1884, ch. 397, 1883–84 Va. Acts 504.
22. Act of Jan. 29, 1882, ch. 41, §1, 1881–82 Va. Acts 37, 38.
23. Act of Feb. 14, 1882, ch. 84, 1881–82 Va. Acts 88.
24. 107 U.S. 769 (1883).
25. Id. at 774.
26. *Green v. Biddle,* 21 U.S. (8 Wheat.) 1, 76 (1823). Accord, *Bronson v. Kinzie,* 42 U.S. (1 How.) 311 (1843).
27. 107 U.S. at 782.
28. Id. at 783 (Matthews, J., concurring).
29. Joint Resolution of Dec. 21, 1883, ch. 3, §1, 1883–84 Va. Acts 7, 7.
30. Act of March 13, 1884, ch. 421, §3, 1883–84 Va. Acts 527, 527.

31. Act of March 15, 1884, ch. 450, §112, 1883–84 Va. Acts 561, 603.
32. Id. §65, 1883–84 Va. Acts at 590.
33. Id. §91, 1883–84 Va. Acts at 596–97.
34. Id. §113, 1883–84 Va. Acts at 603.
35. William L. Royall, *Some Reminiscences* (1909), p. 9.
36. E.g., *Hartman v. Greenhow,* 102 U.S. 672 (1881); *Antoni v. Greenhow,* 107 U.S. 769 (1883); *Virginia Coupon Cases,* 114 U.S. 269 (1885); *In re Ayers,* 123 U.S. 443 (1887); *McGahey v. Virginia,* 135 U.S. 662 (1890); see also *Royall v. Virginia,* 116 U.S. 572 (1886) (representing his own interests as an owner of coupons); *Royall v. Virginia,* 121 U.S. 102 (1887) (same).
37. *Ex parte Royall,* 112 U.S. 181 (1884); *Ex parte Royall,* 117 U.S. 241 (1886).
38. William L. Royall, *History of the Virginia Debt Controversy: The Negro's Vicious Influence in Politics* (1897), pp. 79–80; see also William L. Royall, *Some Reminiscences* (1909), p. 120.
39. 114 U.S. 269 (1885). *Poindexter v. Greenhow,* id. at 270; *White v. Greenhow,* id. at 307; *Chaffin v. Taylor,* id. at 309; *Allen v. Baltimore & O. R.R.,* id. at 311; *Carter v. Greenhow,* id. at 317; *Pleasants v. Greenhow,* id. at 323; *Marye v. Parsons,* id. at 325; *Moore v. Greenhow,* id. at 338.
40. *Poindexter v. Greenhow,* id. at 279.
41. Id. at 288.
42. Id. at 303–4.
43. *Poindexter v. Greenhow,* id. at 270; *Chaffin v. Taylor,* id. at 309; see also *White v. Greenhow,* id. at 307 (reversing judgment of U.S. Circuit Court for the Eastern District of Virginia).
44. *Allen v. Baltimore & O. R.R.,* id. at 311.
45. *Cf.* Francis Church, "Is There a Santa Clause?" *New York Sun,* Sept. 21, 1897 (answering yes).
46. Act of Jan. 21, 1886, ch. 45, 1885–86 Va. Acts 36.
47. Act of Jan. 26, 1886, ch. 49, 1885–86 Va. Acts 40.
48. Act of Feb. 26, 1886, ch. 238, 1885–86 Va. Acts 249.
49. Act of March 1, 1886, ch. 347, 1885–86 Va. Acts 384.
50. Act of Feb. 27, 1886, ch. 266, 1885–86 Va. Acts 312.
51. Act of May 12, 1887, ch. 185, §3, 1887 Va. Acts (extra sess.) 257, 258.
52. Act of March 2, 1833, ch. 57, §2, 4 Stat. 632, 633.
53. 123 U.S. 443 (1887).
54. 135 U.S. 662 (1890).
55. Id. at 684.
56. Id. at 721.
57. Act of Feb. 20, 1892, ch. 325, 1891–92 Va. Acts 533.

58. Ratchford, *op. cit.,* pp. 216–17.
59. William L. Royall, *History of the Virginia Debt Controversy: The Negro's Vicious Influence in Politics* (1897), p. 98.
60. Moore, *op. cit.,* p. 26.
61. *St. Louis Republic,* July 15, 1890, quoted in Charles Fairman, "What Makes a Great Justice? Mr. Justice Bradley and the Supreme Court, 1870–1892," 30 *Boston University Law Review* 49, 75–76 (1950).
62. W. Va. Const. of 1862, art. VIII, §8.
63. Joint Resolution of March 6, 1894, ch. 747, 1893–94 Va. Acts 867.
64. Act of March 6, 1900, ch. 825, 1899–1900 Va. Acts 902.
65. Ratchford, *op. cit.,* p. 219.
66. Ordinance of Aug. 20, 1861, §9, 1861 Va. Acts (extra sess.) 54, 58.
67. James G. Randall, "The Virginia Debt Controversy," 30 *Political Science Quarterly* 553, 556 & n.2, 566 (1915).
68. *Virginia v. West Virginia,* 206 U.S. 290 (1907); 209 U.S. 514 (1908); 220 U.S. 1 (1911); 222 U.S. 17 (1911); 231 U.S. 89 (1913); 234 U.S. 117 (1914); 238 U.S. 202 (1915); 241 U.S. 531 (1916); 246 U.S. 565 (1918).
69. 206 U.S. 290 (1907).
70. Id. at 321.
71. 220 U.S. 1, 35 (1911).
72. Id. at 36.
73. 238 U.S. 202 (1915).
74. Id. at 242.
75. 246 U.S. at 574–579 n. (1918).
76. 246 U.S. 565 (1918).
77. Editorial, "The West Virginia Debt Case: Can the Supreme Court of the United States Issue a Mandamus Against a State Legislature?" 2 *Virginia Law Register* 933 (new series 1917).
78. 246 U.S. at 601.
79. Id. at 603.
80. Act of March 31, 1919, ch. 10, 1919 W. Va. Acts (extra sess.) 19.

VII. Another Exception: Cities and Counties

1. 133 U.S. 529 (1890).
2. Id. at 530.
3. Id. (quoting *Osborn v. The Bank of the United States,* 22 U.S. (9 Wheat.) 738, 857 (1824)).
4. Id.

5. Comment, "The Denial of Eleventh Amendment Immunity to Political Subdivisions of the States: An Unjustifiable Strain on Federalism," 1979 *Duke Law Journal* 1042.
6. Act of Feb. 17, 1873, ch. 13, §19, 1873 Nev. Stat. 54, 58.
7. 74 U.S. (7 Wall.) 118 (1869).
8. Act of March 3, 1845, ch. 27, 1845 Ill. Rev. Stat. 129.
9. 74 U.S. (7 Wall.) at 122.
10. 62 U.S. (21 How.) 539 (1859).
11. Act of Feb. 14, 1848, ch. 479, §12, 1847–48 Ind. Acts 619.
12. *Board of Comm'rs v. Aspinwall,* 65 U.S. (24 How.) 376 (1861).
13. *Riggs v. Johnson County,* 73 U.S. (6 Wall.) 166, 201–02 (1868) (Miller, J., dissenting).
14. 68 U.S. (1 Wall.) 175 (1864).
15. Act of Jan. 28, 1857, ch. 205, 1856–57 Iowa Acts 339.
16. *Iowa ex rel. Burlington & Missouri River R.R. v. County of Wapello,* 13 Iowa 388 (1862) (overruling *Dubuque County v. Dubuque & Pac. R.R.,* 4 Greene 1 (Iowa 1853)).
17. 68 U.S. (1 Wall.) at 206–07.
18. 73 U.S. (6 Wall.) 166 (1868).
19. 74 U.S. (7 Wall.) 175 (1869).
20. Letter from U. S. Grant to John A. Dix (June 20, 1870), reprinted in Charles Fairman, *A History of the Supreme Court of the United States: Reconstruction and Reunion, 1864–88, Part One* (1971), p. 985.
21. 78 U.S. (11 Wall.) 136 (1871).
22. Act of Sept. 24, 1789, ch. 20, §11, 1 Stat. 73, 79; see also Act of March 3, 1875, ch. 137, §1, 18 Stat. 470, 470; Act of Aug. 13, 1888, ch. 866, §1, 25 Stat. 433, 433–34.
23. *Thomson v. Lee County,* 70 U.S. (3 Wall.) 327, 331–32 (1866); see also *City of Lexington v. Butler,* 81 U.S. (14 Wall.) 282 (1872); *Thompson v. Perrine,* 106 U.S. 589 (1883); *Ackley School Dist. v. Hall,* 113 U.S. 135 (1885); *Lake County Comm'rs v. Dudley,* 173 U.S. 243 (1899).
24. John F. Dillon, *The Law of Municipal Bonds* (1876), p. 7.
25. Letter from Samuel F. Miller to William P. Ballinger (Feb. 3, 1878), quoted in Charles Fairman, *Mr. Justice Miller and the Supreme Court, 1862–1890* (1939), p. 232.
26. 13 *Congressional Record* 2097 (speech by Sen. Eugene Hale of Maine).
27. *National Bank v. County of Yankton,* 101 U.S. 129 (1880).
28. Law of Feb. 11, 1881, ch. 54, 1881 Dak. Terr. Sess. Laws 63.
29. Act of May 19, 1828, ch. 68, 4 Stat. 278.
30. Law of Feb. 12, 1881, ch. 137, 1881 Dak. Terr. Sess. Laws 219.
31. Charles Fairman, *A History of the Supreme Court of the*

United States: Reconstruction and Reunion, 1864–88, Part One (1971), pp. 1039–47.

32. Fed. R. Civ. P. 25(d)(1).

33. 20 *Congressional Record* 2195 (1889) (admission of South Dakota).

34. James L. High, *A Treatise on Extraordinary Legal Remedies, Embracing Mandamus, Quo Warranto, and Prohibition* (1874), p. 279.

35. Id. (2d ed., 1884), pp. 314–15; id. (3d ed., 1896), p. 388.

36. Frank W. Hackett, "A Recent Decision of the Supreme Court upon Municipal Bonds," 5 *Harvard Law Review* 157, 159 (1891) (comment on *Merrill v. Monticello*, 138 U.S. 673 (1891)).

37. Charles Fairman, *A History of the Supreme Court of the United States: Reconstruction and Reunion, 1864–88, Part One* (1971), p. 918.

38. Id., p. 922.

39. *Federal Deposit Ins. Corp. v. Cades*, 357 F. Supp. 1111 (E.D. Pa. 1973).

40. *Aerojet-General Corp. v. Askew*, 453 F.2d 819 (5th Cir. 1971), cert. denied, 409 U.S. 892 (1972).

41. *Chesapeake Bay Bridge & Tunnel Dist. v. Lauritzen*, 404 F.2d 1001 (4th Cir. 1968) (immunity waived in this case).

42. *Raymond Int'l Inc. v. The M/T Dalzelleagle*, 336 F. Supp. 679 (S.D.N.Y. 1971); see also *Doris Trading Corp. v. SS Union Enter.* 406 F. Supp. 1093 (S.D.N.Y. 1976); *Litton RCS, Inc. v. Pennsylvania Turnpike Comm'n*, 376 F. Supp. 579 (E.D. Pa. 1974), aff'd mem. sub nom. *Litton Business Sys., Inc. v. Pennsylvania Turnpike Comm'n*, 511 F.2d 1394 (3d Cir. 1975); *S. J. Groves & Sons Co. v. New Jersey Turnpike Auth.*, 268 F. Supp. 568 (D.N.J. 1967).

43. *George R. Whitten, Jr., Inc. v. State Univ. Constr. Fund*, 493 F.2d 177 (1st Cir. 1974); see also *Mifsud v. Palisades Geophysical Inst. Inc.*, 484 F. Supp. 159 (S.D. Tex. 1980); *Huckins v. Board of Regents*, 263 F. Supp. 622 (E.D. Mich. 1967).

44. *Aerojet-General Corp. v. Askew*, 453 F.2d 819 (5th Cir. 1971), cert. denied, 409 U.S. 892 (1972).

45. *Ford Motor Co. v. Department of Treasury*, 323 U.S. 459, 463–64 (1945).

46. *Mt. Healthy City School Dist. Bd. of Educ. v. Doyle*, 429 U.S. 274, 280 (1977).

47. Act of April 20, 1871, ch. 22, 17 Stat. 13.

48. *Monell v. New York City Dep't of Social Servs.*, 436 U.S. 658, 690 n.54 (1978).

49. Act of April 20, 1871, ch. 22, §1, 17 Stat. 13, 13 (codified as amended at 42 U.S.C. §1983 (1982)).
50. *Markham v. City of Newport News,* 292 F.2d 711 (4th Cir. 1961).
51. 178 U.S. 436 (1900).
52. Act of March 9, 1937, ch. 101, §13, 1937 Utah Laws 193, 196.
53. *Kennecott Copper Corp. v. State Tax Comm'n,* 327 U.S. 573, 577 (1946).
54. *Atascadero State Hosp. v. Scanlon,* 105 S. Ct. 3142, 3147 (1985) (state constitution provided for suits against state "in such courts as shall be directed by law"); see also *Pennhurst State School & Hosp. v. Halderman,* 465 U.S. 89, 99 (1984).

VIII. From 1890 to 1908

1. William D. Guthrie, "The Eleventh Article of Amendment to the Constitution of the United States," 8 *Columbia Law Review* 183 (1908).
2. *The New York Times,* Oct. 2, 1907, at 6, col. 1.
3. 42 *Congressional Record* 67, 72 (1907).
4. E.g., S.3732, 60th Cong., 1st Sess., 42 *Congressional Record* 637 (1908); H.R.4000, id. at 116; H.R.7637, id. at 309; H.R.-9195, id. at 362.
5. H.R.J. Res. 250, 59th Cong., 2d Sess., 41 *Congressional Record* 3711 (1907).
6. 8 *Columbia Law Review* at 199 (footnote omitted). (Guthrie actually said that *Davis* was decided in 1872, by which he meant in the October Term that began in 1872 and ended in 1873. The case was in fact decided on April 15, 1873, as appears in 21 L. Ed. 447.)
7. John E. Semonche, *Charting the Future: The Supreme Court Responds to a Changing Society, 1890–1920* (1978), p. 191.
8. William Blackstone, *Commentaries on the Laws of England* (1765–69), vol. 3, p. 256.
9. Id.
10. U.S. Const. art. III, §2, cl. 1.
11. 8 *Columbia Law Review* at 189.
12. 200 U.S. 273, 283–84 (1906).
13. 108 U.S. 76, 91 (1883) (emphasis added).
14. 108 U.S. 436, 447 (1883).
15. 134 U.S. 1, 20 (1890) (emphasis added).
16. 83 U.S. (16 Wall.) 244 (1873).
17. 200 U.S. at 284.

18. 8 *Columbia Law Review* at 188; see also Karl Singewald, *The Doctrine of Non-Suability of the State in the United States* (1910), pp. 29–35. The Supreme Court contemporaneously confirmed the general rule that judicial power cannot be conferred on federal courts by consent. *Louisville & Nashville R.R. v. Mottley*, 211 U.S. 149 (1908).
19. 8 *Columbia Law Review* at 189.
20. Finley Peter Dunne, *Mr. Dooley's Philosophy* (1900), p. 253.
21. 140 U.S. 1 (1891).
22. 154 U.S. 362 (1894).
23. 169 U.S. 466 (1898).
24. *Fitts v. McGhee*, 172 U.S. 516 (1899).
25. 188 U.S. 537 (1903).
26. Id. at 543.
27. U.S. Const. amend. XIII, §2; amend. XIV, §5; amend. XV, §2.
28. 8 *Columbia Law Review* at 197.
29. *Fitzpatrick v. Bitzer,* 427 U.S. 445 (1976) (amend. XIV); *cf. City of Rome v. United States,* 446 U.S. 156 (1980) (amend. XV empowers Congress to override otherwise valid principles of federalism).
30. 157 U.S. 429 (1895); 158 U.S. 601 (1895).
31. U.S. Const. art. I, §2, cl. 3; id. §9, cl. 4.
32. *Hylton v. United States,* 3 U.S. (3 Dall.) 171 (1796); *Springer v. United States,* 102 U.S. 586 (1881).
33. U.S. Const. amend. XVI.
34. Charles Evans Hughes, *The Supreme Court of the United States* (1928), pp. 50–53.
35. 60 U.S. (19 How.) 393 (1857).
36. 75 U.S. (8 Wall.) 603 (1870); 79 U.S. (12 Wall.) 457 (1871).
37. 198 U.S. 45 (1905).
38. 209 U.S. 123 (1908).
39. *McNeill v. Southern Ry.,* 202 U.S. 543 (1906); *Ex parte Wood,* 155 F. 190 (C.C.W.D.N.C. 1907); *Perkins v. Northern Pac. Ry.,* 155 F. 445 (C.C.D. Minn. 1907).
40. Act of April 4, 1907, ch. 97, 1907 Minn. Laws 109; Act of April 18, 1907, ch. 232, 1907 Minn. Laws 313.
41. Law of March 2, 1907, ch. 216, 1907 N.C. Sess. Laws 250.
42. 8 *Columbia Law Review* at 204.
43. 209 U.S. at 160.
44. 109 U.S. 3, 11 (1883).
45. 209 U.S. 205 (1908).
46. 45 *Congressional Record* 7256 (1910).
47. Kenneth Culp Davis, "Suing the Government by Falsely Pretending to Sue an Officer," 29 *University of Chicago Law Review* 435 (1962).

48. Charles Alan Wright, *The Law of Federal Courts* (4th ed., 1983), p. 292.
49. Id.
50. David P. Currie, *Federal Jurisdiction in a Nutshell* (2d ed., 1981), p. 168.
51. Theodore F. T. Plucknett, *A Concise History of the Common Law* (5th ed., 1956), p. 663.
52. *Mostyn v. Fabrigas,* 1 Cowp. 161, 98 Eng. Rep. 1021 (K.B. 1774).
53. Id. at 180, 98 Eng. Rep. at 1031.
54. Jeremy Bentham, *Works* (John Hill Burton ed., 1843), vol. 1, p. 235; vol. 7, pp. 283–87.
55. Charles Dickens, *Oliver Twist* (1838), chap. 51.
56. John W. Salmond, *The First Principles of Jurisprudence* (1893), p. 160. American jurists, less versed in classical Latinity, have tended to say: *"Damnum absque injuria,"* see *Black's Law Dictionary* (5th ed., 1979), p. 354.
57. 2 U.S. (2 Dall.) at 455–56.
58. *Bartlett's Familiar Quotations* (15th ed., 1980), p. 312.
59. Mark Twain, *Letters from the Earth* (Bernard DeVoto ed., 1962), pp. 97–98; accord, Joseph Story, *Commentaries on the Constitution of the United States* (1833), vol. 1, pp. 194–95.

IX. After *Ex Parte Young:* The Eleventh Amendment in the Twentieth Century

1. Charles Alan Wright, *Handbook of the Law of Federal Courts* (4th ed., 1983), p. 292.
2. William D. Guthrie, "The Eleventh Article of Amendment to the Constitution of the United States," 8 *Columbia Law Review* 183, 197 (1908).
3. 256 U.S. 490 (1921).
4. Id. at 498.
5. *Cf. Parden v. Terminal Ry.,* 377 U.S. 184 (1964) (state-owned railroad operating in interstate commerce not protected by sovereign immunity in action against it under Federal Employers' Liability Act).
6. *Maryland Port Admin. v. SS American Legend,* 453 F. Supp. 584 (D. Md. 1978).
7. E.g., *In re Holoholo,* 512 F. Supp. 889, 902–06 (D. Hawaii 1981).
8. Comment, "Eleventh Amendment Immunity and State-Owned Vessels," 57 *Tulane Law Review* 1523, 1535 n.57 (1983).

9. 292 U.S. 313 (1934).
10. Gordon Ireland, "Constitutional Law—Immunity of a State from Suit by a Foreign State—Defaulted State Bonds," 8 *Mississippi Law Journal* 392, 396 (1936).
11. U.S. Const. art. III, §2, cl. 2.
12. 292 U.S. at 322.
13. Id. (footnote omitted).
14. Id. at 330.
15. *Cohens v. Virginia,* 19 U.S. (6 Wheat.) 264, 406 (1821).
16. 292 U.S. at 330.
17. Act of Oct. 21, 1976, Pub. L. No. 94-583, §4, 90 Stat. 2891, 2892–94 (codified at 28 U.S.C. §§1604–05 (1982)).
18. See *Verlinden B.V. v. Central Bank of Nigeria,* 461 U.S. 480 (1983) (Congress may constitutionally authorize suit by foreign corporation against foreign sovereign).
19. *Edelman v. Jordan,* 415 U.S. 651, 663 (1974).
20. John J. Gibbons, "The Eleventh Amendment and State Sovereign Immunity: A Reinterpretation," 83 *Columbia Law Review* 1889, 2004 (1983).
21. 359 U.S. 275 (1959).
22. Act of July 27, 1949, S.B. 153, 1949 Mo. Laws 621; Act of April 8, 1949, ch. 168, 1949 Tenn. Pub. Acts 514.
23. U.S. Const. art. I, §10, cl. 3.
24. Act of Oct. 26, 1949, ch. 758, 63 Stat. 930.
25. Id. at 931 (Compact, art. I, §3).
26. Id. at 930.
27. 377 U.S. 184 (1964).
28. 45 U.S.C. §51–60 (1982).
29. 377 U.S. at 192. As an alternative, the Court held that the state had consented to suit by beginning to operate its railroad twenty years after enactment of the FELA. Id. at 192–93.
30. *Cohens v. Virginia,* 19 U.S. (6 Wheat.) at 380–83.
31. 411 U.S. 279 (1973).
32. Act of June 25, 1938, ch. 676, §16(b), 52 Stat. 1060, 1069 (current version at 29 U.S.C. §216(b) (1982)).
33. See also *Atascadero State Hosp. v. Scanlon,* 105 S. Ct. 3142 (1985) (state has not consented to suit under Federal Rehabilitation Act by accepting funds and participating in programs).
34. 415 U.S. 651 (1974).
35. Id. at 678 (affirming *Ford Motor Co. v. Department of Treasury,* 323 U.S. 459, 466–67 (1945)).
36. 211 U.S. 210 (1908).
37. 8 *Columbia Law Review* at 205.
38. Act of June 18, 1910, ch. 309, §17, 36 Stat. 539, 557.
39. 45 *Congressional Record* 7256 (1910).

40. Act of Aug. 12, 1976, Pub. L. No. 94-381, 90 Stat. 1119.
41. 312 U.S. 496 (1941).
42. 401 U.S. 37 (1971).
43. John J. Gibbons, "Our Federalism," 12 *Suffolk University Law Review* 1087, 1092 (1978).
44. 401 U.S. at 44.
45. Aviam Soifer and H. C. Macgill, "The *Younger* Doctrine: Reconstructing Reconstruction," 55 *Texas Law Review* 1141 (1977).
46. 415 U.S. 651 (1974); accord, *Quern v. Jordan*, 440 U.S. 332 (1979); *Florida Dep't of Health & Rehabilitative Servs. v. Florida Nursing Home Ass'n*, 450 U.S. 147 (1981) (per curiam); *Green v. Mansour*, 106 S. Ct. 423 (1985).
47. 415 U.S. at 663.
48. 465 U.S. 89 (1984).
49. 451 U.S. 1 (1981).
50. 465 U.S. at 105.
51. Id. at 106.
52. Act of April 20, 1871, ch. 22, §1, 17 Stat. 13, 13 (current version at 42 U.S.C. §1983 (1982)).
53. *Tenney v. Brandhove*, 341 U.S. 367 (1951) (absolute immunity).
54. *Pierson v. Ray*, 386 U.S. 547, 553–55 (1967) (absolute immunity).
55. *Imbler v. Pachtman*, 424 U.S. 409 (1976) (absolute immunity).
56. *Pierson v. Ray*, 386 U.S. 547, 555–57 (1967) (qualified immunity).
57. *Scheuer v. Rhodes*, 416 U.S. 232, 238–49 (1974) (qualified immunity).
58. See *United States v. Carolene Products Co.*, 304 U.S. 144, 152–53 n.4 (1938); see also Edward S. Corwin, *Constitutional Revolution, Ltd.* (1941), pp. 111–12, 115.
59. *Brown v. Board of Educ.*, 347 U.S. 483 (1954).
60. Act of Sept. 9, 1957, Pub.L.No. 85-315, 71 Stat. 634.
61. E.g., Act of July 2, 1964, Pub.L.No. 88-352, 78 Stat. 241 (civil rights); Act of Aug. 6, 1965, Pub.L.No. 89-110, 79 Stat. 437 (voting rights).
62. 427 U.S. 445 (1976).
63. U.S. Const. amend. XIV, §5.
64. But see *Atascadero State Hosp. v. Scanlon*, 105 S. Ct. 3142 (1985) (congressional abrogation of Eleventh Amendment must be unequivocally expressed).
65. 446 U.S. 156 (1980).
66. U.S. Const. amend. XV, §2.
67. 8 *Columbia Law Review* at 197.
68. *Employees of the Dep't of Pub. Health & Welfare v. Depart-*

ment of Pub. Health & Welfare, 411 U.S. 279, 313–14 (1973) (Brennan, J., dissenting); *Edelman v. Jordan,* 415 U.S. 651, 687 (1974) (Brennan, J., dissenting); *Pennhurst State School & Hosp. v. Halderman,* 465 U.S. 89, 125 (1984) (Brennan, J., dissenting); *Atascadero State Hosp. v. Scanlon,* 105 S. Ct. 3142, 3150 (1985) (Brennan, J., dissenting); *Green v. Mansour,* 106 S. Ct. 423, 429 (1985) (Brennan, J., dissenting).

69. 105 S. Ct. at 3177 (Brennan, J., dissenting).
70. Martha A. Field, "The Eleventh Amendment and Other Sovereign Immunity Doctrines," 126 *University of Pennsylvania Law Review* 515, 541 n.89 (1978).
71. *Employees of the Dep't of Pub. Health & Welfare v. Department of Pub. Health & Welfare,* 411 U.S. 279, 287 (1973) (proposition is "arguably" true); id. at 297–98 (Marshall, J., concurring in result).
72. *Hunter v. Martin,* 18 Va. 11, 23, 4 Munf. 1, 34–35 (1814), rev'd, 14 U.S. (1 Wheat.) 304 (1816).
73. U.S. Const. art. VI, cl. 3.
74. David P. Currie, *Federal Jurisdiction in a Nutshell* (2d ed., 1981), pp. 167–68.
75. Comment, "Eleventh Amendment Immunity and State-Owned Vessels," 57 *Tulane Law Review* 1523, 1524 & n.1 (1983).
76. Howard Fink and Mark V. Tushnet, *Federal Jurisdiction: Policy and Practice* (1984), p. 140.

X. Epilogue

1. Deut. 15:6 & 28:12.
2. Charles Dickens, *A Christmas Carol* (1843), stave 2.
3. David M. Walker, *The Oxford Companion to Law* (1980), p. 1093.
4. Mass. Const. of 1780, part 1, art. 30; see also *Marbury v. Madison,* 5 U.S. (1 Cranch) 137, 163 (1803).
5. A. V. Dicey, *Introduction to the Study of the Law of the Constitution* (1885), see H. W. Arndt, "The Origins of Dicey's Concept of the Rule of Law," 31 *Australian Law Journal* 117 (1957).
6. See John V. Orth, "On the Relation Between the Rule of Law and Public Opinion" (review essay on Richard A. Cosgrove, *The Rule of Law: Albert Venn Dicey, Victorian Jurist*), 80 *Michigan Law Review* 753 (1982).
7. Grant Gilmore, *The Ages of American Law* (1977), pp. 105, 146 n.7.

183

8. E. P. Thompson, *Whigs and Hunters: The Origin of the Black Act* (1975), p. 266.

9. Morton J. Horwitz, "The Rule of Law: An Unqualified Human Good?" (review of E. P. Thompson, *Whigs and Hunters: The Origin of the Black Act*), 86 *Yale Law Journal* 561, 566 (1977).

10. *Paxton's Case,* Quincy's Mass. Rep. 51, 57 (1761).

11. See John V. Orth, Book Review (A. W. Brian Simpson, *Cannibalism and the Common Law: The Story of the Tragic Last Voyage of the Mignonette and the Strange Legal Proceedings to Which It Gave Rise*), 16 *Albion* 440 (1984).

12. U.S. Const. art. III, §2, cl. 1.

13. E.g., Benjamin Robbins Curtis, *Jurisdiction, Practice, and Peculiar Jurisprudence of the Courts of the United States* (George Ticknor Curtis & Benjamin R. Curtis eds., 1880), pp. 14–18.

14. E.g., Karl Singewald, *The Doctrine of Non-Suability of the State in the United States* (1910).

15. *Cf.* John V. Orth, "Doing Legal History," 14 *Irish Jurist* (n.s.) 114 (1979) (examples from history of English labor law).

Bibliographic Essay

Citations to official sources may be found in the notes and in the table of constitutions and statutes. Citations to cases are in the notes and in the table of cases.

OUTLINE

I. *General*

II. *Ratification of the Eleventh Amendment*
   A. *Chisholm v. Georgia* and the Ratification of the Eleventh Amendment
   B. The "Original Understanding"

III. *Early Interpretation*
   A. Chief Justice John Marshall
   B. The Supreme Court During the Taney Era
   C. Repudiation in the 1830s and 40s

IV. *Reconstruction and American Law*
   A. General
   B. Legal Issues
   C. The Election of 1876 and the Compromise of 1877

V. *The Eleventh Amendment and the End of Reconstruction: Louisiana and North Carolina*
   A. Background
   B. Debt Repudiation
   C. Justice Joseph P. Bradley and Others
   D. The Supreme Court and the Uses of History

VI. *An Exception: Virginia*
   A. Background
   B. Debt Repudiation

185

Note: In citations to periodicals I follow the convenient legal form: volume number first, then title, next page number, and finally the date in parentheses. If the periodical has no volume number, the date takes its place.

I. General

The history of the Eleventh Amendment has attracted little scholarly attention. Brief mention of it is made in Charles Warren's classic, *The Supreme Court in United States History,* 2 vols. (rev. ed., 1926), and in the modern text by Alfred H. Kelly, Winfred A. Harbison, and Herman Belz, *The American Constitution: Its Origins and Development* (6th ed., 1983). David P. Currie provides a lawyerly survey in *The Constitution in the Supreme Court: The First Hundred Years, 1789–1888* (1985). Something may be gleaned from Felix Frankfurter and James Landis, *The Business of the Supreme Court* (1927). Biographies of judges sometimes refer to the Amendment and occasionally provide the context for specific decisions. Every justice is accorded a brief biography with representative judicial opinions and selected bibliography in *The Justices of the United States Supreme Court, 1789–1969,* edited by Leon Friedman and Fred L. Israel, 4 vols. (1969). The only full-length treatment of the history of the Amendment is by Clyde E. Jacobs, *The Eleventh Amendment and Sovereign Immunity* (1972). While useful for the ratification and early interpretation of the Amendment, Jacobs's book is unsatisfactory for the post-Civil War period. Little is said about Eleventh Amendment law after *Ex parte Young* (1908), and the treatment of the period from 1873 to 1908 is handicapped by an unwillingness to look beyond the doctrines manipulated by the Court.

Coincidentally in 1983, three law review articles covered much but not all of the subject: William A. Fletcher, "A Historical Interpretation of the Eleventh Amendment: A Narrow Construction of an Affirmative Grant of Jurisdiction Rather Than a Prohibition Against Jurisdiction," 35 *Stanford Law Review* 1033 (1983), argues that the Amendment was intended to restore the original understanding that the jurisdictional grant in Article III is limited to cases in which the state appears as plaintiff; John J. Gibbons, "The Eleventh Amendment and State Sovereign Immunity: A Reinterpretation," 83 *Columbia Law Review* 1889 (1983), argues that the Amendment was intended to apply only to cases in which federal jurisdiction is based on the character of the parties, not cases with another basis for jurisdiction; and John V. Orth, "The Interpretation of the Eleventh Amendment, 1798–1908: A Case Study of Judicial Power," 1983 *University of Illinois Law Review* 423, shows the way in which the realities of judicial power affected the Court's interpretation of the Amendment without regard to the original understanding.

References to works on the modern law of the Eleventh Amendment are collected in Section IX below.

II. Ratification of the Eleventh Amendment

A. *Chisholm v. Georgia* and the Ratification of the Eleventh Amendment

The relevant decade of American history is well surveyed by John C. Miller's volume in the New American Nation Series, *The Federalist Era, 1789–1801* (1960). The classic account of the famous case in Warren, *op. cit.,* volume 1, chapter 2, is flawed, as shown by Doyle Mathis, "The Eleventh Amendment: Adoption and Interpretation," 2 *Georgia Law Review* 207 (1968). See also Doyle Mathis, "Chisholm v. Georgia: Background and Settlement," 54 *Journal of American History* 19 (1967). The most exhaustive modern account is in Julius Goebel's volume of the Oliver Wendell Holmes Devise *History of the Supreme Court of the United States: Antecedents and Beginnings to 1801* (1971), chapter 16. For an analysis of Iredell's important opinion, see Jeff B. Fordham, "Iredell's Dissent in Chisholm v. Georgia: Its Political Significance," 8 *North Carolina Historical Review* 155 (1931). On John Jay, diplomatist and first Chief Justice, see Richard B. Morris, *John Jay, the Nation, and the Court* (1967), and Samuel Flagg Bemis, *Jay's Treaty: A Study in Commerce and Diplomacy* (1923; rev. ed., 1962). On *Hollingsworth v. Virginia* and its relevance to a recent debate concerning the ratification of the proposed Equal Rights Amendment see Charles L. Black, "Correspondence on Art. I, §7, cl. 3," 87 *Yale Law Journal* 896 (1978). The scanty record on the drafting and ratification of the Eleventh Amendment is conveniently presented by Jacobs, *op. cit.,* pp. 64–74. A brief account of one state's contribution is by Charles K. Darling, "Massachusetts' Part in the Adoption of the Eleventh Amendment to the United States Constitution," 1 *Boston Law School Magazine* (No. 3) 5 (1897).

B. The "Original Understanding"

More or less perfunctory surveys of the evidence concerning the original understanding about state sovereign immunity are included in most works on the Eleventh Amendment. If anything on the subject had been said at the Constitutional Convention it would be in *The Records of the Federal Convention of 1787,* edited by Max Farrand, 4 vols. (1911–37). The standard source for the proceedings of the state ratifying conventions has been *The Debates in the Several State Conventions on the Adoption of the Federal Constitution,* edited by Jonathan Elliot, 5 vols. (2d ed., Philadelphia, 1836–45). This is now being superseded by the multivolume *Documentary History of the Ratification of the Constitution* (1976–   ). The general context is effectively summed up by William P. Murphy, *The Triumph of Nationalism: State Sovereignty, the Founding Fathers, and the Making of the Constitution* (1967). The specific meaning of the judiciary article is quested by Robert N. Clinton, "A Mandatory View of Federal Court Jurisdiction: A Guided Quest for the Original Understanding of Article III," 132 *University of Pennsylvania Law Review* 741 (1984).

It is worth noting that debate about the modern relevance of the original understanding of the Constitution has become a staple of legal literature. Vigorously maintaining that it is almost the only thing that matters is Raoul Berger, *Government by Judiciary: The Transformation of the Fourteenth Amendment* (1977). Arguing that it is nearly irrelevant is Paul Brest, "The Misconceived Quest for the Original Understanding," 60 *Boston University Law Review* 204 (1980). H. Jefferson Powell has recently enlivened the stale debate by investigating whether the Framers understood that their intent would be dispositive, "The Original Understanding of Original Intent," 98 *Harvard Law Review* 885 (1985).

For further references on the Supreme Court's use of history see Section V.D below.

III. Early Interpretation

A. Chief Justice John Marshall

The literature on John Marshall is voluminous, none of it focused on Marshall and the Eleventh Amendment. The classic biography of the great Chief Justice is by the politician and man of letters Albert J. Beveridge, *The Life of John Marshall,* 4 vols. (1916–19). A modern biography, which supplements but does not supplant Beveridge's, is by Leonard Baker, *John Marshall: A Life in Law* (1974). For Marshall's jurisprudential contribution, see Edward S. Corwin, *John Marshall and the Constitution* (1919), and the essays collected in *Chief Justice John Marshall: A Reappraisal,* edited by W. Melville Jones (1956).

For the work of the Supreme Court during the Marshall era, see George Lee Haskins and Herbert A. Johnson's volume of the Holmes Devise History, *The Foundations of Power: John Marshall, 1801–15* (1981); R. Kent Newmyer, *The Supreme Court Under Marshall and Taney* (1968); and G. Edward White, "The Working Life of the Marshall Court, 1815–1835," 70 *Virginia Law Review* 1 (1984). On the interaction of law and politics at the time, see Richard E. Ellis, *The Jeffersonian Crisis: Courts and Politics in the Young Republic* (1971).

On *Marbury,* see Donald O. Dewey, *Marshall versus Jefferson: The Political Background of Marbury v. Madison* (1970); William Van Alstyne, "A Critical Guide to Marbury v. Madison," 1969 *Duke Law Journal* 1; and John J. Gibbons, "The Interdependence of Legitimacy: An Introduction to the Meaning of Separation of Powers," 5 *Seton Hall Law Review* 435, 437–53 (1974). On the background to *Peters* and *Bright,* see Hampton L. Carson, "The Case of the Sloop 'Active,' " 16 *Pennsylvania Magazine of History and Biography* 385 (1892) (including a photograph of Fort Rittenhouse). On *Osborn,* see Bray Hammond's essay on "The Bank Cases" in *Quarrels That Have Shaped the Constitution,* edited by John A. Garraty (1962).

American constitutional law as of the end of the era is comprehensively stated by Marshall's protégé, Justice Joseph Story, in *Commentaries on the Constitution of the United States,* 3 vols. (1833); American law in general is canvassed by Chancellor James Kent, *Commentaries on American Law,* 4 vols. (1826–30).

B. The Supreme Court During the Taney Era

The standard biography of Marshall's successor is by Carl Brent Swisher, *Roger B. Taney* (1935). Swisher also contributed the volume of the Holmes Devise History on *The Taney Period, 1836–1864* (1974). The law of federal jurisdiction at the end of the period is stated by Alfred Conkling, judge and Congressman (and father of the more famous lawyer and politico Roscoe

Conkling), *A Treatise on the Organization, Jurisdiction and Practice of the Courts of the United States* (4th ed., 1864).

C. Repudiation in the 1830s and 40s

For a thorough account of repudiation following the Panic of 1837, see Reginald C. McGrane, *Foreign Bondholders and American State Debts* (1935), chapters 1–13. For the background, see the same author's *The Panic of 1837: Some Financial Problems of the Jacksonian Era* (1924). Short accounts may be found in Benjamin U. Ratchford, *American State Debts* (1941), chapter 5, and William A. Scott, *The Repudiation of State Debts* (1893), chapter 2. On the world of high finance, see Ralph W. Hidy, *The House of Baring in American Trade and Finance: English Merchant Bankers at Work, 1763–1861* (1949). The legal advice Baring Brothers received may be seen in *The Papers of Daniel Webster: Correspondence, Vol. 4: 1835–1839,* edited by Charles M. Wiltse and Harold D. Moser (1980), pp. 404–7. Criticism of Webster's advice was published by an anonymous Junius, *A Letter to Daniel Webster in Reply to His Legal Opinion to Baring Bros.* (1840). A more elaborate legal opinion for the bankers was [Benjamin R. Curtis], "Debts of the States," 58 *North American Review* 109 (1844). A biography of Curtis by his brother George Ticknor Curtis, edited by his son Benjamin R. Curtis, is in volume 1 of *A Memoir of Benjamin Robbins Curtis* (1879); in volume 2, Curtis's article is reprinted. Curtis's lectures on federal jurisdiction at the Harvard Law School were posthumously published in *Jurisdiction, Practice and Peculiar Jurisprudence of the Courts of the United States,* edited by George Ticknor Curtis and Benjamin R. Curtis (1880).

The spirit of the boom days preceding the Panic is recaptured by Joseph G. Baldwin, *The Flush Times of Alabama and Mississippi* (1853).

IV. Reconstruction and American Law

A. General

The Civil War and Reconstruction have generated an immense body of literature. A recent study which includes a thorough bibliography is by James M. McPherson, *Ordeal by Fire: The Civil War and Reconstruction* (1982). Excellent accounts of Reconstruction are provided by John Hope Franklin, *Reconstruction After the Civil War* (1961), and by Kenneth M. Stampp, *The Era of Reconstruction, 1865–1877* (1965). The classic account by William A. Dunning, *Reconstruction, Political and Economic, 1865–1877* (1907), is of interest today mainly for historiographical purposes.

The post-Reconstruction era is surveyed by John A. Garraty in his volume for The New American Nation Series, *The New Commonwealth, 1877–1890* (1968), and by Robert H. Wiebe in his volume for The Making of America Series, *The Search for Order, 1877–1920* (1967); the regional story is told by C. Vann Woodward, *Origins of the New South, 1877–1913* (1951), volume IX in A History of the South.

B. Legal Issues

The classic study by the prominent political scientist John W. Burgess, *Reconstruction and the Constitution, 1866–1876* (1902), is marred by uncritical acceptance of Southern criticism of Northern policy. The same is true of James G. Randall's *The Civil War and Reconstruction* (1937), although David Donald improved the balance in a revised edition in 1969. Useful accounts in The New American Nation Series are Harold M. Hyman and William M. Wiecek's *Equal Justice Under Law: Constitutional Development, 1835–1875* (1982), and Loren P. Beth's *Development of the American Constitution, 1877–1917* (1971). Exhaustive detail is provided by Charles Fairman in his contribution to the Holmes Devise History of the Supreme Court, *Reconstruction and Reunion, 1864–88, Part One* (1971), cover-

192

ing the period to 1873. For a shorter, more focused study, see Stanley I. Kutler, *Judicial Power and Reconstruction Politics* (1968). Federal jurisdiction during Reconstruction is covered by William M. Wiecek, "The Reconstruction of Federal Judicial Power, 1863–1875," 13 *American Journal of Legal History* 333 (1969). See also Drew L. Kershen, "The Jury Selection Act of 1879: Theory and Practice of Citizen Participation in the Judicial System," 1980 *University of Illinois Law Forum* 707; Michael Les Benedict, "Preserving Federalism: Reconstruction and the Waite Court," 1978 *Supreme Court Review* 39; and Alfred Avins, "The Ku Klux Klan Act of 1871: Some Reflected Light on State Action and the Fourteenth Amendment," 11 *St. Louis University Law Journal* 331 (1967). The sequel is recounted by Eugene Gressman, "The Unhappy History of Civil Rights Legislation," 50 *Michigan Law Review* 1323 (1952).

On the *Legal Tender Cases* see Gerald T. Dunne, *Monetary Decisions of the Supreme Court* (1960); Kenneth W. Dam, "The Legal Tender Cases," 1981 *Supreme Court Review* 367; and Charles Fairman, "Mr. Justice Bradley's Appointment to the Supreme Court and the Legal Tender Cases" (2 parts), 54 *Harvard Law Review* 977, 1128 (1941).

The year the Fourteenth Amendment was ratified, Judge Thomas M. Cooley of the Michigan Supreme Court published his *Treatise on the Constitutional Limitations Which Rest upon the Legislative Power of the States of the American Union* (1868), a book of the utmost importance in American constitutional development, especially in the interpretation of the Reconstruction Amendments.

C. The Election of 1876 and the Compromise of 1877

On the momentous election see Paul Leland Haworth, *The Hayes-Tilden Disputed Presidential Election of 1876* (1906; new ed., 1927). On the public perception of Justice Bradley's role, see Sister Marie Carolyn Klinkhamer, "Joseph P. Bradley: Private and Public Opinion of a 'Political' Justice," 38 *University of Detroit Law Journal* 150 (1960). For reflections on the modern relevance of the election, see Joseph R. Wyatt, "The Lessons of the Hayes-Tilden Election Controversy: Some Suggestions for Electoral College Reform," 8 *Rutgers-Camden Law Journal* 617 (1977). The Compromise is dissected by C. Vann Woodward, *Reunion and Reaction: The Compromise of 1877 and the End of Reconstruction* (1951); for recent assessments see Michael Les Benedict, "Southern Democrats in the Crisis of 1876–1877: A Reconsideration of *Reunion and Reaction*," 46 *Journal of Southern History* 491 (1980), and Vincent P. DeSantis, "Rutherford B. Hayes and the Removal of the Troops and the End of Reconstruction," in *Region, Race, and Reconstruction: Essays in Honor of C. Vann Woodward,* edited by J. Morgan Kousser and James M. McPherson (1982). A novelistic account of the election and Compromise is provided by Gore Vidal, *1876* (1976).

The implications of the Compromise for American legal development have gone largely unexamined except in the area of race relations. For the latter see C. Vann Woodward, *The Strange Career of Jim Crow* (1955; 3d rev. ed., 1974); Rayford W. Logan, *The Betrayal of the Negro: From Rutherford B. Hayes to Woodrow Wilson* (new enl. ed., 1965); and Richard Kluger, *Simple Justice: The History of Brown v. Board of Education and Black America's Struggle for Equality* (1976).

V. The Eleventh Amendment and the End of Reconstruction: Louisiana and North Carolina

A. Background

For a short account of Louisiana history, see Joe Gray Taylor, *Louisiana: A Bicentennial History* (1976). The colorful tale of Reconstruction and its sequel may be found in Joe Gray Taylor, *Louisiana Reconstructed, 1863–1877* (1974), and William Ivy Hair, *Bourbonism and Agrarian Protest: Louisiana Politics, 1877–1900* (1969).

The classic account of North Carolina history is R. D. W. Connor, William K. Boyd, and J. G. de Roulhac Hamilton's *History of North Carolina,* 3 vols. (1919). Each author contributed one volume; Reconstruction is covered in volume 3 by Hamilton, a disciple of William A. Dunning. The best modern account is by Hugh Talmage Lefler and Albert Ray Newsome, *North Carolina: The History of a Southern State* (3d ed., 1973). The bicentennial history is by William S. Powell, *North Carolina* (1977).

The successive constitutions of Louisiana and North Carolina, as well as of all other states, are conveniently reprinted in *Sources and Documents of United States Constitutions,* edited by William F. Swindler (1973–82). With respect to North Carolina, however, it must be noted that Swindler treats the extensive amendments to the Constitution of 1868 that were adopted in 1876 as if they resulted in a "Constitution of 1876." In fact, North Carolinians recognize only the Constitution of 1868 between the early Constitution of 1776 and the late Constitution of 1970.

B. Debt Repudiation

The economic facts are scrupulously laid out in the *Tenth Census* (1880), volume 7, "Report on Valuation, Taxation, and Public Indebtedness in the United States." For a careful marshaling of earlier data, see Robert P. Porter, "State Debts and Repudiation," 9 *International Review* 556 (1880). The legal issues are introduced by the editorial note, "Suability of a State," 2 *Virginia Law Journal* 457 (1878). Two exchanges principally concerned with Virginia's repudiation (for which see Section VI.B below) raise legal issues relevant to other Southern repudiations: asking the general question "Can States Be Compelled to Pay Their Debts?" Bradley T. Johnson, a debt-payer, answered yes, 12 *American Law Review* 625 (1878), while W. H. Burroughs, a readjuster, answered no, 3 *Virginia Law Journal* 129 (1879); asking the specific question "Can a State Be Sued in a Federal Circuit Court by Its Own Citizen?" R. W. Hughes, Federal Circuit Court judge for the Eastern District of Virginia, answered yes, 8 *Virginia Law Journal* 385 (1884), while J. R. Tucker, Jr., answered no, id. at 641 (1884). The Supreme Court decisions in 1883 led to comments by John Norton Pomeroy, "The Supreme Court and State Repudiation—The Virginia and Louisiana

Cases," 17 *American Law Review* 684 (1883), and by Francis J. Lippitt, "State Repudiation in the United States Supreme Court," 14 *International Review* 325 (1883). The discussion was continued the following year by George M. Davie, "Suing the State," 18 *American Law Review* 814 (1884), and by D. H. Chamberlain, "The Constitutionality of Repudiation," 138 *North American Review* 294 (1884) (including a reply by John S. Wise). John F. Hume asked "Are We a Nation of Rascals?" 139 *North American Review* 127 (1884), and answered in the affirmative; the same author explained who was to blame in "Responsibility for State Roguery," id. at 563. The hopes and fears of holders of Southern bonds can be glimpsed in the annual reports (from 1874 on) issued by the London-based Corporation of Foreign Bondholders.

On Louisiana's debt, see John V. Orth, "The Fair Fame and Name of Louisiana: The Eleventh Amendment and the End of Reconstruction," 2 *Tulane Lawyer* 2 (1980). On North Carolina's debt, see three articles by Benjamin U. Ratchford: "The North Carolina Public Debt, 1870–1878," "The Adjustment of the North Carolina Public Debt, 1879–1883," and "The Conversion of the North Carolina Public Debt After 1879," in 10 *North Carolina Historical Review* 1, 157, 251 (1933); and John V. Orth, "The Eleventh Amendment and the North Carolina State Debt," 59 *North Carolina Law Review* 747 (1981). A pamphlet by an assistant attorney general of North Carolina, Frank Nash, "The Legal and Constitutional Aspect of Special Tax Bonds Repudiated by the State" (post 1928) is the legal equivalent of Margaret Mitchell's novelistic argument in *Gone with the Wind:* technical (and unconvincing) arguments mixed up with overt racism. The railroad building that was responsible for North Carolina's antebellum debt is described by Cecil K. Brown, *A State Movement in Railroad Development* (1928).

The case for repudiation in South Carolina was first made by the repudiators themselves in the *Report of the Joint Investigating Committee on Public Frauds and Election of Hon. J. J. Patterson to the United States Senate, Made to the General Assembly of South Carolina at the Regular Session 1877–78* (1878); it was later restated in a brief pamphlet by the state Comptroller General, A. J. Beattie, *History of South Carolina Fraudulent Bond Issues* (1929).

For the background to *South Dakota v. North Carolina,* see Carman F. Randolph, "Notes on Suits Between States" (2 parts), 2 *Columbia Law Review* 283, 364 (1902), and Robert F. Durden, *Reconstruction Bonds and Twentieth-Century Politics* (1962). Post-World War I squabbles among the Allies about debt repayment raised the specter of repudiated Southern bonds. See Raymond Turner, "Repudiation of Debts by States of the Union" (including replies by the governors of Arkansas, Georgia, North Carolina, and Virginia), 23 *Current History* 475 (1926); Charles P. Howland, "Our Repudiated State Debts," 6 *Foreign Affairs* 395 (1928); and Bessie C. Randolph, "Foreign Bondholders and the Repudiated Debts of the Southern States," 25 *American Journal of International Law* 63 (1931).

Academic discussion of the issue began with William A. Scott, *The Repudiation of State Debts* (1893), chapters 3 and 4, continued with Reginald C. McGrane, *Foreign Bondholders and American State Debts* (1935), chapter 14, and culminated in Benjamin U. Ratchford, *American State Debts* (1941), chapters 7–9. For a brief statement of the once standard version of the rights and wrongs of repudiation see J. G. de Roulhac Hamilton, "Those Repudiated Southern Bonds," 3 *Virginia Quarterly Review* 490 (1927). A revised version of the political causes and effects is by J. Mills Thornton, "Fiscal Policy and the Failure of Radical Reconstruction in the Lower South," in *Region, Race, and Reconstruction: Essays in Honor of C. Vann Woodward,* edited by J. Morgan Kousser and James M. McPherson (1982).

The Contracts Clause, at issue in so many cases concerning repudiated Southern bonds, is carefully described by Benjamin Fletcher Wright, *The Contract Clause of the Constitution* (1938). For a recent plea to bring the clause back to life see Richard A. Epstein, "Toward a Revitalization of the Contract Clause," 51 *University of Chicago Law Review* 703 (1984).

C. Justice Joseph P. Bradley and Others

Justice Bradley's role in the decision of the *Legal Tender Cases* and his service on the Electoral Commission have already been noted; see Section IV.B and C above. The nearest thing we have to a biography of the Justice are articles by Charles Fairman: "The Education of a Justice: Justice Bradley and Some of His Colleagues," 1 *Stanford Law Review* 217 (1949); "The So-Called Granger Cases, Lord Hale and Justice Bradley," 5 *Stanford Law Review* 587 (1953); "What Makes a Great Justice? Mr. Justice Bradley and the Supreme Court, 1870–1892," 30 *Boston University Law Review* 49 (1950); and "Mr. Justice Bradley," in *Mr. Justice,* edited by Allison Dunham and Philip B. Kurland (rev. ed., 1964). See also John Anthony Scott, "Justice Bradley's Evolving Concept of the Fourteenth Amendment from the Slaughterhouse Cases to the Civil Rights Cases," 25 *Rutgers Law Review* 552 (1971). *Miscellaneous Writings* by the Justice were published posthumously by his son, Charles Bradley, in 1902; along with many harmless and even endearing writings are included the Justice's apologia with regard both to the *Legal Tender Cases* and the Electoral Commission.

Good biographies exist for three of Justice Bradley's colleagues, although all ignore the Southern bond cases: Charles Fairman, *Mr. Justice Miller and the Supreme Court, 1862–1890* (1939); C. Peter Magrath, *Morrison R. Waite: The Triumph of Character* (1963); and Carl Brent Swisher, *Stephen J. Field, Craftsman of the Law* (1930). A group portrait of Miller, Bradley, and Field is provided by G. Edward White in *The American Judicial Tradition: Profiles of Leading American Judges* (1976), chapter 4. Field spoke for and about himself in his *Personal Reminiscences of Early Days in California* (1893), memoirs which in spite of the title cover events in Washington as well as on the West Coast. Justice Miller summarized constitutional law as it then stood in his posthumously published *Lectures on the Constitution of the United States* (1891).

D. The Supreme Court and the Uses of History

Forensic history has attracted less attention than it deserves. Among the few good studies—none dealing with the use of history in construing the Eleventh Amendment—see Paul L. Murphy, "Time to Reclaim: The Current Challenge of American Constitutional History," 69 *American Historical Review* 64 (1963); Alfred H. Kelly, "Clio and the Court: An Illicit Love Affair," 1965 *Supreme Court Review* 119; and Charles A. Miller, *The Supreme Court and the Uses of History* (1969).

VI. An Exception: Virginia

A. Background

The standard history of Virginia is by Virginius Dabney, *Virginia: The New Dominion* (1971). The bicentennial history is by Louis D. Rubin, *Virginia* (1977). On the painful birth of West Virginia see Richard Orr Curry, *A House Divided: A Study of Statehood Politics and the Copperhead Movement in West Virginia* (1964). For a relevant slice of Virginia history see Allen W. Moger, *Virginia: Bourbonism to Byrd, 1870–1925* (1968).

B. Debt Repudiation

(1) BONDHOLDERS V. VIRGINIA, 1872–1890. The bibliography of contemporary comment in Section V. B is also relevant to Virginia's repudiation. In addition see the exchange between the Funder John W. Johnston, "Repudiation in Virginia," 134 *North American Review* 149 (1882), and the Readjuster H. H. Riddleberger, "Bourbonism in Virginia," id. at 416 (1882). See also the editorial article on "The 'Coupon Killers,'" in 7 *Virginia Law Journal* 513 (1883). James C. Lamb, editor of the *Virginia Law Journal,* published *The Virginia Coupon Cases* (1885); it reprints the cases from the official reporter, 114 U.S. 269. For a balanced contemporary assessment, see Morris Gray, "The Coupon-Legislation of Virginia," 23 *American Law Review* 924

(1889). An unbalanced but colorful account is by William L. Royall, the bondholders' lawyer, *History of the Virginia Debt Controversy: The Negro's Vicious Influence in Politics* (1897). See also Royall's eccentric memoirs, *Some Reminiscences* (1909).

For scholarly accounts of the opposing forces see Charles Chilton Pearson's old but still useful study of *The Readjuster Movement in Virginia* (1917) and Jack P. Maddex's detailed description of *The Virginia Conservatives, 1867–1879* (1970). James Tice Moore's sociological approach to the problem, *Two Paths to the New South: The Virginia Debt Controversy, 1870–1883* (1974), is marred by inadequate understanding of the legal issues. For an analysis of the relevance of the Eleventh Amendment, see John V. Orth, "The Interpretation of the Eleventh Amendment, 1798–1908: A Case Study of Judicial Power," 1983 *University of Illinois Law Review* 423, 439–47.

(2) VIRGINIA V. WEST VIRGINIA, 1894–1920. Eminent scholars have been attracted by the dispute: James G. Randall, "The Virginia Debt Controversy," 30 *Political Science Quarterly* 553 (1915); Thomas Reed Powell, "Coercing a State to Pay a Judgment: Virginia v. West Virginia," 17 *Michigan Law Review* 1 (1918); James Brown Scott, *Judicial Settlement of Controversies Between States of the American Union: An Analysis of Cases Decided in the Supreme Court of the United States* (1919), chapter 10. See also an article by the "second auditor" of Virginia, Rosewell Page, "The West Virginia Debt Settlement," 5 *Virginia Law Register* 257 (new ser., 1919).

For a brief modern account see John V. Orth, "The Virginia State Debt and the Judicial Power of the United States," in *Ambivalent Legacy: A Legal History of the South,* edited by David J. Bodenhamer and James W. Ely (1984), p. 106. For the lasting mark the controversies left on the Old Dominion, see A. E. Dick Howard, *Commentaries on the Constitution of Virginia* (1974), pp. 1099–1108.

VII. Another Exception: Cities and Counties

Scholarly treatment of public finance began in 1887 with Henry C. Adams's *Public Debts: An Essay in the Science of Finance;* municipal indebtedness is "scientifically" analyzed in part 3, chapter 3. For a monograph devoted to the subject see A. M. Hillhouse, *Municipal Bonds: A Century of Experience* (1936). A recent examination of the law of municipal corporations is by Gerald E. Frug, "The City as a Legal Concept," 93 *Harvard Law Review* 1059 (1980).

The legal history of municipal indebtedness is a twice-told tale: Charles Fairman told it briefly in 1939 in his biography of Justice Miller, chapter 9, and at great length in 1971 in his volume in the Holmes Devise History of the Supreme Court, *Reconstruction and Reunion, 1864–88, Part One,* chapters 17 and 18. Neither time, however, did he contrast it with the parallel story of state indebtedness. Since Fairman is so severe on *Gelpcke v. City of Dubuque,* it is useful to consult the intelligent defense of the decision by James B. Thayer, "The Case of Gelpcke v. Dubuque," 4 *Harvard Law Review* 311 (1891).

The law of the Eleventh Amendment as it bears on this topic is adequately but tendentiously set out in a law student's Comment, "The Denial of Eleventh Amendment Immunity to Political Subdivisions of the States: An Unjustifiable Strain on Federalism," 1979 *Duke Law Journal* 1042.

The evolution of the law on the subject can be traced in legal treatises. For a benchmark see *The Law of Municipal Bonds* (1876) by the prominent jurist John F. Dillon. Then see the successive editions of Judge Dillon's *Law of Municipal Corporations* (1st ed., 1872; 2d ed., 1873; 3d ed., 1881; 4th ed., 1890; 5th ed., 1911) and of Leonard A. Jones's *A Treatise on the Law of Railroad and Other Corporate Securities, Including Municipal Aid Bonds* (1st ed., 1879; 2d ed., 1890 entitled *A Treatise on the Law of Corporate Bonds and Mortgages;* 3d ed., 1907 with same title as 2d ed.). Contemporary emotions are dispassionately analyzed by Charles Francis Adams, a Brahmin who became an expert on railroads, in "The Granger Movement," 120 *North American Review* 394 (1875).

VIII. From 1890 to 1908

A. Background

The best introduction to the legal ethos of the period is Arnold M. Paul's *Conservative Crisis and the Rule of Law: Attitudes of Bar and Bench, 1887–1895* (1960). Detailed accounts of the Supreme Court's work are provided by William F. Swindler, *Court and Constitution in the Twentieth Century,* 2 vols. (1969–70) (volume 1 covers *The Old Legality, 1889–1932*); John E. Semonche, *Charting the Future: The Supreme Court Responds to a Changing Society, 1890–1920* (1978) (reviewed by John V. Orth, 58 *North Carolina Law Review* 399 (1980)); and David P. Currie's two articles, seemingly the opening chapters in a volume on the Supreme Court's "second hundred years" (for the first volume see Section I above), "The Constitution in the Supreme Court: The Protection of Economic Interests, 1889–1910," 52 *University of Chicago Law Review* 324 (1985), and "The Constitution in the Supreme Court: Full Faith and the Bill of Rights, 1889–1910," id. at 867. A specialized study is by Richard S. Kay, "The Equal Protection Clause in the Supreme Court, 1873–1903," 29 *Buffalo Law Review* 667 (1980). The latter part of the period is scrutinized by William F. Duker in three articles: "Mr. Justice Rufus W. Peckham: The Police Power and the Individual in a Changing World," 1980 *Brigham Young University Law Review* 47; "The Fuller Court and State Criminal Process: Threshold of Modern Limitations on Government," id. 275; and "Mr. Justice Rufus W. Peckham and the Case of *Ex Parte Young:* Lochnerizing *Munn v. Illinois,*" id. 539. See also Stephen A. Siegel, "Understanding the *Lochner* Era: Lessons from the Controversy over Railroad and Utility Rate Regulation," 70 *Virginia Law Review* 187 (1984).

B. *Dramatis Personae*

William D. Guthrie may be glimpsed at work in Robert T. Swaine's *The Cravath Firm and Its Predecessors, 1819–1947,* 2 vols. (1946), volume 1, pp. 359–62, 369, 483, 518–36. He is depicted as an ultraconservative by Benjamin R. Twiss, *Lawyers and the Constitution: How Laissez-Faire Came to the Supreme Court* (1942), pp. 214–17. Guthrie speaks for himself in his collected writings, *Magna Carta and Other Addresses* (1916) (which includes his 1908 address on the Eleventh Amendment).

For a summary of Theodore Roosevelt's criticisms of his Republican contemporaries on the bench, see Jonathan Lurie, *Law and the Nation, 1865–1912* (1983), chapter 4.

C. The Eleventh Amendment

For a balanced view of Eleventh Amendment law at the beginning of the period, see A. H. Wintersteen, "The Eleventh Amendment and the Non-Suability of the State," 39 *American Law Register* 1 (1891). At the turn of the century Joseph Wheless made sovereign immunity the touchstone in "Suits Against a State," 34 *American Law Review* 689 (1900). At the end of the period, prominent lawyers in addition to Guthrie were turning their attention to the topic: Judge Jacob Trieber, a U.S. District Court judge from Arkansas, wrote on the "Suability of States by Individuals in the Courts of the United States," 41 *American Law Review* 845 (1907); Allen Caperton Braxton made the Eleventh Amendment the subject of his presidential address to the Virginia State Bar Association, see volume 20 of the Association's *Reports,* p. 172 (1907); and Herbert S. Hadley, attorney general of Missouri, published on "The Eleventh Amendment" in 66 *Central Law Journal* 71 (1908).

IX. After *Ex Parte Young:*
The Eleventh Amendment in the Twentieth Century

A. General

In the context of overall treatments of constitutional law in the twentieth century, Eleventh Amendment law is succinctly analyzed by Lawrence H. Tribe, *American Constitutional Law*

(1978), and by John E. Nowak, Ronald D. Rotunda, and J. Nelson Young, *Handbook on Constitutional Law* (2d ed., 1983) (reviewed by John V. Orth, 1983 *University of Illinois Law Review* 1039). See also Bernard Schwartz, *A Commentary on the Constitution of the United States, Part I: The Powers of Government,* 2 vols. (1963), volume 1, pp. 399–410.

As an academic discipline in law schools, Eleventh Amendment law is covered in courses on federal jurisdiction. Among introductory treatises, which lawyers still call "hornbooks," the best on the subject is by Charles Alan Wright, *The Law of Federal Courts* (4th ed., 1983). See also Martin H. Redish, *Federal Jurisdiction: Tensions in the Allocation of Judicial Power* (1980), chapter 6. A useful brief summary is David P. Currie's *Federal Jurisdiction in a Nutshell* (2d ed., 1981). The authoritative treatise is by Charles Alan Wright, Arthur R. Miller, and Edward H. Cooper, *Federal Practice and Procedure* (1969–82), 27 vols.; the Eleventh Amendment is treated in volume 13. Among casebooks, the basis of law-school instruction, the best are *Hart and Wechsler's The Federal Courts and the Federal System,* edited by Paul M. Bator, Paul J. Mishkin, David L. Shapiro, and Herbert Wechsler (2d ed., 1973), and David P. Currie, *Federal Courts: Cases and Materials* (1982). A new entrant is by Howard Fink and Mark V. Tushnet, *Federal Jurisdiction: Policy and Practice* (1984). As might be expected with such present-oriented books, supplements and new editions appear regularly.

In the last two decades, interest in the Eleventh Amendment has increased as the Supreme Court has elaborated its doctrine and law professors have sought out ever more esoteric topics for research. See Alan D. Cullison's fancifully titled "Interpretation of the Eleventh Amendment (A Case of the White Knight's Green Whiskers)," 5 *Houston Law Review* 1 (1967); Wayne McCormack, "Intergovernmental Immunity and the Eleventh Amendment," 51 *North Carolina Law Review* 485 (1973); Frederic S. LeClercq, "State Immunity and Federal Judicial Power—Retreat From National Supremacy," 27 *University of Florida Law Review* 361 (1975); Samuel H. Liberman, "State Sovereign Immunity in Suits to Enforce Federal Rights," 1977 *Washington University Law Quarterly* 195; Stewart A. Baker, "Federalism and the Eleventh Amendment," 48 *University of Colorado Law Review* 139 (1977); and Martha A. Field, "The Eleventh Amendment and Other Sovereign Immunity Doctrines" (2 parts), 126 *University of Pennsylvania Law Review* 515, 1203 (1977–78). A few authors actually expressed alarm for the safety of the Amendment: Judge Paul C. Weick, U.S. Court of Appeals (6th Cir.), "Erosion of State Sovereign Immunity and the Eleventh Amendment by Federal Decisional Law," 10 *Akron Law Review* 583 (1977); Philip L. Martin, "The New Interpretation of Sovereign Immunity for the States," 16 *California Western Law Review* 39 (1980); and Peter W. Thornton, "The Eleventh Amendment: An Endangered Species," 55 *Indiana Law Journal* 293 (1980). Law students have produced some useful Notes and Comments. See especially the Comment, "Avoiding the Eleventh Amendment: A Survey of Escape Devices," 1977 *Arizona State Law Journal* 625; wholly analytical, this piece makes an interesting contrast with historical studies. A student Note, valuable for other reasons, is "A Practical View of the Eleventh Amendment—Lower Court Interpretations and the Supreme Court's Reaction," 61 *Georgetown Law Journal* 1473 (1973). See also the Note, "Private Suits Against States in the Federal Courts," 33 *University of Chicago Law Review* 331 (1966), the Note, "Constitutional Law—The Eleventh Amendment—Injustice for All," 77 *West Virginia Law Review* 724 (1975), and the Comment, "The Eleventh Amendment and Federally Protected Rights," 27 *Buffalo Law Review* 57 (1978).

B. Historical

The history of the Eleventh Amendment in the first half of the twentieth century can be reconstructed from a series of scholarly studies, chronologically arranged. The baseline is drawn by Karl Singewald, *The Doctrine of Non-Suability of the State in the United States* (1910). Then see LeRoy G. Pilling, "An Interpretation of the Eleventh Amendment," 15 *Michigan Law Review* 468 (1917); Robert Dorsey Watkins, *The State as a Party Litigant* (1927); and Charles S. Hyneman, "Judicial Interpretation of the Eleventh Amendment," 2 *Indiana Law Journal* 371 (1927).

A student Note describes "The Present Status of the Eleventh Amendment," 10 *Vanderbilt Law Review* 425 (1957).

C. Special Topics

Admiralty is covered by a student Comment, "Eleventh Amendment Immunity and State-Owned Vessels," 57 *Tulane Law Review* 1523 (1983). On *Monaco v. Mississippi,* see Gordon Ireland, "Constitutional Law—Immunity of a State from Suit by a Foreign State—Defaulted State Bonds," 8 *Mississippi Law Journal* 392 (1936).

Waiver, express and implied, is covered in student pieces: Comment, "States—Waiver of State Immunity to Suit with Special Reference to Suits in Federal Courts," 45 *Michigan Law Review* 348 (1947); Note, "Express Waiver of Eleventh Amendment Immunity," 17 *Georgia Law Review* 513 (1983); and Comment, "Implied Waiver of a State's Eleventh Amendment Immunity," 1974 *Duke Law Journal* 925. See also the article by Wendy Robbins, "The Eleventh Amendment: A Constitutional Roadblock to Recovery by State Employees Under Title VII and the FLSA?" 12 *Columbia Journal of Law & Social Problems* 77 (1975).

For a current statement of the law concerning suits against officers as well as a clarion call for change, see Peter H. Schuck, *Suing Government: Citizen Remedies for Official Wrongs* (1983). Again a sense of development can be gained from the chronological arrangement of scholarly studies: Joseph D. Block, "Suits Against Government Officers and the Sovereign Immunity Doctrine," 59 *Harvard Law Review* 1060 (1946); Kenneth Culp Davis, "Suing the Government by Falsely Pretending to Sue an Officer," 29 *University of Chicago Law Review* 435 (1962); Louis L. Jaffe, "Suits Against Governments and Officers" (2 parts), 77 *Harvard Law Review* 1, 209 (1963); David E. Engdahl, "Immunity and Accountability for Positive Governmental Wrongs," 44 *University of Colorado Law Review* 1 (1972); Noel P. Fox, "The King Must Do No Wrong: A Critique of the Current Status of Sovereign and Official Immunity,"

25 *Wayne Law Review* 177 (1979); and David P. Currie, "Sovereign Immunity and Suits Against Government Officers," 1984 *Supreme Court Review* 149. Scholarly comment on a recent case can be found in George D. Brown, "Beyond *Pennhurst*—Protective Jurisdiction, the Eleventh Amendment, and the Power of Congress to Enlarge Federal Jurisdiction in Response to the Burger Court," 71 *Virginia Law Review* 343 (1985); Erwin Chemerinsky, "State Sovereignty and Federal Court Power: The Eleventh Amendment After *Pennhurst v. Halderman*," 12 *Hastings Constitutional Law Quarterly* 643 (1985); David Rudenstine, "*Pennhurst* and the Scope of Federal Judicial Power to Reform Social Institutions," 6 *Cardozo Law Review* 71 (1984); and David L. Shapiro, "Wrong Turns: The Eleventh Amendment and the *Pennhurst* Case," 98 *Harvard Law Review* 61 (1984). Student comment is in 26 *Boston College Law Review* 947 (1985); 18 *Creighton Law Review* 75 (1984); 34 *De Paul Law Review* 515 (1985); 59 *St. John's Law Review* 141 (1984); 53 *University of Cincinnati Law Review* 877, 1107 (1984); 71 *Virginia Law Review* 655 (1985); 60 *Washington Law Review* 407 (1985); and 20 *Willamette Law Review* 823 (1984). See also George D. Brown, "State Sovereignty Under the Burger Court—How the Eleventh Amendment Survived the Death of the Tenth: Some Broader Implications of *Atascadero State Hospital v. Scanlon*," 74 *Georgetown Law Journal* 363 (1985).

The background of the surprising decision in *Edelman v. Jordan* is canvassed by John E. Nowak, "The Scope of Congressional Power to Create Causes of Action Against State Governments and the History of the Eleventh and Fourteenth Amendments," 75 *Columbia Law Review* 1413 (1975). The sequel is sketched by Norman B. Lichtenstein, "Retroactive Relief in the Federal Courts Since *Edelman v. Jordan:* A Trip Through the Twilight Zone," 32 *Case Western Reserve Law Review* 364 (1982), and by a student Note, "Reconciling Federalism and Individual Rights: The Burger Court's Treatment of the Eleventh and Fourteenth Amendments," 68 *Virginia Law Review* 865 (1982).

On the Abstention Doctrine and "Our Federalism," see Judge

John J. Gibbons, "Our Federalism," 12 *Suffolk University Law Review* 1087 (1978), and Aviam Soifer and H. C. Macgill, "The *Younger* Doctrine: Reconstructing Reconstruction," 55 *Texas Law Review* 1141 (1977).

Table of Cases

209

Table of Constitutions and Statutes

Index